THE ESSENCE OF
JAVA PROGRAMMING

THE ESSENCE OF COMPUTING SERIES

Published Titles
The Essence of Artificial Intelligence
The Essence of C for Electronic Engineers
The Essence of Compilers
The Essence of Databases
The Essence of Discrete Mathematics
The Essence of Human–Computer Interaction
The Essence of Java Programming
The Essence of Logic
The Essence of Neural Networks
The Essence of Professional Issues in Computing
The Essence of Program Design
The Essence of Programming Using C++
The Essence of Structured Systems Analysis Techniques
The Essence of Z

Forthcoming Titles
The Essence of Expert Systems
The Essence of IT

THE ESSENCE OF
JAVA PROGRAMMING

Glenn Rowe
University of Dundee

Prentice Hall
LONDON   NEW YORK   TORONTO   SYDNEY   TOKYO
SINGAPORE   MADRID   MEXICO CITY   MUNICH   PARIS

Prentice Hall
An imprint of
Pearson Education Limited
Edinburgh Gate
Harlow
Essex CM20 2JE
England

© Pearson Education Limited 1999

The right of Glenn Rowe to be identified as the author of this Work has been asserted by him in accordance with the Copyright, Designs and Patents Act 1988.

All rights reserved. No part of this publication may be reproduced, stored in a retrieval system, or transmitted in any form or by any means, electronic, mechanical, photocopying, recording or otherwise, without either the prior written permission of the publisher or a licence permitting restricted copying in the United Kingdom issued by the Copyright Licensing Agency Ltd, 90 Tottenham Court Road, London W1P 9HE.

Many of the designations used by manufacturers and sellers to distinguish their products are claimed as trademarks. Pearson Education Ltd has made every attempt to supply trademark information about manufacturers and their products mentioned in this book. A list of the trademark designations and their owners appears below.

First published 1999

Typeset in 10/12pt Times

Printed and bound in Great Britain by
Biddles Ltd, Guildford and Kings Lynn

Library of Congress Cataloging-in-Publication Data

Available from the publisher

British Library Cataloguing-in-Publication Data

A catalogue record for this book is available from the British Library

ISBN: 0-13-011377-8

---
1 2 3 4 5   03 02 01 00 99

Trademark Notice
Motif is a registered trademark of The Open Group
Unicode is a registered trademark of Unicode, Inc
UNIX is licensed through X/Open Company Ltd
Windows is a registered trademark of Microsoft Corp

Contents

Series Preface	**viii**
Preface	**ix**
Who is the book for?	ix
What does the book cover?	ix
Acknowledgements	**xi**
1 Classes and objects	**1**
What's in a program?	1
The object-oriented idea	2
Classes and objects in Java	4
Writing a Java program	8
Running a Java program	11
Exercises	17
2 Creating a window	**18**
Displaying a frame	18
Drawing text in a frame	20
Linking the Clock class with an applet	22
Applets and web pages	25
Simple animation – making the clock tell time	26
Exercises	31
3 Java syntax	**33**
Introduction	33
Primitive data types in Java	34
Variables, declarations, and scope	35
Variables and memory	37
Operators and operands	38
Conditional expressions	45
Loops	54
Exercises	58
4 Constructors, inheritance, and interfaces	**64**
Pointers	64
Constructors	66

Value and reference 67
Inheritance 71
Packages 81
Abstract classes 83
Interfaces 87
Exercises 90

5 The Java AWT and event handling 92
The Java AWT 92
Interacting with a program 94
The Java event model 95
Event handling using adapters and inner classes 100
The simpler Java AWT components 103
A Java AWT example – the game of nim 106
Exercises 117

6 Arrays and strings 119
Arrays and their properties 119
Arrays of objects 125
Strings 130
Unicode, bytes, and chars 132
String tokenizers 133
A String example – counting letters and word sizes 134
Exercises 140

7 Layout managers 143
Arranging components on the screen 143
The FlowLayout manager 144
The GridLayout manager 147
The BorderLayout manager 148
The CardLayout manager 149
Panels 150
Example – a tic-tac-toe game 151
The GridBagLayout manager 161
Exercises 166

8 Graphics and animation 168
The graphics context 168
The paint(), update(), and repaint() methods 170
Colours 170
Fonts 173
Font metrics 176
Scrollbars 179

Canvases	183
Menus	184
Popup menus	186
Example – a checkers game	189
Animation	200
Exercises	204

9 Threads — 206
Doing more than one thing at a time	206
The Thread class and the Runnable interface	207
Multithreading example – the clock revisited	211
Synchronization	219
Exercises	222

10 Exceptions — 223
Dealing with errors	223
Java's built-in exceptions	224
Throwing exceptions	227
Runtime and non-runtime exceptions	227
Defining new exception classes	229
A more general exception class	231
When to use exceptions	232
Exercises	233

11 Saving, loading, and printing — 235
Saving your work	235
Serialization	235
Printing	240
Lightweight and heavyweight components	243
Exercises	244

Appendix Further reading — 246
General	246
The basics of Java	246
The Sun Microsystems library	247

Index — 248

Series Preface

As the consulting editor for the Essence of Computing Series it is my role to encourage the production of well-focused, high-quality textbooks at prices which students can afford. Since most computing courses are modular in structure, we aim to produce books which will cover the essential material for a typical module.

I want to maintain a consistent style for the Series so that whenever you pick up an Essence book you know what to expect. For example, each book contains important features such as end of chapter summaries and exercises, and a glossary of terms, if appropriate. Of course, the quality of the Series depends crucially on the skills of its authors and all the books are written by lecturers who have honed their material in the classroom. Each book in the Series takes a pragmatic approach and emphasises practical examples and case studies.

Our aim is that each book will become essential reading material for students attending core modules in Computing. However, we expect students to want to go beyond the Essence books and so all books contain guidance on further reading and related work.

This is a beginner's book that takes an object first approach to programming in Java; the reader is introduced to interesting object-oriented programs right from the beginning. The emphasis is upon building interactive graphical programs using Java libraries. In spite of the restricted length of the book, all the essential elements of Java are covered. There are examples of substantial Java programs, with associated commentary, each succeeding example consolidating the reader's expertise. I believe that by the end of this book you will have an excellent basic knowledge of Java upon which to build.

Computing is constantly evolving and so the teaching of the subject also has to change. Therefore the Series has to be dynamic, responding to new trends in computing and extending into new areas of interest. We need feedback from our readers to guide us - are we hitting the target? Are there 'hot' topics which we have not covered yet? Feedback is always welcome but most of all I hope you find this book useful!

Ray Welland
Department of Computing Science
University of Glasgow
(e-mail: ray@dcs.gla.ac.uk)

Preface

Who is the book for?

This book is written for the programming novice who wishes to learn one of the most exciting new computer languages in widespread use today. Although no prior experience in programming is required to read this book, you should know your way around a computer, in the sense that you should know how to run pre-existing programs, use the mouse, examine your files, and so on.

What does the book cover?

Although Java is a relatively new computer language, its rate of growth over the past few years has been phenomenal. The original version of Java, version 1.0.2, was reasonably compact, but since then Java has undergone several revolutions. This book covers the 'essence' of Java, version 1.2 (also known as Java 2), although virtually all the code is also compatible with Java 1.1 compilers. At those few locations in the text where changes need to be made to allow the code to compile under Java 1.1, a footnote points out the differences.

There are several main differences between Java 1.0.2 and Java 1.2, however. Some of these differences are fundamental, in the sense that the ways that Java programs interact with the user (via the keyboard and mouse, for example) have been completely changed. Other differences are mainly in the increase in the power of the language and the libraries of pre-written material that you can plug into your own programs.

Since this book is limited in size, and is to be accessible to novices, some sacrifices had to be made. It was simply not possible to provide coverage of *all* the features of Java 1.2 in a book restricted to around 250 pages. The book therefore introduces the basic structures needed to write Java programs, and provides a comprehensive introduction to Java's graphical interface libraries. No attempt has been made to cover more 'advanced' topics such as networking, Java Beans, remote method invocation, servlets, etc.

The book is best read from beginning to end, since many chapters refer to examples and concepts in previous chapters, both in the main text and in the exercises. The book follows the 'objects first' philosophy, in that we begin in Chapter 1 with an introduction to the idea of object-oriented programming, a concept that is central to writing any Java program. Chapter 2 introduces simple graphical programming by setting up a separate window and displaying a clock inside it.

Chapter 3 gets into the details of the language by covering most of the elementary programming tools needed to write Java programs. Chapter 4 extends the idea of object-oriented programming by describing some of the more advanced ways of handling classes and objects provided by Java 1.2.

Chapter 5 introduces the Abstract Windowing Toolkit (AWT), which is Java's core library of graphical interface components. The AWT is used to construct any interface containing standard graphical components such as buttons, menus, text boxes, checkboxes, and so on. It also contains methods for drawing, setting colours, setting up text fonts, and so on.

Chapter 6 introduces arrays and describes how Java handles strings of text. Chapter 7 covers layout managers, which are tools allowing the components from the AWT to be arranged within panels and windows in such a way that the interface appears the same on all computer systems.

Chapter 8 continues the study of graphics and the AWT by studying more advanced methods and techniques, including animation. Chapter 9 introduces threads, which allow a single Java program to run several tasks at once (or at least, *appear* to do this!).

Chapter 10 covers exception handling, and Chapter 11 shows how to save data to and load data from disk files, and how to print out hardcopy.

There are numerous examples of complete Java programs throughout the book. Although some of these programs are fairly long (for a textbook), it was felt that students learn much more from seeing complete programs than from isolated methods or statements. All the source code in the book is available on the web site http://alife.mic.dundee.ac.uk/growe/Books/index.html.

Some suggestions for further reading are made at the end of the book.

Glenn Rowe
February, 1999.

Acknowledgements

Thanks are due to the students in the *Programming for the Internet* class at the University of Dundee, and in particular to Adam Grieve, for reading through the entire manuscript and making many useful suggestions from a student's point of view. Thanks are also due to Marc Nebbett, who read through the manuscript in its early stages and provided helpful comments. Several anonymous referees also provided useful feedback. As always, Jackie Harbor, David Harrison, and the staff at Prentice Hall provided invaluable support along the way.

CHAPTER 1

Classes and objects

What's in a program?

When the idea of programming a computer was first invented (and for quite a while after that), 'writing a computer program' usually meant writing some instructions that would ask for some input, do some calculations, and produce the 'answer' as output. Early computer programs were written mostly to solve mathematical problems, and indeed, many introductory textbooks still use numerical examples to illustrate how to write simple programs.

These days, a computer program is expected to do a lot more than just number crunching. If you have used a computer before, even if you've never programmed one, you will know that programs such as word processors, games, spreadsheets, and so on provide you with an easy-to-use (or 'user friendly' as it's called in the trade), absorbing *environment* in which you can work or play. Most modern programs provide a graphical layout on screen, containing objects like windows (each with its own program running) push-buttons that can be pressed using the mouse, and menus that drop down from the tops of the windows (or sometimes pop up in the middle of the screen). Many programs also include high-resolution images, animations, movie clips, and sound (collectively known as *multimedia*). In fact, for many programs, you never need to use the computer's keyboard at all – everything can be done using the mouse, a joystick, or simply by touching the screen with your finger.

Since the goal of the aspiring software developer (a much trendier title than 'computer programmer') should be to produce programs of this quality, a new approach to teaching introductory programming is needed. That is the goal of this modest book: to make a break with tradition, and teach you *real-life-oriented* and *graphical* programming, right from the start.

The Java language is ideally suited to this task. It is a modern language that has only been in widespread use for three or four years. Its popularity is due to many factors: it's much easier to learn and use than more traditional languages like C or C++; it has graphics built into it; it allows high-powered components to be built into material developed for the World Wide Web; and programs written in Java don't need to be rewritten to run on different types of computer.

The main goal of this book is, of course, to teach you to write programs using Java. However, one thought that I hope you will have in the back of your mind most

2 WHAT'S IN A PROGRAM?

of the time is that the programs you are writing should be ones that reflect some real-life situation, and that do so in a natural, user-friendly way.

The object-oriented idea

Java is an *object-oriented* language. We'll get into some of the properties that such a language has to have a bit later, but for now, it's best to think of an object-oriented language as one in which you design your program by thinking of the real-life *objects* that the program is supposed to represent. These objects have natural relations to each other and can interact with each other in certain ways. The goal of object-oriented programming is to build these relations and interactions into the computer program in an equally natural way.

Since it's usually easier to understand a specific example than an abstraction, let's consider an everyday object and see how we might model it using the object-oriented idea.

For many of us, the first bit of technology we encounter on the average working day is an alarm clock. To make things even more definite, let's assume that you have a digital clock that displays the time using red or green numerals. These clocks will usually have a row of buttons on top that allow you to set the time, both for the clock face and the alarm, and turn the alarm on and off. Some 'turbo' models may have other buttons, such as a 'snooze' button which is supposed to give you an extra 10 minutes' sleep after the first alarm goes off.

Suppose we wanted to write a computer program that modelled the behaviour of a digital alarm clock. (Since most such clocks use a computer chip to implement their features, this isn't such a far-fetched example.) What is the object-oriented way of approaching this task?

First (not surprisingly) we need to identify the *objects* that we want to represent in our program. Since we are trying to model an alarm clock, the clock itself is the obvious candidate for the object we are representing.

In a larger program, in which we wish to model a more complex system, we would probably have several different objects. We will see some examples of this sort of thing later, but in order to get used to how an object is described in the object-oriented model, we will stick with just one object for now. To make things even simpler at this stage, we'll ignore the alarm feature for the moment, and concentrate just on the part of the clock that tells the time.

Having decided that the clock is to be our one and only object, what do we do next? We recognize that the clock has *properties* that describe it (such as the hour, minute and second it is displaying). There are also certain *actions* that can be performed on the clock (such as reading the time, setting the time, etc.).

Let's make these lists of properties and actions[1] a bit more formal. We must decide exactly what properties and actions we want the model of the clock to have.

---

[1] If your knowledge of English grammar is up to scratch, it may be helpful to think of the *object* as a *noun*, the *properties* as *adjectives* describing the object, and *actions* as *verbs* that

Since we will eventually have to write computer code to implement all these features, and computer code is very precise, it is a good idea to be clear in our minds at this early stage exactly what we want the finished program to do.

Here is a table of precisely what we want the clock to have in its property and action lists:

Table 1.1

Properties	Actions
Time: hours	Set hours
Time: minutes	Set minutes
Time: seconds	Set seconds
Time: PM	Update the time
	Read current hours
	Read current minutes
	Read current seconds
	Read PM

In the properties list, we're assuming that the hours, minutes, and seconds values are independent of each other. We're also assuming that the clock may display the time either as a 12-hour clock or as a 24-hour clock, with hour values between 0 (for midnight) and 23 (11 PM). In 12-hour mode, we need a separate indicator to tell if the time is AM or PM (many digital clocks have a little red dot that lights up for PM). We have included a PM property for this purpose.

In the actions list, we have three actions allowing us to set the time – we can set the value of hours, minutes, and seconds separately.

The fourth action updates the time stored in the clock by adding 1 to the 'seconds' value (and adjusting the minutes and hours values if necessary).

The next four actions may seem unnecessary. After all, we already have the values of the current time listed as properties, so why do we need separate actions just to read these values?

The answer to this question actually reveals something quite fundamental about the object-oriented idea. Although the properties listed for an object may be essential to fully define the current state of the object, we are under no obligation to allow just anyone to actually know the values of any of these properties. In other words, we decide what properties are necessary to completely define the clock, and *in addition*, we also decide which of those properties is accessible to the outside world.

To see why this makes sense, suppose that our clock runs off a nine-volt battery, and that if the voltage produced by this battery drops below seven volts, the clock stops operating. In order to design an accurate computer model of the clock, we would need to include the present voltage of the battery as one of the properties. However, an external user of the clock has no way of knowing what this value is

---

act upon the object. However, it has been the author's experience that the standard of English taught in schools these days often does not permit this analogy!

(unless the battery is removed from the clock and checked with a voltmeter, but we're assuming the user doesn't have a voltmeter handy). The first indication that our hapless user has that the battery is running low is when the clock stops. When we write the program that simulates the clock's behaviour, though, we would keep track of the battery's voltage as the program runs, even though we don't show this on screen. In this case, we would add 'battery voltage' as one of the properties, but we would *not* add a corresponding action of 'read battery voltage', since a real-life clock doesn't allow us to do that.

Another way of looking at it is that the only indications of the clock's internal state that we are allowed to see are those provided by the display on the clock face, and the only way we are allowed to change the internal state is by using one of the buttons on the top of the clock.

All of this illustrates the principle of *encapsulation* in object-oriented design. When we invent an object, we decide what properties it has. We must also decide what access to these properties we will allow an external user to have. We can think of *any* object introduced into an object-oriented design in much the same way as we think of the clock. We list all the properties we want the object to have, and then we attach displays and buttons to the object to define what access an external user has to these properties. Anyone wanting to use the object must restrict their use to the actions provided by the 'displays' and 'buttons' defined by the object's designer, just as anyone who wants to use a clock has to use the displays and buttons on the clock.

Encapsulation is one of the central ideas of object-oriented design. Each object you create should be entirely self-contained. Its internal structure is fully defined by the current values of its properties. Its interaction with the outside world (by which we mean its interaction with other objects) is fully defined by the actions provided in its design. No direct access to any of the properties is allowed – *all* access to properties (both reading their current values and changing their values) *must* be done through one of the defined actions. We can think of these actions as providing an *interface* between the internal values of the properties and the outside world.

Classes and objects in Java

The time has come to see how we translate an object-oriented design into working Java code. At this stage, since we have not yet introduced any of the structure (formally known as *syntax*) of the Java language, readers may have to accept a few things on faith. What is important here, however, is not so much that you understand what all the curly brackets and semicolons mean; rather that you see the correspondence between the design we worked out in the last section and the formal code we are about to write.

Right, then. Let's dive in and see what the Java code for an alarm clock object might look like. We'll begin with the properties list:

```
1   public class Clock
2   {
3     private int timeHours, timeMinutes, timeSeconds;
4     private boolean timePM;
5   }
```

Let's examine this code one line at a time. The line numbers to the left of the code listings in this book are *not* part of the code – they are there to allow the text to refer to the code.

In line 1, we see the way an object is defined in Java. As with an ordinary language such as English, Java contains a vocabulary of words that have pre-defined meanings (though there are only a few dozen of these compared to the hundreds of thousands of English words). You make use of these words to give meaning to your program. In line 1, the word `public` is one of these special Java words (known as *keywords*) – it tells you that the object about to be defined is to be publicly available.

Also on line 1, we see the word `class`, which is another Java keyword. The word `class` is used in Java to begin the definition of an object. (There is actually a technical difference between a 'class' and an 'object' which we'll get to a bit later. For now, we can think of them as more or less the same thing.) The last word on line 1 is `Clock`, which as you might guess, is *not* a Java keyword – this is a word that we invented to provide a name for the class. We are allowed to use any combination of letters and numbers as names for classes (and other items) provided that we steer clear of Java's keywords. Since there really aren't very many keywords, you will soon learn them all, and thus avoid using them for your own class, property, and action names. It is important, though, to choose names for your classes, properties, and actions that clearly describe what they represent.

Java is a *case-sensitive* language, which means that the case (upper or lower) of the letters used in the names of classes, properties, and actions makes a difference. For example, the class name `Clock` is different from the names `clock` or `CLOCK`. All Java keywords are entirely lower-case, so if you want to be certain of avoiding a keyword when you choose a name for your own classes, properties and actions, make sure you use one or more upper-case letters in the name.

Thus, in summary, line 1 tells us that we are about to define a publicly available class named `Clock`.

All of the code that we write to fully define the class must be enclosed between two *braces* or 'curly brackets,' which we see on lines 2 and 5.

Now let's look at line 3. The word `private` is another Java keyword which tells us that the contents of this line will be available *only* to the current class; that is, only to the `Clock` class. The keyword `int` (short for 'integer') tells us that we are about to define one or more properties that will be represented by integers. Finally, the words `timeHours`, `timeMinutes` and `timeSeconds` provide names for three properties. The first property, `timeHours`, as you might have guessed, is to be used to represent the hours portion of the current time. Similarly, `timeMinutes` and `timeSeconds` represent the minutes and seconds portions of the current time. The

6 WHAT'S IN A PROGRAM?

semicolon at the end of line 3 marks the end of that particular property list. Note that *all* property lists must end with a semicolon.

Line 4 should be reasonably transparent, with the exception of the word `boolean`. A `boolean` value in a Java program is one that can take only the values `true` and `false`. Thus, the quantity named `timePM` is defined as a `boolean` value – if it is `true`, the current time is PM; if it is `false`, the time is AM.

Lines 3 and 4 therefore define the list of properties that the `Clock` class will use. We haven't yet provided any code that implements the actions, but we'll get to that in a minute.

Just before we do, though, it is worth emphasizing how the encapsulation principle is realized in the class definition above. The `Clock` class itself is declared as `public` to show that it is to be accessible to every other object that may (ultimately) be defined in our program. All the properties defined inside the class are specified as `private`, which means that they are accessible only *within* the `Clock` class. In order for us to have any access to these quantities, we must provide some actions that allow this.

We will now add enough code to allow us to read and set the hour value of the current time. The class so far looks like this:

```
1   public class Clock
2   {
3      private int timeHours, timeMinutes, timeSeconds;
4      private boolean timePM;
5
6      public int getTimeHours()
7      {
8         return timeHours;
9      }
10
11     public void setTimeHours(int newTimeHours)
12     {
13        timeHours = newTimeHours;
14     }
15  }
```

Lines 1 through 4 are the same as before, but we have added new code in lines 6 through 14 (line 15 is just the closing brace that ends the class definition). As before, let's examine this section line by line.

Line 6 begins a typical action definition. The technical term for an action in Java is a *method*, so we'll use that terminology from now on. The `public` keyword, as before, means that the method is available to other objects outside the current class. We will see an example later in this chapter where a separate object needs to refer to (or *call*, as it's usually said) the actions within the `Clock` class. Only `public` methods are accessible to these external objects. This continues the implementation of the encapsulation principle – remember that all the properties are `private` (no direct access to them by external objects is permitted), but the actions are to be public, since this is the way external objects are allowed access to the properties stored within the Clock class.

The next word in line 6 is int, which we've also seen before – recall that it is an abbreviation for 'integer'. To understand what int is doing here, look ahead to the next word: getTimeHours. This is our own name for this particular method, and describes what the method does: it retrieves the current value of the timeHours property. Since timeHours is an int (as defined on line 3), the getTimeHours method must produce an int as its result. That is what the int in line 9 indicates – the getTimeHours method *returns* an int as the result of its action.

The last thing to notice about line 6 is the pair of parentheses (with nothing inside them) at the end. The presence of parentheses or round brackets (with or without something between them) is what distinguishes a method from a property: methods *always* have parentheses after their name. Their purpose will become clear when we consider the other method below. When we refer to a method in the text of this book, we will always include the parentheses as part of the name. For example, when referring to the getTimeHours method, we will always write it as getTimeHours().

Since methods in Java have to actually do something (as opposed to properties, which just exist and have values), we need a way of stating what actions a method must perform. The getTimeHours() method's only purpose is to retrieve the current value of timeHours, so that is what is done in lines 7 through 9. The actions for a method are always enclosed in braces (lines 7 and 9), with the code for the actual actions being sandwiched between them.

The instruction on line 8 comprises a single Java *statement*. A statement can be thought of as a command, which will cause the computer to do something when it is executed. Statements must end with semicolons, just like property lists.

The statement on line 8 retrieves the value of timeHours and returns it using the Java keyword return. (Don't worry yet about where it gets returned *to* – at this point, just see that the method does its job of finding the current value of timeHours and making it available.) The timeHours value that is returned on line 8 is the int referred to on line 6. Note that this method is allowed access to the private property timeHours, since both the getTimeHours() method and the timeHours property belong to the same class. Thus the getTimeHours() method serves as a public interface between the private timeHours property and the outside world. If we had not provided this interface method, the timeHours property would remain inaccessible, since it is a private property.

Finally, let's look at the other method, on lines 11 through 14. This method is also declared as public, so it is accessible to external objects. The second word, void, is however a new Java keyword. Since it occurs in the same relative position as the int keyword did in the getTimeHours() method, you might guess that it serves a similar purpose, in that it should define the type of data that is returned by the setTimeHours() method. In a sense, you would be right, except that void indicates that *no* data is returned by this method. If you read the name of the method, setTimeHours(), you will see why this is the case. This method is designed to set the value of `timeHours` to a new value, so no data is being read, so no return value is needed.

However, since the purpose of the `setTimeHours()` method is to allow an external object to set the `timeHours` property to a new value, we need some way to tell the method what that new value is. This is the purpose of the `int newTimeHours` bit contained inside the parentheses at the end of line 11. Parentheses in a method definition contain a list of data being sent *to* a method. Empty parentheses mean that *no* data is being sent to the method (as with the method on line 6). The list of data inside the parentheses is similar to a property list, except that the data type must be specified for *each* item in the list, and there is no semicolon at the end. The `int` lets the method know that the type of data that is being sent to it is an integer, and the `newTimeHours` is just the name we have invented for that integer.

The value (or values) between the parentheses is called the *argument* of the method. This doesn't mean that there is a disagreement between the value and the method in which it is found; the term 'argument' is a leftover from the mathematical origins of computer languages.

When we refer in the text of the book to a method that expects an argument, we will write it in the same way as a method without arguments. That is, we will refer to the `setTimeHours` method as `setTimeHours()`, with an empty pair of parentheses after the name. This saves space in the text, since some methods have lengthy argument lists.

Line 11, then, defines a method that is `public` (available to external objects), `void` (returns no data), and receives a single `int` value which is called `newTimeHours`. We'll see a bit later how an external object would use the `setTimeHours()` method, and in particular, how it can send a value for `newTimeHours` to the method. For now, just assume that the method is used from some external object and that the required data is provided.

Finally, line 13 *assigns* the value of `newTimeHours` to `timeHours`. (The = sign used in line 13 isn't quite the same thing as an = sign in a mathematical equation. We'll explore how it works in detail a bit later, but for now, just think of it as assigning the value on its right-hand side to the property on its left-hand side.)

The other actions (except for updating the time, which we'll consider later) listed in Table 1.1 can be coded in a similar way, and are left as exercises for the reader.

Writing a Java program

We have seen how to design an object or class by listing its properties and actions, how to encapsulate an object by restricting its properties to be private and providing public interface methods, and how to translate this design into Java code. What we have yet to do is actually use this code in a real Java program.

Before actually writing any code, you must become familiar with what is called the Java *development environment* on your computer. This is basically the software package or set of tools that you will use to write the Java code and run the program that it produces.

There are a number of commercially available Java development packages around (for example, Microsoft's Visual J++, Symantec's Café and Visual Café, Borland's JBuilder, IBM's Visual Age for Java, and so on). Before you rush out and buy one of these, however, consider the following points:

- This book is written for version 1.2 of the Java language. Some commercial tools only support the earlier version 1.0 (usually sub-version 1.0.2) or one of the sub-versions of Java 1.1. There are many major differences between versions 1.0 and later versions, so some (in fact, most) of the code in this book will not work with a package that only supports version 1.0. There are relatively few differences (at the level of Java covered in this book) between versions 1.1 and 1.2.
- All you really need to develop Java software is available for free from Sun Microsystems. Look for the *Java Development Kit* (often abbreviated JDK) on Sun's web page (at URL http://www.javasoft.com/), download and install the package, and you should be ready to go. Complete, on-line documentation for the Java libraries that we will be using later in the book is also available from the same site. This documentation is at least as important as the JDK itself – there are a great many features available in Java, so it is important to get into the habit of browsing through the documentation to see what is there.
- The only thing not included in the JDK is a text editor, which you will need to actually write the Java source code. There should be a text editor already available on whatever computer system you are using (for example, notepad on a Windows system, emacs on UNIX or Windows), so you should be able to get all the tools you need without any cost.
- All the software in this book was developed using public domain (free) software: the JDK and associated documentation from Sun, and the emacs editor (a product of the Free Software Foundation, who produce a lot of very good and very useful software, much of it under the GNU banner) for Windows 95. Most UNIX setups have emacs installed already. If you want information on installing emacs on Windows 95 or Windows NT, visit the web site http://xarch.tu-graz.ac.at/autocad/lsp_tools/ntemacs-faq.html (or do a web search for the phrase "emacs for Windows").

This is probably a good place to reiterate what this book assumes about your computer knowledge. Although we don't assume that you've done any programming before, we *do* assume that you have some familiarity with your computer system. In particular, we assume that you know how to navigate around the file structures, create and delete files and directories, run pre-existing programs, and so on.

It is always a good idea to create a new directory for each new program that you write. That way, all the files (and you will create quite a few) for each project will be

10 WHAT'S IN A PROGRAM?

together in their own location, so you won't get them mixed up with files from other projects.

So, if you haven't already done so, create a new directory on your computer for Java programs. Within that directory, create another directory called `Clock`, and use that directory for what follows.

All Java code must be written into files with a `.java` extension. Furthermore, the name of the file must be the same as the name of the Java class it contains. (It is possible to write more than one class in a single file, but for now, we'll assume you write each class definition in a separate file.)

Start up your text editor, and create a new file called `Clock.java`. Enter the code for the `Clock` class given above into this file and save it. (You can either type the code in directly from the book, or download the code from the Web site mentioned in the Preface to this book.) Before you can do anything with the code, it must first be translated into a form that the computer can understand. This process is known as *compiling* the program. The JDK includes a program called the Java compiler which is what you must use to compile your program into a form of machine code. To compile your `Clock.java` file, open up a window into which you can type commands (such as an MS-DOS window on a PC, or an ordinary command window in UNIX), make sure you are in the `Clock` directory, and type the command:

```
javac Clock.java
```

If all goes well, the computer should pause for a second or two, and the compilation should finish with no errors. If you *do* get errors at this point, there are two main causes.

Firstly, you may not have set up the JDK correctly. This is most likely the cause if you get a 'bad command' or 'command not found' error. The computer is saying that it can't find the `javac` program. You need to adjust the list of directories searched by the computer when a command is issued to solve this problem. If you're unsure how to do this, ask someone who has a bit more experience with your type of computer.

Secondly, you might have made a typing error in entering the code into the file. In this case, you should get an error message that looks something like this:

```
Clock.java:4: ';' expected.
   private boolean timePM
                         ^
1 error
```

This error was generated intentionally by leaving the semicolon off the end of line 4 in the code above. The Java compiler reports the error by giving you the filename (`Clock.java`), followed by the line number (4), followed by the error message (';' expected). It then prints out the offending line and attempts to identify where it thinks the error has occurred by placing a caret (^) underneath the line.

Although the Java compiler is reasonably user-friendly with its error messages, it sometimes gets confused and tells you that an error occurs on a particular line, when in fact the error is somewhere else in the file. After you develop a proper programming style, however, you should become quite skilled in interpreting compiler error messages, even if at first you find them a bit obscure.

When writing computer code in Java (or in any language), it is very important that you make frequent use of the compiler to check your code. Don't wait until you've written the entire program before you run the compiler for the first time. If you do, you will probably get dozens of error messages that will drive you to despair. Many of these error messages could be due to only a single error, such as a missing brace or semicolon. If you get into the habit of compiling your code after every 4 or 5 lines you add, you will (usually) avoid long lists of error messages, and if you do get errors, you will have a pretty good idea of where they are in the code.

So do take the time now to make sure you've typed in the Clock.java file correctly, and that your JDK is properly installed.

When the compilation finishes with no errors, have a look at the files in your Clock directory. You will see that the compiler has created a new file called Clock.class. This is the machine-readable version of the Clock class. It is this file that is actually run by the computer when you want to run your Java program.

If you try to run the Clock.class file (we'll get to how you run class files in a minute), you will get an error, since the Clock class that we have defined above doesn't contain all the components needed to make it into a runnable program. We'll fix that now.

Running a Java program

Java programs are a bit unusual in that they can be run in two different ways: either as stand-alone programs, or as components embedded in a Web page. Stand-alone Java programs are called *applications*, while programs that run inside Web pages are called *applets*. We'll begin by running an application.

A Java application must have a special method called main() in order to run. We could add a main() method to the Clock class, but it is better practice to create a new class which controls the running of the program. In your text editor, create a new file called TestClock.java and enter the following code:

```
1   import Clock;
2
3   public class TestClock
4   {
5      private Clock clock;              // The Clock object
6
7      // Initializes the clock object
8      void setup()
9      {
10        clock = new Clock();
```

12 WHAT'S IN A PROGRAM?

```
11        clock.setTimeHours(12);
12     }
13
14     /* Prints out the current time.
15        This method makes use of the library methods
16        print() and println()
17     */
18     void showTime()
19     {
20        System.out.print("The current hour is ");
21        System.out.println(clock.getTimeHours());
22     }
23
24     // The program starts with the main() method
25     public static void main(String argv[])
26     {
27        TestClock myClock = new TestClock();
28        myClock.setup();
29        myClock.showTime();
30     }
31  }
```

We'll explain what this code does in a minute, but for now, compile the code in the same way as before:

```
javac TestClock.java
```

(You can compile both your .java files at once if you like, by giving the command `javac TestClock.java Clock.java`.) Now, run the program by using the command:

```
java TestClock
```

If all goes well, you should see the output

```
The current hour is 12
```

printed on the screen.

It is now time to explain what this new file `TestClock.java` does.

Line 1 is an `import` statement (`import` is another Java keyword). It imports the definition of the `Clock` class so that it is available within the `TestClock.java` file. Since the code in the file `TestClock.java` refers to the `Clock` class (on line 5, for example), the compiler needs to know how a `Clock` class is defined when it is compiling the file `TestClock.java`. In practice, if the files are in the same directory, the compiler will find the file `Clock.java` automatically, so the `import` statement isn't needed, but it doesn't hurt to have it there anyway to remind yourself that reference is made to the `Clock` class.

Line 3 defines a new class called `TestClock`. This is the class we will use to test out the `Clock` class, so we need to include an object of type `Clock` in this class.

Line 5 *declares* the object of type `Clock`. It is at this point that we need to clarify the distinction between the *class* and the *object*. Up to now, we've used the terms more or less interchangeably, but, as promised, there is a subtle distinction.

Think of it this way. When we defined the `Clock` class, we specified the properties and actions that are possessed by the type of clock we want our program to represent. We have, in effect, written a blueprint for a particular type of clock. We can then use that blueprint to produce as many *actual* clocks as we like, just as a factory uses a blueprint to manufacture clocks in real life.

In the same way, a class definition is a set of instructions for building an actual object. The declaration statement on line 5 begins the process of building a `Clock` object. It tells the compiler to create an object called `clock`, and that the blueprint for building the object is provided by the `Clock` class definition.

Merely declaring an object doesn't actually build it, however. It is rather like placing an order with the factory for an object of type `Clock`. The factory will put your order in a 'to do' pile and wait for further instructions from the foreman as to when to build it.

These instructions are provided by the `setup()` method, beginning on line 8. The statement on line 10 contains the Java keyword `new`, which instructs the computer to build an object of type `Clock`. The = sign here has the same meaning as earlier: take the object on the right-hand side and assign it to the object on the left-hand side. (Don't worry about the empty pair of parentheses at the end of line 10 for now. This will be explained later, when we talk about *constructors*.) Thus the effect of line 10 is to actually build an object according to the blueprint provided by the `Clock` class definition, and assign this newly constructed object to `clock`. The `clock` now contains a `Clock` object which may be used in any way allowed by the methods in the `Clock` class definition.

Line 11 shows how the `setTimeHours()` method is used. Note the form of this statement: the object name (`clock`) appears to the left of a 'dot' (or 'period' or 'full stop'), and the `setTimeHours()` method itself appears to the right. The dot serves to connect the object with the specific method that is to be invoked for that object.

The compiler will examine the object to the left of the dot first, and attempt to determine its class. Since this is the `clock` object, its data type is the class `Clock`, as the compiler can tell from line 5. Then the compiler tries to find the definition, within the `Clock` class, of the method to the right of the dot. That is, once the compiler knows that it is dealing with the `Clock` class, it will search the class definition, looking for a `setTimeHours()` method (which in this case, it will find).

Once it finds the method, it reminds itself of the form the method takes. Let us remind ourselves as well. The `setTimeHours()` method looks like this:

```
public void setTimeHours(int newTimeHours)
{
   timeHours = newTimeHours;
}
```

The first thing the compiler will check is that it is legal for an external class such as `TestClock` to access the `setTimeHours()` method. Since the method is declared as `public`, this is allowed.

Next, it will see from the definition of `setTimeHours()` that an `int` value is required within the parentheses. (As we mentioned earlier, the list of parameters that must be passed to a method is called its *argument list*, with each parameter being called an *argument*.) Looking back at line 11 above, we see that an `int` value (12) is indeed provided. When the program is run, the value 12 will be assigned to the `int` object `newTimeHours` when the `setTimeHours()` method is called. The statements inside the `setTimeHours()` method will then be run, with the result that the `timeHours` value will be set to 12.

The technique of *calling* a method, and passing *arguments* to that method is very common in Java programming. It is therefore important that you fully understand what is required when you make such a call.

When a method is called, the compiler will look at the method's definition to see how many arguments that method requires, and what type (`int`, `boolean`, etc.) each argument is. Next, it will check that the code that makes the call to this method has the *same* number of arguments, and that these arguments are of the *same* type, and in the same order. For the `setTimeHours()` method, a single argument is required, and that argument must be an `int`. Some methods, such as `getTimeHours()` take no arguments at all, while others may take more than one. It all depends on how the methods are defined within their enclosing class.

It is also important to realize that, for simple data types like `int`s and `boolean`s, when an argument *is* required, a copy of the value being sent to the method is made and assigned to the name given in the method's definition. In line 11 above, we used a constant value of 12 in the call to `setTimeHours()`, so this value is copied to `newTimeHours` within the `setTimeHours()` method. We could equally well have chosen any other `int` value to pass to `setTimeHours()`: there is nothing special about 12.

What we could *not* do, however, is attempt to pass a non-`int` value, such as the `boolean` constant `true`, as an argument to `setTimeHours()`. Since the data type of `true` is not `int`, the compiler would detect a mismatch between the data types of the value being sent to the method and the value required in the method definition. In the same way, we couldn't get away with leaving the argument out altogether, or in trying to pass more than one argument.

In summary, the effects of line 11 are:

- The `clock` object is examined to see what data type (class) it is. It is of class `Clock`.
- The `Clock` class definition is searched for the definition of the method `setTimeHours()`. This is found.

RUNNING A JAVA PROGRAM   15

- A check is made to see if it is legal for an external class (`TestClock`) to access the `setTimeHours()` method. The method is declared as `public` in the `Clock` class definition, so this is OK.
- The argument list required by the `setTimeHours()` method is compared with the arguments given in line 11. Since the method requires a single argument of type `int` (an integer), and an `int` (12) is provided, this is OK.
- The integer value (12) is assigned to the argument `newTimeHours` within the `setTimeHours()` method.
- The value of `newTimeHours` is assigned to the `timeHours` property of the `clock` object.

The `showTime()` method on lines 18 through 22 prints out some information on the screen. Again, don't worry at the moment about the `System.out.print` and `System.out.println` statements. For now, just accept that line 20 prints out the text 'The current hour is', but does not start a new line afterwards. Line 21 prints out its argument, and *does* print a new line afterwards. This is the only difference between a `print` and a `println`.

Line 21 calls the `getTimeHours()` method to retrieve the value of `timeHours` for the clock object. You should be able to trace through the steps followed by the computer to retrieve this value. They are very similar to those for setting the value back on line 11. In particular, note that the `return timeHours` statement inside the `getTimeHours()` method sends the current value of the `timeHours` property for the clock object back, and this is printed by the statement in line 21.

We have now seen how to communicate with a method in both directions. On line 11, we sent some data to a method by passing it an argument. On line 21, the method sent some data back to the code that called it by using the `return` statement. Communication in both directions is governed by strict rules. When sending data to a method through its argument list, the number and types of the arguments must match. When a method sends data back to the code that called it, it may only send back a single data item, and the type of that item is determined by the *return type* as specified in the definition of the method. If you refer back to the definition of the `getTimeHours()` method, you will see that its return type is specified as an `int`.

Finally, have a look at the `main()` method, starting on line 25. You will see several words in this line that are unfamiliar – don't worry about them for the moment. Just remember that the definition of the `main()` method *always* starts this way, so you can copy this line to other Java programs.

The most important thing to remember about the `main()` method is that it is *essential* to have one class in an application that contains a `main()` method that starts with *exactly* the code given in line 25. To run an application, use the `java` command followed by the name of the class containing the `main()` method, just as we used the command '`java TestClock`' above. If you have used other classes in your application, you don't need to include them as part of the `java` command – they will be found automatically when your program runs. (A `main()` method is *not*

16 WHAT'S IN A PROGRAM?

required for Java programs that are only to be run as *applets*, that is, only within a web page.)

The structure of the `main()` method will seem a bit odd, in that an object of class `TestClock` is declared and initialized *inside* the `main()` method itself, even though `main()` is contained *within* the `TestClock` class. The reason for this is that `main()` is not allowed to access directly any of the other methods or objects belonging to the class in which it occurs.[1] The form for the `main()` method used here is a good one to apply whenever you write a `main()` method in any other class. That is:

- Inside the `main()` method, declare an object of the same class as that within which the `main()` method is found.
- Call any methods of the class within which `main()` is found by using this *local* object that you created in step 1.

For example, after creating the local `TestClock` object called `myClock` on line 27, we use `myClock` to call the `setup()` and `showTime()` methods on lines 28 and 29.

Line 7 is a *comment*. That part of a line following a double slash // is ignored by the compiler. Comments can occupy an entire line, as in line 7, or just the last portion of a line as in line 5. A second form of comment, illustrated on lines 14 through 17, may span several lines. Any text opening with /* and ending with */ is also ignored by the compiler.

It is a good idea to put a few comments in your code to explain what you're doing. Don't overdo it, however – too many comments can be more distracting than helpful. We won't put many comments in the code in this book, since you've got the accompanying text to explain what's going on, but when you write code yourself, you should always put in a few comments to help yourself and others understand how the code works. Useful places to put comments are:

- At the beginning of each method, to explain what that method does.
- Next to each declaration statement, to explain what each object is used for.
- Before a block of code that implements some instructions that may not be obvious. Since we haven't written any really substantial code yet, we haven't seen a case like this.

You should experiment with the code above by changing various things and seeing what effects they have. For example, try leaving out the 'clock.' at the start of line 11, try misspelling the name of the `setTimeHours()` method, try using a non-integer value (such as 3.14) as the argument to `setTimeHours()` (or leaving the argument out completely), and try declaring the `setTimeHours()` method as `private` back in the definition of `Clock`. All of these changes should result in

---

[1] And the reason for *that*, in turn, is somewhat technical, so is best left to Chapter 6. Basically, it is because `main()` must be a `static` method. Static methods may refer only to other `static` methods (or `static` properties).

compiler errors, but it is instructive to see what the compiler tells you in each of these cases.

Exercises

1. Add the interface methods required to set and get the other parameters in the `Clock` class: `timeMinutes`, `timeSeconds`, and `timePM`.
2. Add code to the `setup()` method in the `TestClock` class that sets the values of `timeMinutes`, `timeSeconds`, and `timePM` to values of your choice.
3. Add some code to the `showTime()` method in the `TestClock` class that allows the full time (hours, minutes, seconds) to be printed out. The time should be printed with colons separating each component of the time, as in 9:15:18.
4. Add more code to the `showTime()` method that prints out the value of the `timePM` parameter. Since it is a `boolean` value, it will be printed as either `true` or `false`, so print out a line that states something like 'PM: <value>', where <value> should be the value of the `timePM` parameter (true or false).
5. Define a new class called `DayMonth`, and define two `int` properties called `day`, and `month`. Add a 'set' and 'get' method for each of these properties.
6. Add a declaration of a `DayMonth` object called `dayMonth` in the `TestClock` class. Initialize this object to a day and month of your choice. Add code to the `showTime()` method to print out the day and month on a separate line from the time.
7. Experiment with the error messages that are obtained from the Java compiler by introducing some intentional errors into the code for `TestClock`. In particular, try the following (one at a time!):

    (a) Leave out the '`clock.`' at the beginning of line 11.
    (b) Misspell the name of a method.
    (c) Send a non-integer value (e.g. 43.21) to a method such as `setTimeHours()` that expects an int argument.
    (d) Leave out the argument to `setTimeHours()`.
    (e) Put 2 or more int arguments into the call to `setTimeHours()`.
    (f) Put an argument into the call to `getTimeHours()`.
    (g) Omit the initial `//` from the start of a comment line.
    (h) Declare `setTimeHours()` as private.
    (i) Leave the closing `}` off a method.
    (j) Leave the closing `}` off the end of a class file.
    (k) Omit one of the parentheses in a method's argument list.
    (l) Type `==` in place of a single `=` in the `setTimeHours()` method.

CHAPTER 2
Creating a window

Displaying a frame

Up to now, all the output from our Java programs has been displayed in a simple text window – either a command (DOS) window on a PC, or a command line window on a UNIX machine. Very few 'real-life' Java programs work this way. Since Java was designed with a comprehensive library of graphical features, virtually all Java programs make extensive use of this Graphical User Interface, or GUI (pronounced 'gooey').

Although Java's GUI programming features are much easier to use than those in many other languages, there is still a lot to learn, so we won't cover everything in this single chapter. Our goals for this chapter may be split into two main areas:

- To learn how to display a *frame* (basically, a window created by the Java program) and write some text into it;
- To learn some more about Java syntax, in particular about simple *variable declarations*, *conditional statements*, and *loops*.

Our ultimate goal in this chapter is to create a small window which displays the time, updating it every second, so that it looks like a digital watch. We will use our Clock class for this, but most of the additions to the code will be made in the TestClock class that we introduced in Chapter 1.

First, let's see how to display a frame. Create a new file called TestClock2.java and enter the following code[1] in it:

```
1   import java.awt.*;
2
3   public class TestClock2
4   {
5      public static void main(String argv[])
6      {
7         // Declare a Frame object
8         Frame clockFrame = new Frame("Clock");
9         clockFrame.setSize(100, 100);
```

---

[1] This code is the first in the book to rely on the Java version 1.1 or 1.2 libraries. If you attempt to run this program using Java version 1.0.2, it will not compile.

```
10           clockFrame.setVisible(true);
11       }
12   }
```

Compile and run the code in the usual way. If all goes well, you should see a small square window appear. In the title bar of the window should be the word 'Clock' (you may have to make the window wider in order to see the complete title; if so, just resize the window in the normal way for your computer). Let us now examine the code to see how this was done.

Line 1 is an `import` statement similar to those we saw in Chapter 1. This time, though, we are importing something called `java.awt.*`. This is one of the pre-written packages provided with any installation of Java. The Java AWT, or Abstract Windowing Toolkit, contains a great many classes that may be used in the construction of GUIs. Whenever you want to use one of these classes, you must `import` the classes before you can use them. In this program we make use of only one (so far) AWT class: the `Frame`, used on line 8.

Since the AWT contains a lot of classes, and most Java programs that have even a simple graphical interface use a fair number of these classes, the `import` statement provides a shorthand way of importing all the classes in a given package. The `*` symbol in the `import` statement in line 1 means 'include *all* classes in the `java.awt` package'.

Line 8 declares and initializes a `Frame` object called `clockFrame` (since we'll be using it to display the clock), which is basically just a window with a title bar. You can initialize the text that appears in the title bar by including it as an argument to the `Frame()` method, as shown on line 8. (Technically, the `Frame()` method is a *constructor*, but we'll leave that until Chapter 4.)

Having created the `Frame`, lines 9 and 10 set its size and display it on the screen. You can see that this is done by calling the `setSize()` and `setVisible()` methods. Both of these methods are provided as part of the `Frame` class, so you don't need to write them yourself. This is a very common technique in Java programming. It is a good idea to get into the habit of browsing through the Java documentation (which is usually available as part of the Java development package you are using, or on a Web page). You will find a great many classes already written for you, and the documentation will give you a list of all the methods that have been provided for each class. Many of these methods are of the 'set' and 'get' variety that allow you to change or retrieve the values of some of the properties of the object.

In this case, line 9 sets the dimensions of the `Frame` object to 100 by 100 pixels. The first argument to `setSize()` specifies the width of the frame, and the second, the height. Line 10 sets the visibility (which determines whether or not the `Frame` appears on screen) to `true`. In Java, `true` and `false` are reserved words, so you can't use them for object names.

Another thing about this program that is different from the command-line program in Chapter 1 is that, once you start it running, the window it produces remains on screen until you do something to get rid of it. In the program in Chapter 1, once all the statements in the program had been executed, the program stopped

20 CREATING A WINDOW

and the command prompt returned. This time, once the window appears, it stays there, and your command prompt doesn't come back.

When we get to the point where we can write more sophisticated programs, we will include a method whereby you can shut down a frame-based program smoothly, but for now, stop the program by making sure the window into which you typed the 'java TestClock2' command (*not* the window created by the Java program!) is active, and then typing 'Control-C' (hold down the key marked 'Control' or 'Ctrl' and then press the 'C' key once). This method should kill the frame and restore your command prompt in both MS-DOS and UNIX.

Drawing text in a frame

Obviously, an empty frame, even if it does have a title bar, isn't going to hold your interest for long. We need to be able to draw something inside the frame. To do this, we make a few changes and additions to our `TestClock2` class to produce `TestClock3`:

```
1   import java.applet.*;
2   import java.awt.*;
3
4   public class TestClock3 extends Applet
5   {
6     public static void main(String argv[])
7     {
8       Frame clockFrame = new Frame("Clock");
9       TestClock3 testClock = new TestClock3();
10      clockFrame.add("Center", testClock);
11      clockFrame.setSize(100,100);
12      clockFrame.setVisible(true);
13    }
14
15    public void paint(Graphics g)
16    {
17      g.drawString("Hello, world", 25, 25);
18    }
19  }
```

Line 1 imports the `java.applet` package, and line 4 now has the words `extends Applet` added at the end. Since we mentioned earlier that an applet was a Java program that runs in a web browser, you might think we are going to produce such a program here.

In a sense, we are, since `TestClock3` *could* be run in a web browser, but we are still going to run it as an application. The `Frame` object that gets created in the `main()` method essentially mimics the web browser by becoming the window in which the applet will be displayed.

We convert the `TestClock3` class into an applet by adding the `extends Applet` terms at the end of line 4. `extends` is another Java keyword (which we will investigate more fully when we study inheritance in Chapter 4 – for now you can think of `TestClock3` *inheriting* all the properties and methods of the pre-defined `Applet` class, which essentially makes a `TestClock3` object an `Applet` object), and `Applet` is another pre-written class that comes as part of the `java.applet` package (hence the `import` statement on line 1).

Looking at the `main()` method, we see that a `Frame` object is created on line 8, just as in the `TestClock2` class. On line 9, we create a `TestClock3` object named `testClock`. This object becomes the applet that is to be displayed within the `Frame` (or that would be displayed in a web browser if this program were being run as a true applet). The `testClock` object is added to `clockFrame` on line 10 (the `add()` method is another pre-written method belonging to the `Frame` class). The first argument of the `add()` method specifies the orientation of the applet – here we specify that it should be centered in the frame. The second argument is the name of the applet we wish to add to the frame.

After the applet has been added to the frame, we set the size of the frame and display it, just as in `TestClock2`.

However, if you run this program, you will find the message 'Hello, world' written in the frame when it appears on screen. This must obviously have something to do with the `paint()` method on line 15, but how does `paint()` get called, since there is no reference to it in the `main()` method?

The `paint()` method is one of several methods in the `Applet` class that gets called automatically when an applet starts up. The `Applet` class comes with a pre-written version of `paint()` that doesn't actually do anything. Why? By having the automatic call to `paint()` built in to the startup procedure for an applet, Java makes it possible for the programmer to produce a customized version of `paint()` that will draw whatever is desired. If no customized version of `paint()` is found, the default version, which doesn't draw anything, is called instead.

What is really happening is that, when `clockFrame` appears on screen, it displays the applet `testClock` that was added to it on line 10. When the applet is displayed, its `paint()` method is called automatically, which results in the 'Hello, world' text being drawn.

Actually, `paint()` gets called whenever it is necessary to redraw the applet. Try running the `TestClock3` program, then cover up the frame it produces with another window, then uncover it again. Note that the 'Hello, world' text reappears when the frame re-emerges from underneath the other window. This happens not because the computer has 'remembered' what was in the window before it was covered up, but because the `paint()` method is called again when the window needs to be redrawn.

The `paint()` method always begins with the code shown in line 15 – the method takes a single argument which is a `Graphics` object. The `Graphics` class is another class defined in the `java.awt` package. We will study it in more detail in Chapter 8. For now, it is sufficient to remember that all drawing operations must take place using methods from the `Graphics` class.

The `drawString()` method, used in line 17, draws the string passed to it as its first argument ('Hello, world' here) at the horizontal and vertical co-ordinates given by its last two arguments (25 and 25 here).

To make sure you understand how this program works, try changing the dimensions of `clockFrame`, and changing the position at which the text is displayed. What happens if the frame isn't large enough to hold all the text?

Linking the Clock class with an applet

We now have the basic tools needed to link the `Clock` class to an applet, and thus display the time as text drawn within a window. We'll assume in this section that interface methods for setting and getting each of `timeHours`, `timeMinutes`, and `timeSeconds` have all been written – their forms are all identical to the methods given in Chapter 1 for `timeHours`.

The aim in this section is to apply the principles in the preceding sections so that we may produce a program that asks the user for values with which to initialize the hour, minute and second of the clock, and then to display these values in the applet within the frame. In a 'proper' GUI interface, we would place on the applet text boxes into which the user could type the required data, and a button that could be pushed to start the clock going. Since we're not quite up to the stage where we can handle text boxes and push buttons, we will have to content ourselves with entering the data at a command prompt, and then viewing the result in the window.

The code for the new class, named `TestClock4`, is as follows.

```
1   import Clock;
2   import java.applet.*;
3   import java.awt.*;
4   import java.io.*;
5
6   public class TestClock4 extends Applet
7   {
8     private Clock clock;
9
10    public static void main(String argv[])
11    {
12      Frame clockFrame = new Frame("Alarm clock");
13      TestClock4 testClock = new TestClock4();
14      testClock.init();
15      clockFrame.add("Center", testClock);
16      clockFrame.setSize(400,100);
17      clockFrame.setVisible(true);
18    }
19
20    public void paint(Graphics g)
21    {
22      String currentTime;
23
```

```
24        currentTime = clock.getTimeHours() +
25          ":" + clock.getTimeMinutes() +
26          ":" + clock.getTimeSeconds();
27
28        g.drawString(currentTime, 25, 25);
29      }
30
31      int readInt()
32      {
33        int timeData = 0;
34        String timeString;
35
36        BufferedReader readData =
37          new BufferedReader(new InputStreamReader(System.in));
38        try {
39          timeString = readData.readLine();
40          timeData = Integer.parseInt(timeString);
41        } catch (IOException e) {
42          System.out.println("Read error: " + e.toString());
43        }
44        return timeData;
45      }
46
47      public void init()
48      {
49        clock = new Clock();
50
51        System.out.println("Enter initial hour: ");
52        clock.setTimeHours(readInt());
53        System.out.println("Enter initial minute: ");
54        clock.setTimeMinutes(readInt());
55        System.out.println("Enter initial second: ");
56        clock.setTimeSeconds(readInt());
57      }
58    }
```

Compile and run this program to test it out. You should be asked for initial values for the hour, minute, and second in the same window where you typed the command to start the program itself. After entering the initial value for the second, the frame should appear and display the time you entered in the form 12:00:00 (with each pair of numbers separated by a colon).

You may be a bit intimidated by the length of this program, given that it still doesn't do very much. However, most of the new code is required just to read in the initial values for the hour, minute, and second. Unfortunately, although Java is easier to use than many other languages for producing graphics, it isn't as straightforward as it could be for data input.

Since we are using an Clock object this time, we import the class on line 1. In addition to importing the java.applet and java.awt packages, we also import java.io, the I/O (input/output) package, which is needed for reading in data from the command line.

24 CREATING A WINDOW

We declare an `Clock` object on line 8. The `main()` method is almost the same as it was in `TestClock3`, except for an extra call to the `init()` method on line 14. The `init()` method is another of those methods that is automatically called at certain times in an applet's life. In this case, `init()` is called the first time an applet is loaded into a web browser, and should contain any code that is needed to set things up within the applet before it is displayed. Since we are running the applet within a `Frame`, and not from within a web browser, we need to write in the call to `init()` ourselves.

The `init()` method is defined starting on line 47. We initialize the `clock` object on line 49. The remaining code within `init()` deals with reading in the initial values for the hour, minute, and second. A bit of explanation may be needed here, so let's take line 52 as an example.

If you look back at the definition of the `setTimeHours()` method given in Chapter 1, you will see that it expects an `int` to be passed to it as its argument. In this case, that `int` should be a value typed in by the user, rather than the constant value of 12 that we used in Chapter 1. How do we obtain this value?

You will see that the argument passed to `setTimeHours()` on line 52 is itself a call to another method, `readInt()`. The `readInt()` method is defined starting on line 31, and its purpose is to read the data typed in by the user and return it as an `int` value. The fact that the code in `readInt()` looks somewhat frightening is, at the moment, beside the point – what matters is that `readInt()` does in fact return a single `int` value (note on line 31 that its return value type is given as `int`, and that the last statement in the method is a `return` statement, on line 44). It is this value that is passed directly to the `setTimeHours()` method on line 52.

If this process confuses you a bit, we could rewrite line 52 as the following lines of code:

```
int newHour;
newHour = readInt();
clock.setTimeHours(newHour);
```

That is, we create an `int` data object called `newHour`, call the `readInt()` method to read an `int` from the user, and then pass this `int` to `setTimeHours()` as its argument. Rather than go to the trouble of using the intermediate quantity `newHour`, on line 52 we just call `readInt()` and pass the value it returns directly to `setTimeHours()`.

The code within the `readInt()` method itself need not concern you unduly at this stage and is provided only to allow you to read `int`s from the command line (something you won't be doing very often once we get a full GUI up and running anyway). It is therefore acceptable to treat `readInt()` as a 'black box' (a method which works, but you don't need to understand how).

The only remaining change is in the `paint()` method (line 20). On line 22, we create a `String` object (another pre-defined class which holds textual data) called `currentTime`. Lines 24 to 26 construct the text that is to be written into the `Frame`. The three 'get' methods of the `Clock` class are called to retrieve the values of the hour, minute, and second stored in the `clock` object. We can use the + sign to join together separate strings and `int`s to make a longer string, so we join together the hour, minute, and second with a colon between each pair of numbers. Finally, on line 28, we print out the `currentTime` string using the `drawString()` method we encountered back in `TestClock1`.

Applets and web pages

As we mentioned earlier, Java programs come in two forms: applets and applications. An application is a stand-alone program which can be run on any computer that supports Java, whereas an applet can only be run within a web browser (or other specialized program for viewing applets, such as the *appletviewer* program that comes with the JDK).

Since this book is not about designing web pages, we won't consider the implications of running Java applets in any depth. The reader is referred to books on web site design with Java for more information. However, since many readers' motivation for learning Java may be its use in writing applets, we will give a brief description of how to run a Java program as an applet.

All web browsers and applet viewers require an HTML (HyperText Markup Language) file that contains an instruction to load a Java program as an applet. HTML is itself a language that is used for constructing web pages, but a basic web page that will load a Java class file named `TestClock4.class` is as follows. The file should be named something like `TestClock4.html` and should be stored in the same directory as the Java class files.

```
<html>
<body>
<applet code="TestClock4.class" width=300 height=100>
</applet>
</body>
</html>
```

The HTML file can then be loaded into a web browser such as Netscape Communicator or Microsoft Internet Explorer, which will then take over the management of displaying the Java applet within the web page.

The third line defines an *applet tag*, specifies the file from which the code is to be read, and specifies the width and height of the area on the web page that is assigned to the applet. These instructions give the web viewer enough information to mimic the action of the `main()` method in a Java application.

In order for a Java program to run as an applet, the class referred to in the applet tag in the HTML file must extend the `Applet` class (as the `TestClock4` class did on line 6 in the listing above). When a Java program is run as an applet, the `main()` method is ignored. The web browser will begin execution by looking for the `init()` method. After `init()`, it will look for a `start()` method. The `init()` method is run only once, the first time the applet is loaded into the browser. The `start()`

method is run each time the user returns to the page containing the applet in the same browsing session. The `start()` method is optional.

Most of the programs in this book should work equally well as applications or applets. Applets are, however, subject to several security restrictions, so that any actions that would allow the applet direct access to the hard drive of the user's computer (such as saving and loading files) are not allowed. However, any programs that operate entirely autonomously should run as applets.

Simple animation – making the clock tell time

As our final version of the clock program (at least in this chapter!), we will now make the display update itself every second, so that it can be used as a genuine clock. In the process, we will get an introduction to a few aspects of Java syntax, such as conditional statements and loops. This section is slightly cheeky in that we will be using aspects of Java syntax that are new and will not be properly introduced until the next chapter. However, with a little study, it should be possible for you to understand what the code in this section is doing, and it will add some meaning to the in-depth examination of these aspects of syntax when you meet them in Chapter 3.

First, we need to formalize the instructions needed to tell time. Such a formal specification of a problem is known as an *algorithm*. A computer program is, itself, a very formal specification of a set of instructions, since it is sufficiently precise and unambiguous that a computer can follow it without getting lost. The programs we have seen so far are all, therefore, algorithms in the strictest sense. However, the things we were trying to get the computer to do in these programs were all simple enough that we didn't need to think too much about the steps that needed to be followed.

The process of telling time is not a horrendously difficult problem, but it is sufficiently involved that it is worth thinking through the steps before we sit down to write out the Java code.

First, since we are using hours, minutes, and seconds, we want the display to change every second. This means we start by taking the values for hours, minutes and seconds that were input by the user at the startup phase, display that, then add 1 to the number of seconds and display the time again, then add 1 to the number of seconds and display the time again, and so on. We keep adding 1 to the number of seconds until the number of seconds equals 60, at which point we must add 1 to the minutes value and reset the number of seconds to 0. We continue in the same fashion, incrementing the seconds value by 1 until it reaches 60, then adding to the minutes value and resetting the seconds value to 0, until the minutes value itself reaches 60. Then we add 1 to the hours value and reset the minutes value to 0. If we are using a 24-hour clock, we will keep incrementing the hours value until it reaches 24, at which point we will reset it to 0 and start the whole cycle over again (we're not keeping track of days, so that's as far as we have to go).

The preceding paragraph is a rather imprecise statement of the problem in ordinary English, and as it stands, would be fairly difficult to translate directly into computer code. We need some sort of intermediate 'language' that is more precise than English, but not quite as abstract as Java code. Such a language is called *pseudo-code*, and is used in most introductory programming courses to teach the process of translating an algorithm from ordinary English into the final product of a computer program.

Since this book's main purpose is to teach the elements of Java, and is not designed to be a complete course on programming, there isn't enough room here to give a full course on pseudo-code. We can, however, get a good idea of how it works by applying it to the problem of telling time. Consider the following specification of the algorithm:

```
1    While the clock is still running: {
2        Display the current time
3        Add 1 to the seconds value.
4        If seconds >= (greater than or equal to) 60 then: {
5            Add 1 to the minutes value.
6            Reset seconds to 0.
7            If minutes >= 60 then: {
8                Add 1 to the hours value.
9                Reset minutes to 0.
10               If hours >= 24 then: {
11                   Reset hours to 0.
12               } // End of If hours...
13           }   // End of If minutes...
14       }   // End of If seconds...
15       Wait 1 second (of real time!).
16   } // End of while...Go to step 2.
```

This is a pseudo-code algorithm for telling time. It illustrates two central features of computer programming: *conditional expressions* and *loops*.

With the passing of each second, the clock must execute a series of instructions. However, the important point to notice about these instructions is that they are the *same* for each second. Therefore, once we have written out, in full, the instructions that need to be followed to change from the starting time (the time typed in by the user when the program starts) to the time one second later, all we need to do is repeat the same set of instructions to go to the next second, and the second after that, and so on.

Rather than writing out the instructions over and over again, we simply tell the computer to repeat the set of instructions as long as is necessary. This constitutes a *loop*. In pseudo-code, we define a loop with a statement beginning with the word 'while', which should be interpreted as meaning 'as long as some condition is true, carry out the following instructions'.

Here, line 1 says to carry out the instructions that follow 'as long as the clock is still running'. How we interpret that condition when writing the actual computer program is still left open. We might decide to let the clock run forever (or until the program is stopped manually, by typing Control-C, for example), or we might want the clock to run for some specified time and then do something else, such as ring a bell (like a timer that you might use to tell how long to boil an egg). In the latter case, if we wanted to boil the egg for 5 minutes, say, we would make line 1 more precise by stating 'while minutes < 5'.

We enclose within braces (curly brackets { }) the instructions that we wish to be repeated while our condition is true. The opening brace appears at the end of line 1. It turns out that these braces are also required in real Java code, so it's a good idea to get used to using them in the pseudo-code as well. The closing brace that matches this opening brace occurs on line 16 (which we have marked with a Java-style comment), so that all statements from line 2 to line 15 are to be repeated as long as the condition in line 1 is true.

To reinforce the fact that certain statements are contained within a 'while' statement, we *indent* these statements relative to the opening while statement. Note that all the lines from line 2 through to line 15 are indented relative to the lines that enclose them (lines 1 and 16). When we translate the pseudo-code into Java, we will preserve this indentation. Although the Java compiler ignores indentation when it compiles your code, it should be considered essential that you properly indent your code when you write it, in order to make it readable by humans. Proper code indentation will make it much easier for you to spot errors in the logic of your program due to such things as unterminated loops or conditional statements.

The first things that we do inside the 'while loop' are display the current time (line 2) and then increment the seconds value (line 3). After this, we must check the new value of seconds to see if it has reached 60. For that, we need a conditional statement.

A conditional statement is usually represented with an 'if' statement such as line 4. In line 4, we say that 'if seconds >= 60 then' do what follows. Conditional statements use the same conventions as loops to indicate which statements are to be included within the condition: the included statements are enclosed within braces, and should be indented relative to the opening if statement. You can see that line 4 ends with the opening brace for that if statement, and that the matching closing brace occurs on line 14. All statements within these braces are indented relative to line 4.

If the condition tested in line 4 is true (that is, if the value of seconds is >= 60), then we proceed with the statements within the if statement (that is, we carry on with lines 5, 6, etc.). If the condition tested in line 4 is *false*, though, we skip over all the statements within the if statement. That means we skip down to the end of the 'if seconds' block of statements (line 14), and carry on from there. (Lines with only a single brace on them serve only as place markers and don't actually contain any instructions.)

Returning to the case where the condition tested on line 4 is true, we carry out lines 5 and 6 to increment the minutes value and reset the seconds value to 0. Then, we must check the minutes value to see if it has reached 60, so we encounter another if statement on line 7. This statement works just the same way as the first if statement. Line 7 ends with the opening brace that encloses the statements belonging to this if statement, and is matched by the closing brace on line 13. If the value of minutes has not reached 60, statements 8 through 12 are skipped, otherwise they are executed. The final if statement, on line 10, works the same way.

Having specified the algorithm more precisely, we can now proceed to translate it into Java code. To do this, we should consider where (in which class) the code for updating and displaying the time should go. If you refer back to Table 1.1 in Chapter 1, where we listed the properties and actions belonging to the Clock class, one of the actions was an 'update time' action, which we have so far not implemented. We will now define more precisely the effect of this action, which will be coded in Java as an updateTime() method within the Clock class.

Since the process of adding one second to the current time is an action that affects only the internal state of the clock, it makes more sense to have this method as part of the Clock class, rather than part of an external class. However, control over the number of times the time is updated more properly belongs in an external class, since we might want the clock to run forever (as in the pseudo-code example above), or we might want to use the clock as a timer, which stops after a fixed number of seconds has elapsed.

For these reasons, we will therefore write the code for lines 3 through 14 in the pseudo-code above into the updateTime() method, and write the surrounding code (lines 1, 2, 15, 16) in an external method, contained in a variant of the TestClock4 class we considered earlier.

The updateTime() method must therefore be added to the Clock class (we can do this by just inserting the code directly into the class we defined earlier):

```
1    public void updateTime()
2    {
3      timeSeconds++;
4      if (timeSeconds >= 60) {
5        timeSeconds = 0;
6        timeMinutes++;
7        if (timeMinutes >= 60) {
8          timeMinutes = 0;
9          timeHours++;
10         if (timeHours >= 24) {
11           timeHours = 0;
12         }
13       }
14     }
15   }
```

Even though we have not yet formally studied the Java syntax for condition statements or loops, the code in the updateTime() method should be fairly easy to follow.

The translation of the pseudo-code algorithm itself begins on line 3, where 1 is added to timeSeconds. This is done by putting a double plus sign ++ after timeSeconds. As we'll see in the next chapter, this is a special Java syntax that adds 1 to the object to which it is attached. The remainder of the code in this method should be fairly obvious, as it follows the pseudo-code algorithm exactly.

The final class, called `TestClock5`, is similar to `TestClock4`, except for the `main()` method, and the addition of a new method called `tellTime()`, which completes the pseudo-code algorithm by providing the loop to make the clock run indefinitely. We give only these two methods here:

```
1   public static void main(String argv[])
2   {
3      Frame clockFrame = new Frame("Alarm clock");
4      TestClock5 testClock = new TestClock5();
5      testClock.init();
6      clockFrame.add("Center", testClock);
7      clockFrame.setSize(100,100);
8      clockFrame.setVisible(true);
9      testClock.tellTime();
10  }
11
12  void tellTime()
13  {
14     while (true) {
15        clock.updateTime();
16        try {
17           Thread.sleep(1000);
18        } catch (InterruptedException e) {
19        }
20        repaint();
21     }
22  }
```

The only change to `main()` is the addition of line 9, which starts the clock after initializing it and its enclosing frame.

The `tellTime()` method starting on line 12 provides the loop to keep the clock running forever. The condition to be tested by the `while` statement is set to the Java keyword `true`, which is a constant value. The statement essentially reads: 'while true is true...,' which is, of course, always true, so the loop never stops. Once this program starts, the only way it can be shut down is by manual intervention (usually by pressing Control-C).[1] In a more sophisticated program, we would include a button or menu item that would allow the program to be shut down more gracefully, but we need a few more GUI tools to allow us to do that. Lines 16 through 19 are Java's way of making a program wait for one second of real time before continuing. The `sleep()` method (part of the built-in `Thread` class which we will consider in chapter 9) forces the program to wait for an amount of time given in *milliseconds* (thousandths of a second), so we pass it the argument 1000 to get a one-second

---

[1] Usually, the creation of so-called *infinite loops* is considered to be bad programming practice (or just an error in the logic of the program), but in the case of a clock, we actually want it to run forever.

delay. Don't worry about the `try` and `catch` statements here – we will explain those when we consider *exceptions* in Chapter 10.

Note that lines 15 through 20 are indented relative to the opening `while` statement on line 14, indicating that they are the statements that are to be repeated as long as the `while` statement remains active. Also, notice that this block of statements is surrounded by an opening brace (end of line 14) and a closing brace (line 21), just as in the pseudo-code above. As mentioned earlier, although the indentation is not noticed by the Java compiler, the braces *are essential* for the program to compile properly. The indentation should also be considered essential, since it greatly increases the human-readability of the code.

Finally, the `repaint()` method on line 20 does what you might expect: it clears the current drawing area by painting it over with the current background colour, and then calls the `paint()` method again to update the display. The result is a digital watch type of display which changes every second.

Exercises

1. Modify the code in `TestClock3` so that the title bar of the `Frame` contains your name rather than the word 'Clock'.
2. Make the size of the `Frame` in `TestClock3` 200 pixels wide by 50 pixels high.
3. Add a second line of text to `TestClock3` reading 'How are you today?'. The second line should be drawn underneath the 'Hello, world' message.
4. In `TestClock4`, add two `int` variables called `textX` and `textY`, which will be used to specify the location at which `currentTime` is printed by the `paint()` method. Add code to the `init()` method requesting values for `textX` and `textY`, and arrange for `paint()` to use these values to position `currentTime` within the `Frame`.
5. The pseudo-code given in the text assumes that we are using a 24-hour clock. Modify the pseudo-code to use a 12-hour clock with an AM/PM flag. That is, assume that the clock is set up with a specific time and with the `timePM` flag set to either `true` or `false`. The pseudo-code algorithm should then handle how the clock display changes from any initial setting.
6. Modify the code in the text to incorporate the `timePM` flag as specified by your pseudo-code from question 5. You will need to make several changes to the code to do this:
   (a) Add code to the `init()` method requesting the initial value of the flag (you can use `readInt()` to do this if you specify that 0 means AM and 1 means PM – you can then use an `if` statement to test the input value and set `timePM` to `true` or `false` as required).
   (b) Set the flag in the `Clock` object.
   (c) Modify the `updateTime()` method to mirror your pseudo-code algorithm from question 5.

(d) Modify the `paint()` method to add 'AM' or 'PM' after the time. Decide which string to draw by using the `getTimePM()` method to retrieve the current value of the `timePM` flag from the `Clock` object, and then use an `if` statement to test the value and choose the correct string to draw.

7 Write a new Java program to produce a multiplication table. The user should be asked for a single `int`, and the table of the products of that number with every integer from 1 to 12 should be printed within a `Frame` using the `drawString()` method, with each product on a separate line. (The product of two `ints` is found using the * operator, as in `num1 * num2`.)

CHAPTER 3
Java syntax

Introduction

Chapters 1 and 2 have introduced you to the idea of object-oriented programming, and given you an idea of how a very simple graphics application, including a bit of animation, can be written. Except for the last version of the clock program presented in Chapter 2, however, all our programs have relied on simple input and output, with a few calls to pre-defined methods from the Java libraries in between.

As we saw with the final program in Chapter 2, if we want our Java applets and applications to do anything substantial, we need to learn how to write code that can actually do something with the data it is given. We introduced the idea of conditional statements and loops, but we have not yet given you a 'proper' treatment of how to write Java code – the so-called *syntax* of the language.

Just as with a human language like English, computer languages have their own rules of grammar. Unlike English, however, where even grammatically incorrect sentences can usually be understood by a native speaker of the language, making a grammatical error in a computer language means that the program will not be accepted by the compiler. You can think of a compiler as a very strict schoolmaster – any mistakes are very quickly and severely punished.

This chapter is, therefore, a description of many of these strict rules that must be learned in order for you to be able to write Java code that is understandable to both computers and humans. Most of the rules have a basis in logic, and the best way of learning the rules is to understand the logic underlying them, rather than just attempting to memorize them. For this reason, we will consider what actually happens in the computer when each of the syntactical features is used.

Having said this, though, you must realize that there is no substitute for just 'messing around' with your own programs. By all means study the examples given in this book, but you should also think up your own simple problems and try to write Java programs that solve them. Experiment both with the code in this book and your own programs – try a different way of implementing a loop or a conditional statement, try introducing deliberate errors to see what happens, and so on. You can't do the computer any lasting damage by trying this – at worst, the computer may lock up so you need to reboot it.

Primitive data types in Java

No matter how complex a program you write, all information in a computer is ultimately stored as a sequence of *binary data* – a sequence of zeroes and ones. A so-called *higher level* computer language like Java really just provides an easier-to-use interface that allows you to write binary code using terms that are more familiar to you. Java allows you to construct object-oriented structures such as classes and objects, and provides features such as loops and conditional statements, methods, and so on, but all of this is translated into a binary code by the compiler so that the computer can carry out your instructions.

As we've seen in the previous chapters, Java classes are composed of smaller program units such as methods and properties. At the bottom end of the scale, Java provides some built-in data types which can be thought of as *primitive data types*, since they are not composed of any smaller units within the Java language. The property fields of all Java classes must ultimately be built out of these primitive data types.

We have already encountered one of these types: the `int`. In this section, we'll examine all of them. They are shown in the table:

Data type	Contents	Size	Range
boolean	true/false	1 bit	true or false
char	character	16 bits	Unicode character set
byte	signed integer	8 bits	–128 to +127
short	signed integer	16 bits	–32768 to +32767
int	signed integer	32 bits	–2147483648 to +2147483647
long	signed integer	64 bits	–9223372036854775808 to +9223372036854775807
float	floating point	32 bits	$\pm 3.40282347 \times 10^{38}$ to $\pm 1.40239846 \times 10^{-45}$
double	floating point	64 bits	$\pm 1.79769313486231570 \times 10^{308}$ to $\pm 4.9406564581246544 \times 10^{-324}$

The first column of the table shows the Java keyword that is used to refer to that data type. The second column shows the type of data that may be stored in that data type, while the last two columns show the amount of computer memory (in bits) occupied by a single item of data, and the range of values that can be stored.

The individual data types are:

- `boolean`: A `boolean` (named after George Boole, an English mathematician) data type can store only true or false values. Its most common use is as a value to be checked by conditional statements or loop termination conditions, as we'll see later.
- `char`: A single keyboard character can be stored in a `char` data type. The most common format in which character data is stored in a computer is the ASCII code (American Standard Code for Information Interchange). An

ASCII character, however, requires only 8 bits of storage, but the Java `char` is allocated 16 bits. This is because Java was designed to support the new Unicode character encoding standard, which will allow a larger number of characters to be encoded, thus providing support for many different international alphabets, as well as mathematical symbols.
- `byte`, `short`, `int`, `long`: These four data types all store signed (positive or negative) integer data. The only difference between these types is in the number of bits allocated to each type, and therefore in the range of values that each can store.
- `float`, `double`: The final two data types store *floating-point* data. A floating-point value may store numbers with a sign (+ or −), a *mantissa*, and an *exponent*. In a number like $+3.72812 \times 10^6$, the mantissa is 3.72812 and the exponent is 6. (In the computer, of course, the mantissa and exponent are stored in binary, so the number is first converted from base 10 to base 2, which makes the numerical values of the mantissa and exponent different, but the idea is the same.)

Variables, declarations, and scope

In Chapter 1, the distinction between a *class* and an *object* was made. Remember that a class provides the description or blueprint necessary to actually build an object.

In a similar way, the eight primitive data types above are descriptions of how particular types of data are to be stored in the computer. To make use of one of these data types, we need to create an actual instance of it, just as we need to create an *object* to bring a *class* to life. We do this by means of a statement such as line 3 or 4 in the `main()` method of the `TestClock5` class on page 30. Such a statement is called a *declaration*, because we are declaring to the compiler our intention to create an instance of a particular class. For example, line 3 in the `main()` method declares an object named `clockFrame` (and then initializes it by using the `new` keyword, but that isn't technically part of the declaration).

In addition to being an object, `clockFrame` may also be called a *variable*. This is because the object to which it refers need not remain constant throughout the lifetime of the program. In the `main()` method in the `TestClock5` class, we initialize it immediately to be a new object of type `Frame`, but we could reassign it to a different `Frame` object later on if we wanted to. The only constraint is that `clockFrame` can only refer to a `Frame` object, and not to any other data type.

Technically speaking, the primitive data types listed above are not classes (in fact, they are the only data types in Java that aren't), so a specific instance of one of these data types isn't called an object. An instance of a primitive data type may be declared in the same way as that of a class, but is just called a variable. In addition, we may define a *constant* instance of a primitive data type. We have already used several examples of constants in previous Java code. For example, line 7 in the code on page 30 calls the `setSize()` method to set the dimensions of a `Frame` object to the constant values of 100 by 100 pixels: the 100 is an example of a constant instance of an `int`.

In line 14 on page 30, the keyword `true` used as the termination condition of the `while` loop is a `boolean` constant. Constants need not be declared, since their actual value is given explicitly in the code, so the compiler can use that value directly.

We have already used variable declaration when creating the `Clock` class in Chapter 1. If you glance back at page 6, lines 3 and 4 of the `Clock` definition are variable declarations, using the `int` and `boolean` primitive data types. These declarations are within the `Clock` class, but outside any of the methods in that class.

Another example of variable declaration occurred in the `main()` method of the `TestClock5` class, which we defined on page 30. Line 3 in the `main()` method declares a variable called `clockFrame`, which is of data type `Frame`, but this time the variable is declared *within a method*. The `testClock` variable is accessible only within the method in which it is declared.

From the last two examples, it is clear that variables can be declared at various places in a Java program, and that the location of the declaration determines which parts of the program may refer to these variables. The parts of a program which may refer to a given variable are called the *scope* of that variable. It is very important that you understand the concept of scope, since many programming errors are the result of attempting to access variables outside their scope, or of giving a variable a larger scope than it needs. We will now clarify the rules regarding the scope of variables, and state some guidelines that should be used when declaring variables.

First, any variable that is declared within a class, but outside of any method in that class, has *class-wide scope* – it is accessible to all methods within that class. We have seen examples of this with the variables that were defined as property fields in the `Clock` class. We have freely referred to these variables in methods such as `getTimeMinutes()`, `updateTime()`, and so on.

On the other hand, variables such as `clockFrame` and `testClock` as used in the `main()` method on page 30 are declared *inside the method*. Such variables are said to be *local variables* and have only *method-wide scope*. That is, only statements within the method may refer to these variables. A statement in another method that tried to use, say, `clockFrame` in one of its statements would result in a compiler error.

Java allows variables to be declared at almost any place within a program. It is possible to declare variables that are local to only one portion of code within a method, such as within one particular loop. Opinions vary on whether the use of these 'sub-local' variables is good programming practice. It is certainly possible to write most programs using only the two types of declaration that we have seen so far: variables declared as class properties, and variables local to a particular method.

How do you decide which variables should have each type of scope? A general guideline is that only those variables which represent properties of a class, as decided when the class was originally designed, should be given class-wide scope. This is consistent with the principles of object-oriented design: to design a class, you first construct a list of the properties and methods which belong to the class, and then write the code to implement these decisions. All other variables should be declared as local variables within those methods where they are needed.

Variables and memory

What exactly does a variable declaration *do*? Why are declarations needed at all? (In fact, in some computer languages, declarations are *not* required. Merely using a variable for the first time in a statement causes it to be created.)

To understand variable declaration, we need to say a little bit about how the computer's memory is managed when a program is run. When you run your Java program, enough free space in memory must be found to load the instructions to be executed. In addition, free space must also be found to store the data that is to be used by the program. The available free space in a computer's memory is called the *heap*.

The execution of your program (and all other programs running on your computer) is managed by a 'master program' called the *operating system*. It is the responsibility of the operating system to ensure that each program running on the computer gets its fair share of resources (time and memory) in order to run properly. Popular operating systems are programs like UNIX, Linux, MS-DOS, Windows 95, and Windows NT.

The memory in your computer can be thought of as a long sequence of bits (or, more commonly, *bytes*, where 1 byte is 8 bits). Each byte has a numerical *address*, much like the houses along a street have numbers to identify them. You can access a particular memory location (to either read what is stored there, or store something new there) if, and only if, you know its address.

For a program like the `TestClock5` program in Chapter 2, as execution of the program proceeds, the operating system must find enough space in the heap for all the variables you have declared, and it must keep track of which variable has been assigned to which memory location.

For example, suppose you are executing a method that contains the declaration statement:

```
int a, b, c;
```

The operating system will first determine how much space each of these variables requires (since they are `int`s, we see from the table earlier in this chapter that they require 32 bits, or 4 bytes, each), then examine the heap to see if it can find that much free space. If it can, it will reserve three blocks of 4 bytes each, and record the addresses of these three locations in an internal table. When these variables are referred to later in the code (for example, a statement such as `a = 42` stores the `int` constant 42 in the memory allocated to `a`), the operating system looks up the name of the variable in its table, finds out where that variable is stored in memory, and then accesses that memory location to either read the value stored there, or write a new value at that location.

You should now be able to understand how the scope of a variable is implemented in practice. Variables with class-wide scope are created when an instance of the class is created, and remain in existence until the object is destroyed. Variables that are local to a method are created only when that method starts executing, and are destroyed (removed from memory) when that method finishes. It should now be clear why it is illegal for other methods to make reference to variables that are local to a given method – those variables simply don't exist when the method in which they are defined isn't running, so it would be impossible to refer to them.

Operators and operands

Knowing how to create a variable is all well and good, but to actually *do* something with a variable, we need some *operators*.

In a computer language, an operator is a symbol or keyword that has two main properties:

- It *operates* on one or more items of data (which can be constants, variables, or more complex expressions). The data on which an operator operates is called the *operand* or *operands*.
- It *returns* a value after the operation is finished. In this sense, an operator is similar to a non-void method – they both perform some actions or calculations and then return a value.

Although operators in Java come in a wide variety of styles, all of them have the two properties just stated. Recognizing this fact avoids the necessity of having to learn special rules for different types of operators.

There are two other properties of operators that are important to understand: *precedence* and *associativity*. Both of these concepts are actually familiar to you from your school days, although you may not recognize them.

The precedence and associativity of an operator are only used if that operator occurs in an expression with other operators. For example, given that the + and * symbols are the addition and multiplication operators respectively, we could have a compound expression such as 3 + 5 * 8. If you were asked to evaluate this expression, you would give an answer of 43, rather than 64. This is because you were taught years ago that multiplication and division should always be done before addition and subtraction, so you would multiply 5 * 8 *before* adding the 3, thus getting 43. If you had just processed the expression reading from left to right, you would do the addition first, getting 8, then multiply 8 * 8 to get 64.

The rule of doing multiplication before addition can be stated as 'multiplication has a higher *precedence* than addition'. In a Java statement, it is possible to combine most operators in a single expression, so all operators are assigned a precedence, allowing the program to know the order in which they should be applied.

You probably also know the rule that precedence can be overridden by using parentheses. For example, in the above calculation, if we really did want to do the addition first, we can write the expression as (3 + 5) * 8. The same is true in Java – if we want to override the precedence of any operator, we can enclose an expression in parentheses to make sure it is done first.

The *associativity* of an operator applies in a compound statement containing 2 or more occurrences of the *same* operator (or operators with the same precedence). It determines whether the expression is evaluated from left-to-right or right-to-left. For example, in an expression such as 1 + 2 + 3, it is possible to do the calculation in the order (1 + 2) + 3 or 1 + (2 + 3). The former case is left-to-right (the leftmost addition is done first) while the latter is right-to-left.

Operators can be grouped into several main families. The main groups are:

- assignment operators
- arithmetic operators
- logical operators

Arithmetic and logical operators in Java have left-to-right associativity, while assignment operators have right-to-left. There are a few other operators that don't fit naturally into one of these main groups, but we'll consider them as we meet them.

Operators can also be classified according to the number of operands they require. The majority of Java operators require two operands (usually, one on each side of the operator, as in 4 + 8). Such operators are called *binary operators*. The word 'binary' should be interpreted in its original sense as indicating 'two', and not in the sense that binary operators operate on binary numbers.

Less common, but still important, are operators that take only a single operand. These are called *unary operators*. We have seen an example of a unary operator in the updateTime() method we added to the Clock class in Chapter 2: there, we used the ++ operator to increase some of the variables by 1. Since this operator only expects a single operand, it is unary.

A somewhat curious example is the - operator, which can be both binary and unary, depending on its context. As a binary operator, it represents subtraction, as in 10 - 3. As a unary operator, it returns the negative of its operand, as in - 5, which represents the integer 'negative 5'.

Finally, there is a single *ternary operator* in Java, which takes three operands. We will meet this operator when we discuss conditional statements later in this chapter.

Assignment operators

The most common assignment operator in Java is the equals sign =. It is very important to realize that the assignment operator in Java does *not* have the same meaning as an equals sign in an algebraic equation. For example, in algebra, we might encounter the equation:

$$x + 7 = 3 - x$$

which states that 'adding 7 to x is equivalent to subtracting x from 3'. We can go on to solve the equation, discovering that x is -2.

In Java, we might encounter the statements:

```
1   int x, y;
2
3   x = 1;
4   y = 4;
5   x = y;
6   x = x + 2;
```

The first line declares x and y to be int variables. The second statement *assigns* the constant value 1 to the variable x. That is, the value 1 is written into the memory location reserved for the variable x.

The assignment operator works by evaluating the expression on its right and *assigning* the result of this evaluation to the variable on its left. The left operand of the assignment operator isn't even considered until after the right operand has been worked out.

To fully understand the difference between an assignment in Java and an equation in algebra, consider the remaining statements in the Java code snippet above. Line 4 assigns the value 4 to the variable y, so it works the same way as line 3. Line 5 assigns the value of y to the variable x. That is, the operating system encounters the symbol y, looks up the memory location allocated to y, retrieves the value stored there (which will be 4, as assigned in line 4), and then writes that value to the location assigned to the variable x. The value of 1 that was previously stored at the x location is overwritten, and lost.

If lines 3, 4, and 5 had been interpreted as a sequence of algebraic statements, rather than assignment statements, line 5 would simply be false, since x is not equal to y. In Java, however, line 5 is not a *test* for equality (we'll see how to do that when we consider logical operators), it is an *assignment* statement.

Line 6 brings home the distinction even more. As an algebraic statement, line 6 is impossible, since it states that x is equal to x + 2, which has no solution. However, in Java, this statement is perfectly acceptable. It is interpreted by evaluating the right operand of the = operator, to obtain the value 4 + 2 (remember that x was assigned the value 4 on line 4). The sum, 6, is then *assigned* to the left operand of the = operator, that is, to the variable x.

The assignment operator has the lowest precedence of any operator in Java, so it is always the last operation to be performed in any statement. In line 6, for example, we can be sure that the addition will occur before the assignment.

We mentioned above that all operators have operands, and that they all *return* a value. What value is returned by an assignment operator? And, more to the point, why? It would seem that a statement like

```
x = 7;
```

wouldn't need a return value, since once it has performed its operation of assigning 7 to x, its work is done.

In fact, all assignment operators *return the value they assign*. Thus the statement x = 7 returns the value 7. What is this used for? Consider the multiple assignment statement:

```
y = x = 7;
```

Since assignment operators have right-to-left associativity, the right-most assignment (x = 7) is done first. After it finishes, it returns the value 7, so that the statement becomes reduced to:

```
y = 7;
```

which can be performed in the usual way. In other words, the return value of an assignment statement can be used in other expressions.

One more example should illustrate the point:

```
x = 5 + (y = 12);
```

The parentheses force the assignment y = 12 to be done first, thus assigning the value 12 to the variable y. This assignment returns the value 12, which can then be added to 5 giving 17. The final assignment statement then assigns 17 to x. Thus the final effect of this statement is two-fold: 12 is assigned to y, and 17 to x.

Arithmetic operators

Java provides the standard operators +, -, *, and / for addition, subtraction, multiplication, and division, respectively. These operators work the same way as in ordinary arithmetic. To add two constants, for example, we write 7 + 9 in Java (and on paper).

One caution is needed concerning the division operator /. If both its operands are ints, it will always return an int as the quotient. This is not always what you expect. For example, in the code:

```
int a, b;
float c;

a = 4;
b = 8;
c = a / b;
```

we would probably expect c to be assigned the value 0.5. However, we find that c is actually equal to 0. Why? The division of a / b must return an int, since both a and b are ints. If b doesn't divide a evenly, the / operator will simply return the largest integer that is less than or equal to the actual quotient. In this case, the actual quotient is 0.5, and the largest integer less than this is 0.

This example illustrates a more general point. The `int` and `float` (and all the other numerical data types) are distinct data types in Java, and you cannot expect automatic conversion from one to the other. Conversion *will* be done in some cases, but you must understand the rules that are applied.

When using a binary arithmetic operator, the data type of the returned value is always taken to be the more precise of the two operands' types. For example, if b had been declared as a `float` in the above example, the division *would* return a `float` value of 0.5, even though a is an `int`. The 'precision' of a data type is taken to mean the accuracy and range with which it can represent numbers. The `byte` is the least precise, followed by `short`, `int`, `long`, `float`, and `double`. If an expression mixes these data types, the returned value is always the more precise of the two. In a compound expression such as (a / b) + c, remember that operators are always evaluated in some sequence (according to precedence and associativity rules) and the rule of the data type being returned at each stage is applied at each stage. Thus, in (a / b) + c, if a and b are `int`s with values of 4 and 8 respectively, and c is a `float` with a value of 0.5, the value returned by the compound expression would be a `float`, but its value would be 0.5, not 1. This is because the division a / b is a purely `int` operation and will return 0, which is then converted to a `float`, and added to 0.5 to produce the final result.

We have already met the ++ operator in the previous chapter, where we saw that its effect is to increase the value of its operand by 1. There is a corresponding -- operator which *decreases* its operand by 1.

These two operators are both unary operators, but they each have two different forms. If the operator *precedes* its operand (in which case it is called a *prefix* operator), the return value of the operator is the value of the operand *after* applying the operator. If the operator *follows* its operand (in which case it is called a *postfix* operator), the return value of the operator is the value of the operand *before* applying the operator. For example:

```
int a, b;

a = 12;
b = ++a;
```

This code results in b being assigned the value 13 (with a also having the value 13 after the last statement). The ++ operator is used as a *prefix* operator, so the return value is the value of its operand (a) *after* the operator has its effect. On the other hand:

```
int a, b;

a = 12;
b = a--;
```

results in b being assigned the value 12 (and a ending up with the value 11). The -- operator is used as a *postfix* operator (it follows its operand) so its return value is the value of a *before* the operator is applied.

This distinction only matters, of course, if the return value of the ++ or -- operator is actually used. On their own, the two statements

    a++;

and

    ++a;

are equivalent.

There is one more arithmetic operator that is often used: the *modulus* or *remainder* operator, given the symbol % (percent). This is a binary operator that expects two int (or short or long) operands, and returns the remainder when the first operand is divided by the second. For example, 14 % 5 returns 4, since 14 divided by 5 produces a quotient of 2, with a remainder of 4.

Finally, there is a group of operators that combine arithmetic operations with assignments. All five binary arithmetic operators (+ - * / %) have corresponding assignment operators of the form +=, -=, *=, /=, %=. Their effect is best illustrated with an example. The statement:

    a += 7;

is equivalent to:

    a = a + 7;

That is, the += operator adds its right operand to its left operand, and stores the result in its left operand. Its return value is the final value stored in the left operand. So, for a slightly more involved example:

    int a, b, c;

    a = 8;
    b = 9;
    c = (a += 3) * (b -= 7);

In the last line, the following operations are carried out:

- a += 3 adds 3 to a, and returns the value 11.
- b -= 7 subtracts 7 from b, and returns the value 2.
- The * operator multiplies 11 by 2, and assigns 22 to c.
- At the end of the code, a has the value 11, b has the value 2, and c has the value 22.

Logical operators

A logical operator in Java may be binary or unary, but *always produces a boolean result*. That is, the value returned by a logical operator is always `true` or `false`. Logical operators are used pretty well exclusively in conditional statements (`if` statements and the like) and loops.

The logical operators are:

- `<, <=, >, >=` for *less than, less than or equal to, greater than, greater than or equal to*, respectively.
- `==, !=` for *equal to* and *not equal to*, respectively.
- `!` (exclamation mark) for *not*.
- `&&` (two ampersands) for *and*.
- `||` (two vertical bars) for *or*.

If you've studied elementary Boolean logic before, the meanings of these operators will be familiar. If not, read on.

The first group of operators will be the most familiar. The `<` operator, for example, is used to compare two arithmetic expressions, and returns `true` if the left operand is less than the right operand. For example, 6 < 9 is `true`. The expression 9 < 9 is `false`, since 9 is not less than 9, but 9 <= 9 is `true` since 9 is less than or equal to 9.

The equality tests `==` and `!=` are used in a similar way, at least for primitive data types. We'll see when we study the nature of objects in Java a bit more deeply that these two operators often do *not* mean what you expect when applied to complex data types, but with primitive data types, for example, 6 == 9 is `false`, and 6 != 9 is `true`.

Be careful not to get the `==` (logical equality operator) and `=` (assignment operator) confused. The first operator *tests* its two operands to see if they are equal and returns a `boolean` result. The second operator *assigns* its right operand to its left operand and returns the value assigned. In most cases, the compiler will report a confusion of the two operators as an error, since if you use the `=` operator where you intend to use the `==` operator, it will usually return a value of an incorrect data type (that is, not a `boolean` type). However, if by chance the two operands of the `=` operator happen to be `boolean` themselves, the return value will also be `boolean`, and will not produce a syntax error. Running the program, however, will probably not produce what you intended!

Understanding the last three operators (`!` `&&` `||`) requires an understanding of logic. While the comparison operators we've studied in the preceding paragraphs can act on operands of various data types, the last three operators all require `boolean` operands.

The `!` (not) operator is a unary operator and inverts the value of its operand. For example, the expression !(6 < 4), meaning '6 is not smaller than 4', produces `true`, since 6 < 4 is `false`, and the `!` inverts the `false` to `true`.

The `&&` (and) operator is binary, and requires two `boolean` operands. It returns `true` *only* if *both* its operands are also `true`. In ordinary English, you can think of the *and* operation in the sense that it requires both its left operand *and* its right operand to be `true`. That is, the expression (6 > 4) && (9 == 8 + 1) returns `true`. (Strictly speaking, the parentheses aren't necessary, since the precedence of the `&&` operator is the lowest in the expression, but having them there increases readability.) Alternatively, the expression (6 < 4) && (9 == 8 + 1) returns `false`. Even though its second operand is `true`, the first operand is `false`, making the result of the overall `&&` operation `false`.

The `||` (or) operator also requires two `boolean` operands. This time, it returns `true` if either its left operand *or* its right operand (or both) is `true`. The only way for the `||` operator to return `false` is if both its operands are `false`. Replacing the `&&` operator with the `||` operator in the preceding paragraph would produce `true` in both cases.

We can summarize the effects of the binary operators in a *truth table*:

First operand	Second operand	&&	||
true	true	true	true
true	false	false	true
false	true	false	true
false	false	false	false

In the table, the third column gives the result of the `&&` operator when its operands are as stated in the first two columns, and the fourth column gives the results for the `||` operator.

Conditional expressions

We met a conditional expression, in the form of an `if` statement, in the `updateTime()` method in Chapter 2. Here, we will spell out the syntax of the `if` statement and that of the other conditional statements in Java.

The idea behind any form of conditional statement is that the program should make a two-way choice based on the value of some `boolean` variable or expression. That is, if the `boolean` expression is `true`, the program should do one thing, and if it is `false`, it should do another. The two choices are implemented in actual Java code by jumping from the place where the `boolean` expression is tested to one of two locations, depending on the value of the expression.

There are three main types of conditional statement in Java:

- The `if...else` statement;
- The `switch` statement;
- The `? :` operator.

The if...else statement

The if...else statement has two main forms. The first form is a simple if statement, omitting the else:

```
if (boolean expression)
{
   // do statements between braces if expression is true
}
// other statements following closing brace
```

The Boolean expression is evaluated, and if it is true, the statements between the braces are executed, followed by the statements following the closing brace. If the Boolean expression is false, the statements between the braces are skipped, and the program jumps directly to the statements following the closing brace.

The second form begins with an if statement, but adds an else clause after the closing brace:

```
if (boolean expression)
{
   // do statements between braces if expression is true
} else {
   // do statements between braces if expression is false
}
// other statements following closing brace
```

In this case, the Boolean expression is evaluated as before and, if it is true, the statements between the first pair of braces are executed. After these statements are finished, the program jumps to the statements following the closing brace (that is, it skips over the statements between the second pair of braces).

If the Boolean expression is false, the statements between the pair of braces after the else statement are executed, followed by the statements after the closing brace.

In other words, *either* the first block of statements *or* the second block of statements is executed when the program runs, but *not both*.

The final form of the if...else statement is really just an extension of the second form. If we have more than one Boolean expression that we wish to test, we can add another if clause after the else to extend the statement:

```
if (first boolean expression)
{
   // do statements if first expression is true
} else if (second boolean expression) {
   // do statements if second expression is true
} else if (third boolean expression) {
   // do statements if third expression is true
} else {
   // do statements if all expressions are false
```

CONDITIONAL EXPRESSIONS

```
}
// other statements following closing brace
```

Here we are testing three different Boolean expressions in turn. If the first expression is `true`, the first block of statements is executed, and then the program jumps to the statements following the final closing brace. If the first expression is `false`, the second Boolean expression is evaluated. If *it* is `true`, the second block of statements is executed, with the program jumping to the statements after the final closing brace. Similarly for the third Boolean expression. Only if all three expressions are `false` does the program reach the final `else` statement, and thus execute the block of statements between the final pair of braces.

Notice the logical distinction between the statements in the last example and the following block of statements:

```
if (first boolean expression)
{
  // do statements if first expression is true
}
if (second boolean expression) {
  // do statements if second expression is true
}
if (third boolean expression) {
  // do statements if third expression is true
} else {
  // do statements if all expressions are false
}
// other statements following closing brace
```

The only difference between this example and the preceding one is that we have removed the `else`s before the second and third `if`s. In this case, the first Boolean expression is tested as before. If it is `true`, the first block of statements is executed. This time, though, since there is no `else` after this block of statements, the Boolean expression in the second `if` statement is evaluated. If it proves to be `true` as well, the block of statements within the second `if` statement will also be executed. Similarly for the third `if` statement.

The final `else` statement applies only to the third `if` statement: the block of statements it contains will only be executed if the third Boolean expression is `false`.

An example – error handling

As a simple example of the use of the `if...else` statement, we will add some code to the `TestClock5` class from Chapter 2 which allows it to detect incorrect input from the user.

Such error detection is an important part of a good *human – computer interface*. The field of human – computer interaction, or HCI, is concerned with analyzing

48 JAVA SYNTAX

those features of a software package which make it both easy and pleasing for humans to use. Even in relatively simple programs such as those we have studied so far, it is possible to include some aspects that make the program easier to use.

If you go back to TestClock5 and run it again, try entering a value for the hour that is incorrect, such as 37 or -3. You will find that the program happily accepts any such value, and when the clock is displayed on screen, displays an impossible time. Clearly, it would be better if the program could detect such errors when the user inputs them, and ask for correct values instead.

The code that follows is a new version of the program, called TestClock6, that includes these checks. We have added a method called readCheckData() and altered the init() method. All other parts of the code are the same as in TestClock5, so we have not reproduced them here.

```
1    int readCheckData(int min, int max)
2    {
3       int readData;
4
5       do {
6          readData = readInt();
7          if (readData < min) {
8             System.out.println("Please enter a value >= " +
9    min);
10         } else if (readData > max) {
11            System.out.println("Please enter a value <= " +
12   max);
13         }
14      } while (readData < min || readData > max);
15      return readData;
16   }
17
18   public void init()
19   {
20      clock = new Clock();
21
22      System.out.println("Enter initial hour: ");
23      clock.setTimeHours(readCheckData(0, 23));
24      System.out.println("Enter initial minute: ");
25      clock.setTimeMinutes(readCheckData(0, 59));
26      System.out.println("Enter initial second: ");
27      clock.setTimeSeconds(readCheckData(0, 59));
28   }
```

The readCheckData() method accepts two arguments: min and max. The method will read in an int from the keyboard and test that this value is within the range from min to max (both endpoints are included in the range). The method declares a *local* int variable named readData, and uses this variable on line 6 to store the value read by the readInt() method, which we used in TestClock5 to read in an `int` from the keyboard. (Ignore the `do` statement on line 5 for now; we'll get to that in a minute.)

The value of `readData` is tested with an `if` statement on line 7. If `readData` is less than `min`, an error message is printed. On line 9, a similar check is made to see if `readData` is greater than `max`.

By the way, lines 8 and 10 show a use for the + operator that we haven't mentioned yet. The `System.out.println()` method expects a single text string as an argument, but we would like it to print out the string "Please enter a value >= " followed by the current value of `min`. Since this value will change from one call of the method to another, we cannot hard-code the value into the `println()` statement. The + operator has a special meaning in Java when one of its operands is a text string and the other operand is a primitive data type such as `int`. It will convert the non-textual data to a text string, and then join the two strings together, producing a single larger string. If both operands of the + operator are text strings, they are simply joined together.

Now we will consider lines 5 and 12 together. We are anticipating the next section in the chapter by introducing the `do...while` statement here, but its meaning should be clear enough. We want the user to enter a correct value, so we keep asking for it until we get it. This suggests a loop, but of a slightly different form than the loop we used back in `TestClock5` for updating the clock in the `tellTime()` method.

In the `readCheckData()` method, we want to keep asking for an input value until the user enters a correct number. Since we don't know what number the user will enter in advance, we cannot open the loop with a `while(some condition)` statement, since we don't have any condition to test yet. In other words, we want a loop that will run at least once before the condition is tested. This means that we want the test to occur at the end of the loop, rather than at the start. This is what the `do...while` loop allows. The `do` statement on line 5 is just a place-holder to mark the beginning of the loop. All statements between the braces on lines 5 and 12 will be executed at least once, and then the condition specified within the `while` statement on line 12 will be tested. If this condition is `true`, the loop will execute again. If the condition is `false`, the loop ends, and execution continues with line 13.

The condition being tested on line 12 illustrates three of the logical operators introduced earlier in this chapter. The condition can be read in English by translating the symbols into words: "while `readData` is less than `min` or `readData` is greater than `max`". That is, the loop will be repeated until the user enters a value that is >= `min` and <= `max`, as desired.

A common error made by novice programmers when using the || and && operators is to shorten the condition in the second operand. For example, you might be tempted to write line 12 as:

```
while (readData < min || > max);
```

since, in English, it is common to say "while `readData` is less than `min` or greater than `max`".

This is not correct Java syntax. Think of it this way: a logical operator like > requires two operands to compare with each other. Both these operands must always be present whenever the operator is used. In our attempt to shorten line 12, the left operand of the > operator is missing: it can't be the || symbol, since the > operator requires a constant (like 12, 42, or 3902) or a variable (like `readData`) as an operand, not another operator like ||. In fact, the Java compiler makes it quite clear what is wrong, and even points out where the missing term should be. The compiler's error message for the line above is:

```
TestClock6.java:92: Missing term.
    } while (readData < min  ||   > max);
                                ^
```

Finally, the `init()` method is changed to call `readCheckData()` instead of `readInt()` directly. In each case, the acceptable range of values is passed to the method.

The switch statement

The `if...else` statement on its own really provides all the functionality you need to implement conditional statements, but there are two other bits of Java syntax that are often used, simply because they are more convenient in certain cases. The first of these is the `switch` statement.

A `switch` statement is most useful in a situation where one of several options is to be chosen, depending on the value of a single variable or expression. A common example of this is a program which prints a menu of choices and asks the user to select one of them. Different instructions are to be followed depending on the user's choice.

For example, let's alter `TestClock6` so that, instead of asking for the initial hour, minute and second every time the program is run, we print a menu offering the user the five choices:

- Set the hour
- Set the minute
- Set the second
- Start the clock
- Quit the program

The user must enter a number from 1 to 5 to select one of these options. The program will then examine the number, and take the appropriate action. We should also include some code to handle the case where the user enters a number less than 1 or greater than 5.

We could implement the menu easily enough using a chain of `if...else` statements, but the `switch` statement offers a slightly more compact method. In

CONDITIONAL EXPRESSIONS 51

TestClock7, we alter the init() method to include a menu, and illustrate the use of the switch statement.

```
1   void printMenu()
2   {
3      System.out.println("1. Set the hour");
4      System.out.println("2. Set the minute");
5      System.out.println("3. Set the second");
6      System.out.println("4. Start the clock");
7      System.out.println("5. Quit the program");
8      System.out.print("\nEnter your choice: ");
9   }
10
11  public void init()
12  {
13     int choice;
14     clock = new Clock();
15
16     do {
17        printMenu();
18        choice = readCheckData(1, 5);
19        switch (choice) {
20        case 1:
21           System.out.println("Enter initial hour: ");
22           clock.setTimeHours(readCheckData(0, 23));
23           break;
24        case 2:
25           System.out.println("Enter initial minute: ");
26           clock.setTimeMinutes(readCheckData(0, 59));
27           break;
28        case 3:
29           System.out.println("Enter initial second: ");
30           clock.setTimeSeconds(readCheckData(0, 59));
31           break;
32        case 4:
33           return;
34        case 5:
35           System.exit(0);
36        default:
37           System.out.println("Error: should not reach here.");
38        }
39     } while (choice >= 1 && choice <= 3);
40  }
```

We have introduced a new method called printMenu() which just prints out the menu and prompts the user to enter a choice. In line 8, note that the first character printed by the print() method is typed \n: these two characters together (the backslash character \ and the n) comprise the code for a 'newline' character, and will result in a blank line between the line printed by line 7 and the 'Enter your choice:' printed by line 8.

In the new `init()` method, we use another do...while loop to process the menu selections. We want to keep asking for input until the user either starts the clock or stops the program, so the `while` statement on line 39 keeps going as long as `choice` is in the range 1 through 3. Note the logical statement that is used here: translated into English, it says 'while `choice` is greater than or equal to 1 and `choice` is less than or equal to 3'. We use the logical AND operator `&&` here, since we require both its operands to be `true` in order for the loop to continue.

Inside the loop, line 17 prints the menu, and line 18 reads the user's choice. We use the `readCheckData()` method, so we can be sure that `choice` is in the range 1 through 5.

Line 19 begins the `switch` statement. The argument of the `switch` statement (`choice` in this case) is the value that will be used to make the decision as to which part of the `switch` statement to execute. We provide the choices using a series of `case` statements, as on line 20. Line 20 is essentially equivalent to saying 'if `choice == 1`', but is obviously more compact.

Notice the syntax of a `case` statement: the statement itself must end with a colon (*not* a semicolon!), and there are no braces surrounding the block of code contained within that particular `case`. This is because a `case` statement works in a somewhat different way from other statements.

To see what happens, let's suppose the user has entered 1 as the `choice` value, and so wishes to set the initial value of the hour. Line 20 will match the value of `choice`, and the program will continue with line 21. (If the value of `choice` had been something else, the program would skip down to line 24, and test to see if `choice == 2`.) Lines 21 and 22 are executed, then the `break` statement on line 23 is encountered.

A `break` statement causes the program to break out of the enclosing `switch` statement immediately, without checking any more `case` statements. Thus, from line 23, the program will jump to line 38, which contains the closing brace of the `switch` statement.

If the `break` statement on line 23 had been omitted, execution would 'fall through' to line 25 *without the `case` statement on line 24 being considered.* In other words, once a `case` statement has been matched, execution will continue from that point onwards until a `break` statement is reached, or until the end of the `switch` statement is found. So, if we had left out the `break` on line 23, but left in the break on line 27, a `choice` of 1 would result in the user being asked to enter both the hour and minute, but not the second. Omitting a `break` inside a `switch` is a common mistake, and can lead to obscure problems when running the program. (Sometimes, however, you can use this behaviour of the `switch` statement to your advantage.)

Menu option 4 should start the clock running. As we know from earlier versions of this class, the clock will start running as soon as the `init()` method finishes, so we simply `return` from the `init()` method to start things off.

Option 5 must stop the program without starting the clock. The library method `System.exit()` may be used for this purpose. The `exit()` method requires a single `int` argument, which may or may not be used by the operating system on which you are running your Java code. Don't worry about the parameter for now – you can use any value you like, though 0 is traditional.

Finally, we come to line 36. The `default` statement is a catch-all statement, roughly equivalent to an `else` clause at the end of an `if` statement. If the value of `choice` didn't match any of the `case` statements, the code in the `default` section would be executed. In our case, since we guaranteed that `choice` has a value between 1 and 5 by using the `readCheckData()` method on line 18, it should be impossible for the `default` statement ever to be reached, but it is a good idea to put one in anyway. This is because we could have made an error in the `readCheckData()` method so that an erroneous value might have slipped through, or we could have inadvertently left out a `break` statement earlier in the `switch` statement, in which case the execution might fall through to the `default` area. Either way, if we see the text on line 37 printed out, we know something has gone wrong.

The ? : operator

The final technique available in Java for performing conditional operations is the `?:` operator. This is the only *ternary* operator in Java, requiring three operands. The general form of the `?:` operator is:

```
boolean expression ? return if true : return if false
```

That is, the first operand, which appears to the left of the `?` symbol, must be a `boolean` constant, variable, or expression. The value of this operand is calculated first, and if it is `true`, the second operand (between the `?` and the `:`) is evaluated and its return value becomes the return value of the entire `?:` operator. Conversely, if the first operand returns `false`, the third operand (following the `:`) is evaluated and returned.

In other words, the `?:` operator is equivalent to the statements:

```
if (boolean expression)
   do if true;
else
   do if false;
```

As such, it is just a shorthand notation for an `if...else` statement. It is a matter of personal programming style whether you use this operator much, but if you do, it is best to restrict its use to cases where all three operands are fairly short. Otherwise, the code can become hard to read (by humans, that is).

A good example of a case where the `?:` operator is useful is in finding the maximum or minimum of two numbers:

```
int num1, num2, min, max;
```

```
num1 = readInt();
num2 = readInt();
min = num1 < num2 ? num1 : num2;
max = num1 < num2 ? num2 : num1;
```

Here, we read in values for `num1` and `num2` using the `readInt()` introduced earlier. Then, we find the minimum and maximum of these two numbers. The calculation of `min`, for example, evaluates the `boolean` expression `num1 < num2`. If this returns `true`, then `num1` is the smaller of the two numbers, and is returned as the minimum value. Otherwise, `num2` is smaller, and is returned if the `boolean` expression is `false`.

Loops

We've already seen two types of loops (the `while` loop and the `do...while` loop) in examples in this and the previous chapter. In this section, we will spell out the rules for using these loops, and introduce the third form of Java loop: the `for` loop.

The while loop

The syntax for the `while` loop has the form:

```
while (boolean expression is true) {
   do statements between braces
}
```

The Java keyword `while` opens the `while` loop, and must be immediately followed by a Boolean expression (that is, an expression that returns a `boolean` value) inside parentheses. If this expression returns `true`, the statements between the braces will be executed. After the last statement inside the braces, the `boolean` value is calculated again, and if it is still `true`, the statements within the braces will be executed again. This cycle continues until one of two things happens:

- the Boolean expression returns `false`;
- a statement between the braces causes the loop to stop.

In rare instances, as we've seen in the `TestClock` series of classes, an *infinite* loop (one that never ends) is required, but most of the time, the loop should stop after a finite number of iterations. When you are constructing a loop, you should carefully work out what the stopping condition should be, and make sure you have programmed this into your code. If you do write an infinite loop by mistake, it may cause the computer to 'lock up', or, if the loop contains a `print()` or `println()` statement, to print out an endless amount of text. Depending on your operating system, you may be able to stop the program by typing Control-C (as we've done to stop the clock program above), or you may need to take more drastic action, such as rebooting your computer. It is a good idea to make sure you know how infinite loops can be halted before you write a program containing a loop, since no matter how careful you are, you will probably write an infinite loop by mistake at some point.

To see how easy it is to make such a mistake, suppose we try to write a program that prints out the squares of the numbers from 1 to 10, one per line. Our first attempt at writing a Java method to do this might be:

```
void printSquares(int lower, int upper)
{
  int counter;

  counter = lower;
  while (counter <= upper) {
    System.out.println("The square of " + counter + " is "
      + counter * counter);
  }
}
```

The two arguments passed to the method give the lower and upper numbers to be used in the table of squares, so to calculate a table of squares from 1 to 10, we would call the method using the statement printSquares(1, 10). The counter variable serves as a marker to keep track of which number is being squared, and is initialized to lower before it is used in the loop. The while loop continues running as long as counter <= upper, and prints out the square of counter on a separate line for each value.

All of this is fine, except that if you trace through the code, you will find that the value of counter never changes, with the result that you will get an infinite sequence of lines giving the square of lower. To fix this, we need to increment counter by 1 after the println() statement. A revised version is:

```
void printSquares(int lower, int upper)
{
  int counter;

  counter = lower;
  while (counter <= upper) {
    System.out.println("The square of " + counter + " is "
      + counter * counter);
    ++counter;
  }
}
```

Now that counter increases by 1 on each pass through the loop, it will eventually reach the value of upper, after which the loop will stop.

You may wonder what this method would do if the values of lower and upper that were passed to it were logically incorrect, say, by having upper less than lower. The boolean expression in the while loop will handle this case automatically. Since counter is set to lower before the loop starts, if upper were less than lower, the condition counter <= upper would be false the first time the while statement was encountered, and the statement inside the loop would never be executed.

The do...while loop

The while loop always tests its boolean condition *before* executing the loop for the first time. Sometimes, we would like to run through the loop at least once before testing the condition. For example, as we saw in TestClock7 above, when we offer the user a menu, we must print the menu and read the user's choice at least once. If the user's first choice is to start the clock or exit the program, then the loop is never repeated, but if the user decides to set part of the time, we must repeat the menu. In that case, a check at the end of the loop, rather than at the beginning, is preferable.

The syntax of a do...while loop is:

```
do {
    // do statements between braces
} while (boolean expression is true);
```

The do portion of the loop is merely a bookmark: it doesn't perform any calculations. All statements between the braces are executed following the do statement, and then the boolean expression in the while statement is evaluated. If this returns true, the loop is repeated.

As a simple example, we rewrite the printSquares() method above, but this time we ask the user for the number to be squared each time we go through the loop. We will continue printing out squares until the user enters 0.

```
void printSelectedSquares()
{
  int numToSquare;

  do {
    System.out.print("Enter number to square (0 to stop):");
    numToSquare = readInt();
    if (numToSquare != 0) {
      System.out.println("The square of " + numToSquare +
      " is " + numToSquare * numToSquare);
    }
  } while (numToSquare != 0);
}
```

The for loop

You may have noticed that, when using one of the types of loops described above, we often have to *initialize* a variable before starting the loop, and *update* that variable at the end of each iteration. For example, in the (proper) `printSquares()` method, we initialized the `counter` variable to `lower`, the first number that was to be squared, before entering the `while` loop, and updated `counter` by adding 1 to it at the end of each iteration.

Since initializing and updating a loop counter is such a common operation when dealing with loops, Java provides a special loop syntax that allows these two steps to be included as part of the loop statement. This is the `for` loop, whose syntax has the form:

```
for (initialization expression;
     boolean expression;
     update expression)
{
    // do statements as long as 2nd expression is true
}
```

The initialization expression is executed once only, before the loop itself is started. Its return value is not used.

The `boolean` expression is also evaluated before the loop is executed for the first time. If this expression returns `true`, the statements between the braces will be executed. In this respect, the `boolean` expression is just like the expression in a `while` loop: it must be `true` in order for the loop to continue.

Finally, the update expression is only evaluated *after* each iteration of the loop. This means that if the Boolean expression is `false` the first time the `for` statement is encountered, the update expression will never be executed, and the statements between the braces will be skipped.

As a simple example of a `for` loop, we'll rewrite the first `printSquares()` method that printed out a table of squares between a lower and upper limit.

```
void printSquares(int lower, int upper)
{
  int counter;

  for (counter = lower; counter <= upper; ++counter)
  {
    System.out.println("The square of " + counter + " is "
      + counter * counter);
  }
}
```

This method has exactly the same effect as the original version using the `while` loop, but notice how much more compact the code is. The `for` statement begins by setting `counter` to `lower` (the initialization expression). It then tests the `boolean` expression to ensure that `counter` is less than or equal to `upper`. If this is `true`, then the statement between the braces (the `println()` statement) is executed. After that, the update expression is evaluated, which increments `counter` by 1. Then the `boolean` expression is checked again and if it is still `true`, the loop gets done once

58 JAVA SYNTAX

again. Eventually, counter will be incremented as far as upper + 1, at which point the Boolean expression will return false, and the loop will stop.

Exercises

1 Consider the three variables declared as:

        int num1, num2, num3;

   If num1 is set to 6 and num2 is set to 13, find the value of num3 after each of the following statements:

   num3 = num2 / num1;

   num3 = num1 / num2;

   num3 = num1 % num2;

   num3 = num2 % num1;

2 Assuming all variables are ints, answer the following (remember that each operator has a return value in addition to its effects on its operands!):
   (a) What value does othernum have after the statements:

   num = 10;
   othernum = num++;

   (b) What value does num have after the statements:

   num = 10;
   othernum = ++num;

   (c) What value does thirdnum have after the statements:

   num = 10;
   thirdnum = (othernum = --num);

   (d) What value does thirdnum have after the statements:

   num = 10;
   thirdnum = (othernum = --num);
   fourthnum = (thirdnum += othernum++);

   (e) What value does fourthnum have after the statements:

   num = 10;

```
thirdnum = (othernum = --num);
fourthnum = (thirdnum += othernum++);
```

(f) What value does `othernum` have after the statements:

```
num = 10;
thirdnum = (othernum = --num);
fourthnum = (thirdnum += othernum++);
```

3 Assume all variables are `int`s and answer the following:
(a) What is the value of `othernum` after the statements:

```
num1 = 5;
num2 = 15;
othernum = (num1 *= (++num2));
othernum /= (num2 -= 10);
```

(b) What is the value of `othernum` after the statements:

```
num1 = 5;
num2 = 15;
othernum = (num1 *= num2++);
othernum /= (num2 -= 10);
```

(c) What is the value of `othernum` after the statements:

```
num1 = 5;
num2 = 15;
othernum = (num1 *= num2++);
othernum %= (num2 %= 10);
```

4 After the statements:

```
num1 = 10;
num2 = 20;
if(num2 > num1 && !num1)
   num3 = num1 + num2;
else if (!(num2 - 2*num1))
   num3 = num1 - num2;
```

what is the value of `num3`?

5 What is the value of `num3` after the following statements?

```
num1 = 10;
num2 = 20;
num3 = 0;
if(num2 = num1)
   num3 = num1 + num2;
```

60 JAVA SYNTAX

6 After the statements:

```
num1 = 10;
num2 = 20;
num3 = 0;
if((num2 = 3*num1) < 0)
    num3 = num1 + num2;
```

what is the value of num2?

7 After the statements:

```
num1 = 10;
num2 = 20;
num3 = 0;
if((num2 = 3*num1) < 0)
    num3 = num1 + num2;
```

what is the value of num3?

8 After the statements:

```
num1 = 10;
num2 = 20;
num3 = 0;
if(num1 == num2 && num1 = num2)
    num3 = num1 + num2;
```

what is the value of num1?

9 After the statements:

```
num1 = 10;
num2 = 20;
num3 = 0;
if(num1 = num2 && num1 == num2)
    num3 = num1 + num2;
```

what are the values of num1 and num3?

10 After the statements:

```
num1 = 10;
num2 = 20;
num3 = 0;
if(num1 == num2 || num1 = num2)
    num3 = num1 + num2;
```

what are the values of num1 and num3?

11 Assume that num1 has been given a value before this code is run. Trace through the code and answer the question at the end.

```
    num2 = 20;
    num3 = 30;
    switch(num1) {
    case 1:
      num3 = num1 + num2;
      break;
    case 2:
      num3 = num1 + 2*num2;
    case 3:
      num2 -= num1;
      num3 = num1 + 4*num2;
    case 4:
      num2 += num3;
      num3 = num1 + 5*num2;
      break;
    default:
      num3 = 0;
      break;
    }
```

Find the values of num2 and num3 if num1 is (a) 1; (b) 2; (c) 4; (d) 5.

12 Consider the statements:

```
    num2 = 20;
    num3 = (2*num1 == num2) ? num1 + num2 : num1 - num2;
```

What is the value of num3 if num1 is (a) 10; (b) 60?

13 Consider the nested conditional operator statement:

```
    num1 = (num2 >= num3+num4) ?
    (num3 > num4 ? num4 : num3)
    : (num2 > 2*num3+num4 ? num2 : 2*num2);
```

(a) What value is num1 if num2, num3, and num4 are all set to 1?
(b) What value is num1 if num2 is 1, num3 is -1, and num4 is 2?
(c) What value is num1 if num2 is -2, num3 is -2, and num4 is 1?

14 Consider the following loop:

```
    int num1 = 2;
    int result = 0;
    while(num1 <= 10) {
      result += num1;
      num1 += 2;
    }
```

What are the values of result and num1 after the loop finishes?

15 The following loop is proposed to provide a shorter version of the loop in the previous question (the line numbers are used in the questions which follow; they are not part of the code):

62 JAVA SYNTAX

```
1. int num1 = 2;
2. int result = 0;
3. while (num1 <= 10)
4.    result += (num1 += 2);
```

(a) What are the values of `result` and `num1` after the loop finishes?
(b) Which of the following changes to this code would give the same value for `result` as in question 14?
  (i) Replace line 1 with `int num1 = 0;`
  (ii) Replace line 2 with `int result = 2;`
  (iii) Replace line 3 with `while (num1 < 10)`
  (iv) (i) and (iii) together.

16 Another form for this loop is as follows:

```
1. int num1 = 0;
2. int result = 0;
3. do {
4.    result += num1;
5.    num1 += 2;
6. } while (num1 <= 10);
```

(a) What are the values of `result` and `num1` after the loop finishes?
(b) How many iterations of the loop are done?
(c) Which of the following changes will allow the number of loop iterations to be reduced while retaining the same final values for `result` and `num1`?
  (i) Replace line 1 with `int num1 = 2;`
  (ii) Replace line 2 with `int result = 2;`
  (iii) Replace line 4 with `result += (num1 += 2);` and delete line 5.
  (iv) Replace line 6 with `while (num1 < 10);`

17 Consider the following loop:

```
int num1, result;
result = 1;
for (num1 = 1; num1 < 6; num1++)
   result *= num1;
```

What values do `result` and `num1` have when the loop finishes?

18 Consider the code fragment:

```
num1 = 10;
for (sum = 0; num1 != 0 && sum/num1 >= 0; --num1)
   sum += num1;
```

(a) What are the values of `sum` and `num1` when the loop finishes?
(b) If the termination condition in the `for` loop is changed to:

```
sum/num1 >= 0 && num1 != 0
```

which of the following is true?
(i) The values of sum and num1 after the loop finishes are unchanged.
(ii) One extra iteration of the loop will occur.
(iii) The loop becomes an infinite loop.
(iv) A runtime error due to division by zero will occur.

19 Consider the nested loops:

```
int num1, num2, sum = 0;
for (num1 = 1; num1 < 6; num1++) {
  for(num2 = 1; num2 <= num1; num2 += 2) {
    sum += num1 + num2;
  }
}
```

In this nested loop, the outer loop sets the value of num1 to 1, then the inner loop iterates over values of num2 from 1 to num1, adding 2 to num2 at each stage. When this inner loop finishes, control passes back to the outer loop, where num1 is incremented to 2. The inner loop is run again, and so on.
(a) What are the values of sum, num1, and num2 after the statements finish?
(b) How many times is the statement sum += num1 + num2 executed?

CHAPTER 4

Constructors, inheritance, and interfaces

Pointers

Recall from our discussion in the preceding chapter (see page 37) that a variable declaration causes the operating system to find and reserve enough free memory for a variable of a given data type. For primitive data types such as `int` and `float`, the name of the variable is stored, together with the address (location in memory) of the reserved memory, in a special table so that, when reference is made to that variable later in the program, it can be found in the computer's memory.

You may also have noticed a subtle distinction between the declaration of a variable of a primitive data type and of an object variable, which is declared as a specific instance of a class. A primitive variable can be declared and then used immediately, as in the statements:

```
int number;
number = 42;
```

An object, on the other hand, must be declared *and initialized* before it can be used:

```
Clock clockObject;
clockObject = new Clock();
clockObject.setTimeHours(12);
```

The middle statement, using the `new` keyword, is essential. If it is omitted, you will get a compiler error stating that '`clockObject` may not have been initialized'. (The first two statements can be combined into the single statement `Clock clockObject = new Clock();`.)

This may seem odd to you. Why do you need only a single declaration to create a primitive variable, but a declaration *and* an initialization to create an object? After all, the steps involved in creating an object should be pretty much the same as those for creating a primitive variable: you need to reserve enough memory for all the class variables (such as `timeHours`, and so on) that are needed by the object, and store the addresses of these variables, together with the object name, in a table so they can be found later.

This *is* more or less what happens, but it happens in two steps. Since a class can contain a large number of class variables (and other information), it is more efficient to store all this information together in a single block of memory, in such a way that the internal structure of the information is the same for each instance of the class. For example, the Clock class (page 6) contains three int variables and a boolean variable. In any given instance of Clock, the four variables would always be stored in the same order. That way, if we know the address of the beginning of the memory block in which a Clock object is stored, we can find each variable by adding an offset to this address. For example, if timeHours is always stored first, it will be found at the start address of the memory block. If timeMinutes is stored next, it will be found at an offset of 4 bytes from the start, since the first variable (an int) takes up 4 bytes. The rest of the variables can all be found in the same way.

Therefore, when we declare a variable such as clockObject above, all we really need to store in it is the address of the start of the memory block where the full object is stored. The clockObject variable itself can then be thought of as a *pointer* to an actual Clock object. This is, in fact, what the declaration

```
Clock clockObject;
```

really does. It does *not* actually create a full Clock object; it just declares a place in which the *address* of a Clock object can be stored. The actual object hasn't been created yet.

The second statement:

```
clockObject = new Clock();
```

is where the creation of the Clock object takes place. The Java keyword new is actually an operator, whose effect is to allocate space for a new object. It is a unary operator, requiring only a single argument which tells it the name of the class of which the new object is an instance. (Actually, the argument is a *constructor* for the class, but more on that in the next section.) The return value of the new operator is the memory address of the beginning of the block of memory that was reserved. Thus the statement clockObject = new Clock() reserves space for a new Clock object, and assigns the address of this space to the clockObject pointer variable.

The new operator performs what is known as *dynamic memory allocation*. The term 'dynamic' means that the new operator allocates memory *while the program is running*, and not statically when the program is compiled.

In summary, the creation of an object is a two-stage process:

- A *pointer* to the correct data type is declared.
- The new operator is used to allocate space for the new object, and the address of this space is stored in the pointer variable.

It is possible that the new operation might fail, if there is not enough free memory available. In this case, the new operator returns the special value null (effectively, zero). All pointer variables are automatically initialized to null when they are declared, so the declaration Clock clock declares a pointer to a Clock object, and sets its value to null to indicate that an actual Clock object has not yet been assigned to it.

Constructors

As we saw in the last section, an object must be initialized before it can be used. At a minimum, the initialization process must allocate enough memory for the object. Often, we also wish to assign initial values to some of the class variables. In the Clock objects we have used in the TestClock series of programs, we initialize the values of timeHours, timeMinutes and timeSeconds before starting the clock. Up until now, we have asked the user to provide this information, but it would be convenient to have a default value provided automatically (rather like the flashing 12:00 you see on video recorders until their time is set).

We could assign initial values for hours, minutes, and seconds by making explicit calls to the setTimeHours() and related methods, but there is an easier and more compact way: use a *constructor*.

A constructor is a special method which is called automatically whenever an object is created using the new operator. A constructor is written just like any other method in a class, but with a few extra rules:

- The name of a constructor is always the same as the name of the class in which it is defined. Thus the constructor for the Clock class must be named Clock().
- A constructor *never* has a return type specified (not even void), and can therefore neither return a value, nor contain a return statement.

Constructors may contain an argument list, or they may take no arguments. If no constructor is written for a class, the compiler provides a default constructor which takes no arguments, and does nothing. The reason this is done is that whenever an object is created with the new operator, a constructor *must* be called, so if the programmer doesn't provide one, the compiler must step in and provide a default version. This explains how we got away without writing a constructor for the Clock class, but still managed to create a Clock object with the new Clock() operation.

As an example of a constructor, let us provide one for the Clock class that initializes the time to 12 hours, 0 minutes and 0 seconds. The following code can be inserted into the Clock class from Chapter 3, immediately after the variable declarations (after line 4 in the code on page 6, for example):

```
Clock()
{
```

```
    timeHours = 12;
    timeMinutes = timeSeconds = 0;
}
```

This constructor takes no arguments, and initializes the variables as required. When a `Clock` object is created with a statement such as:

```
Clock clockObject = new Clock();
```

this constructor will be called and the variables will be initialized automatically.

If we would like a bit more flexibility, we can write a second constructor which takes arguments, allowing the programmer to specify initial values for the hours, minutes, and seconds:

```
    Clock(int newTimeHours, int newTimeMinutes,
        int newTimeSeconds)
    {
      timeHours = newTimeHours;
      timeMinutes = newTimeMinutes;
      timeSeconds = newTimeSeconds;
    }
```

We can now create a second `Clock` object, and preset the time to, say, 10:30:45, as follows:

```
Clock presetClock = new Clock(10, 30, 45);
```

Both these constructors can be included in the same `Clock` class at the same time. You can have as many constructors in a single class as you like, provided that their argument lists are all different (since the only way the compiler can tell which constructor you want to call is by comparing argument lists).

Value and reference

We have seen in this chapter that Java treats primitive variables and objects in a fundamentally different way. Primitive variables are always created by a simple declaration, and may be used (read from and written to) immediately after declaration. Objects, on the other hand, are always created in two steps. First, a pointer to the object is declared, and then the `new` operator is used to allocate memory for that pointer to point to.

This distinction between primitive variables and objects manifests itself in another way as well. We have seen several examples of methods with argument lists, which allow values to be passed to the method for its internal use. So far, we have only passed primitive variables to methods, and have not tried to alter these variables within the method. We shall now examine what happens when we pass

68 CONSTRUCTORS, INHERITANCE, AND INTERFACES

objects as arguments to methods, and what happens when we try to change the value of either type of argument within the method.

First, consider a simple method that takes a primitive argument:

```
void passByValue(int primitive)
{
  System.out.println("value at start: " + primitive);
  primitive++;
  System.out.println("value at end: " + primitive);
}
```

This method is called by the following code:

```
int testValue = 1;

passByValue(testValue);
System.out.println("testValue after call: " + testValue);
```

Before reading on, try to predict what will be printed by the three `println()` statements.

Clearly, `testValue` starts out with the value 1, which is what is passed to `passByValue()`, so the first `println()` statement within the method prints out:

```
value at start: 1
```

Then, `primitive` is increased by 1 by the `primitive++` statement, so the second `println()` statement prints:

```
value at end: 2
```

So far, so good. But what does the final `println()` statement produce? You might guess that `testValue` will be 2 after the call to `passByValue()`, but in fact it is still 1. Why?

When a primitive variable such as `testValue` is passed to a method, the method makes its own local copy of this variable. In other words, the argument of `passByValue()` is treated as a declaration (`int primitive`), a variable named `primitive` is created, and space is allocated for it in memory. The variable is initialized to whatever value is passed to the method when that method is called. From that point on, *all operations on that variable are applied only to the local copy within the method.* The original variable, `testValue`, remains unaltered because it is in a physically different area of memory, and is, in fact, a totally different variable.

It is for this reason that passing `testValue` to the `passByValue()` method does not change its value. The value of `testValue`, that is, 1, is assigned to the newly created variable `primitive` within the method, and all operations on `primitive` within `passByValue()` are independent of the original `testValue` variable.

This technique of passing variables to a method is called *passing by value* (hence the name of the method `passByValue()`). In Java, *all* primitive data types are *always* passed by value, so it is impossible to alter a primitive variable by passing it to a method.

The situation is a bit different when you pass an object as an argument to a method. Consider the following method:

```
void passByReference(Clock passClock)
{
   int hour = passClock.getTimeHours();
   passClock.setTimeHours(hour + 1);
}
```

This method is now called by the code:

```
Clock testClock = new Clock();
testClock.setTimeHours(12);
passByReference(testClock);
System.out.println("Final hour value: +
   testClock.getTimeHours());
```

This code declares and initializes a `Clock` object named `testClock` in the first line. It then sets the hour to 12, and calls `passByReference()`, passing `testClock` as an argument to the method.

Within the method, the current hour value is retrieved from `passClock` and stored in a local `int` variable named `hour`. The hour value of `passClock` is then set to `hour + 1`.

Back in the second code fragment, the hour value of `testClock` is retrieved and printed out. What value will it show, 12 or 13? In this case, the changes made within the `passByReference()` method stick, and the value displayed is 13.

Although this behaviour may seem different to that for the `passByValue()` method above, if we analyze what's going on a bit more deeply, we see that it is actually the same thing in both cases. How can that be?

Recall that, when an object is declared, it is actually a *pointer* to the object that is being created, and not the object itself. It is only when the object is created using the `new` operator that a value is assigned to the pointer. In the statement:

```
Clock testClock = new Clock();
```

the `new` operator allocates some memory for a `Clock` object and stores the *address* of that object in the `testClock` variable. When `testClock` is passed to the `passByReference()` method, a copy of the *pointer* is made to the method's `passClock` variable. As with the `passByValue()` method, `passClock` and `testClock` are independent variables, both of which contain the same value. The difference here is that, this time, these variables contain a *pointer* to a location in memory, rather than an actual data value. The net effect is that, although passClock and testClock are separate variables, they both point to the same area in memory. That area is where the Clock object that was created by the new operator is stored.

We can now understand why changes to passClock within passByReference() remain after the method finishes. The statement

```
passClock.setTimeHours(hour + 1);
```

assigns the value hour + 1 to the timeHours variable in the Clock object pointed to by passClock. This Clock object is the *same* object as that pointed to by testClock, so the effect is to change the timeHours value of testClock as well.

The technique of passing a pointer to a variable, rather than passing a copy of the variable itself, is called *passing by reference*.

To drive home the difference, consider the final example below:

```
void makeNewClock(Clock passClock)
{
   int hour = passClock.getTimeHours();

   passClock = new Clock();
   passClock.setTimeHours(hour + 1);
}
```

This method is now called by the code:

```
Clock testClock = new Clock();
testClock.setTimeHours(12);
makeNewClock(testClock);
System.out.println("Final hour value: +
   testClock.getTimeHours());
```

The only difference between this example and the preceding one is that we have inserted the statement

```
passClock = new Clock();
```

in the makeNewClock() method. This statement allocates memory for a new Clock object (different from the one assigned to testClock), and then assigns its memory address to passClock. The timeHours value of this *new* object is then set to hour + 1. Since this new object is not the one to which testClock is a pointer, its timeHours value is left unchanged, and the final println() statement prints out a value of 12 for the hour, not 13.

Automatic garbage collection

In the past few sections, we've seen that memory for a new object can be dynamically allocated using the new operator. Is there any way this memory can be *deallocated*, that is, released from the control of the program so that it can be reused later?

The answer is that Java, unlike most other computer languages that allow dynamic memory allocation, takes care of this deallocation automatically, so the programmer doesn't have to worry about it. Java keeps track of the number of pointers that point to a particular block of memory that was allocated using new, and when the block of memory no longer has any pointers that point to it, it is deallocated. This process is called *automatic garbage collection*.

For example, consider the following code:

```
Clock myClock = new Clock();
myClock.setTimeHours(12);
myClock = new Clock();
myClock.setTimeMinutes(10);
```

The first line declares a Clock pointer called myClock, allocates some memory for a new Clock object, and assigns the memory location to myClock. The next line sets the timeHours variable to 12. The line after that creates *another* Clock object with the new operator, and assigns the address to myClock. At this point, myClock no longer points to the first block of memory that was allocated on the first line. Java will notice this (possibly not immediately, but soon) and deallocate the memory from the first new operation.

As a slightly more complicated example, glance back at the last example in the preceding section. A Clock object called testClock is allocated and passed to the makeNewClock() method, where passClock gets a copy of this address. Just after makeNewClock() starts, the block of memory has *two* pointers pointing to it (the original testClock and the passClock pointer inside makeNewClock()).

Within makeNewClock(), the passClock pointer gets reassigned to a new block of memory. The original block of memory, however, still has testClock pointing to it, so it is not deallocated. When makeNewClock() finishes, the passClock variable is deleted from memory, so the memory that it pointed to when the method finished now has no pointers pointing to it, so it is deallocated.

Inheritance

Up to now, we have concentrated on developing a series of classes that represent a digital clock. We've added a few graphical enhancements along the way, but the basic object that results from any of these classes is still just a simple digital clock that displays the time to the nearest second.

Suppose we now want to design a class that represents a particular type of clock, such as an alarm clock, or a clock that also displays the day of the week and the date of the month, or a clock that contains a stopwatch. All of these clocks are variants of the basic digital clock we've designed above, in that they all tell the time of day.

Each specialized clock adds in one or two extra features not present in the basic model.

We could design classes for each of these specialized clocks in the same way as for the basic `Clock` class above: list the properties and actions we want the class to have, and translate these into variables and methods in a Java class. However, one of the main features of any object-oriented language is the ability for a new class to *inherit* the variables and methods of another class. In that way, we avoid having to write out all these variables and methods again.

Let us consider a specific example to see how inheritance works in Java. Suppose we wish to extend the `Clock` class so that it represents an alarm clock. The alarm clock should tell time in the same way as the original `Clock` class (by means of a digital display), but should also allow the user to set a time for the alarm to go off. A real alarm clock would also allow the alarm to be enabled or disabled, and would allow the alarm time to be changed while the clock is running. These features require that we interact with the Java program while an animation is running, which is something we aren't able to do yet. (Once an animation starts, it takes control of the whole application, unless we use a separate *thread* for the animation, but more on that in Chapter 9).

When the clock's time reaches the time at which the alarm is set to go off, we need to decide what the clock will do. A real alarm clock, of course, makes an annoying sound to wake you up. It is possible to play sounds in Java, but in the current version of the language, audio is supported only if the program is run as an *applet* (within a web page), and not as an *application* (a stand-alone program). We will therefore content ourselves with a change in the appearance of the display (for example, a change in the colour of the text) when the alarm goes off.

We need to decide in which classes these new features should be placed. In our `TestClock` series of classes above, we divided the work so that the `Clock` class kept track of the time, and the class in which a `Clock` object was declared extracted the values for the hour, minute, and second from the `Clock` object, and handled the display of these values on the screen. We will maintain that division with the `AlarmClock` class, so we will place the values for the hour, minute, and second at which the alarm is due to go off in this class, and leave the display of the alarm itself to another class which declares an `AlarmClock` object. This is not the only way in which the classes could be designed. We could also justify placing both the data for the clock and its display in the same class.

The code for the `AlarmClock` class looks like this:

```
1   import Clock;
2
3   public class AlarmClock extends Clock
4   {
5      private int alarmHours, alarmMinutes, alarmSeconds;
6      private boolean alarmTriggered;
7
8      AlarmClock()
9      {
```

```
10        alarmHours = 12;
11        alarmMinutes = 0;
12        alarmSeconds = 15;
13        alarmTriggered = false;
14      }
15
16      AlarmClock(int newAlarmHours, int newAlarmMinutes,
17         int newAlarmSeconds)
18      {
19        alarmHours = newAlarmHours;
20        alarmMinutes = newAlarmMinutes;
21        alarmSeconds = newAlarmSeconds;
22        alarmTriggered = false;
23      }
24
25      public void setAlarmHours(int newAlarmHours)
26      {
27        alarmHours = newAlarmHours;
28      }
29
30      public int getAlarmHours()
31      {
32        return alarmHours;
33      }
34
35      // Other 'set' and 'get' methods
36
37      public boolean isAlarmTriggered()
38      {
39        return alarmTriggered;
40      }
41      public void updateTime()
42      {
43        super.updateTime();
44        if (alarmHours == timeHours &&
45           alarmMinutes == timeMinutes &&
46           alarmSeconds == timeSeconds)
47        {
48          alarmTriggered = true;
49        }
50      }
51    }
```

Much of this code should be familiar from the Clock class, so we will highlight the new features relating to the use of inheritance.

On line 1, we import the definition of the Clock class, since we are about to inherit it in the new AlarmClock class. The class that is inherited by the new class is called the *base class*, while the class that does the inheriting is called the *derived class*.

74 CONSTRUCTORS, INHERITANCE, AND INTERFACES

Actually, we need to make a small change in the `Clock` class first. The first few lines of this class must be changed to:

```
public class Clock
{
   int timeHours, timeMinutes, timeSeconds;
```

Notice that we have removed the keyword `private` from the beginning of the declarations of the time values. Recall from Chapter 1 that the `private` keyword allows the variable or method to which it is attached to be accessed only by methods within the same class. If we had left the `private` keyword attached to the variable declarations in the `Clock` class, they would not be accessible to any methods in the class which inherits it.

Regrettably, this means that any other class can, in theory, access these variables as well. Java does not, at present, support a special keyword which allows a variable to be accessed only by its own class or any class that inherits this class. Other object-oriented languages, such as C++, *do* provide such a keyword (usually `protected`), but the `protected` keyword in Java means something quite different. However, whenever you use a `Clock` or `AlarmClock` object in an external class, if you are careful to use interface methods (such as `getTimeHours()` and `setTimeHours()`) to refer to class variables, no difficulty should arise.

Since one of the main advantages of inheritance is the provision of classes which may be used as base classes for other specialized classes, it is common practice to omit the `private` keyword from class variables. When a class is originally designed, it is not always possible to predict whether that class will be used as a base class at some future time. If we hard-coded all the variables to be `private`, we would need to modify the class before other classes could be derived from it. For this reason, the `private` keyword is not used as often in Java as a strict object-oriented approach would dictate. We shall omit it from most of the variable declarations in the rest of the book, although it should be kept in mind that access to class variables should still only be allowed through proper interface methods.

We will discuss the meanings of `public`, `private`, and `protected` more fully when we consider the Java package concept later in this chapter.

Returning to the code for the `AlarmClock` class, we see that line 3 defines this class, and says that it `extends Clock`. The Java keyword `extends` means that the `AlarmClock` class inherits the `Clock` class, so that all non-private variables and methods in that class are accessible to the `AlarmClock` class as well. We will see in a minute just what this statement means in practice.

Lines 5 and 6 declare some new variables for the `AlarmClock` class, but since `AlarmClock` inherits the `Clock` class, an `AlarmClock` object also has variables called `timeHours`, `timeMinutes`, and `timeSeconds`, and may use these variables as if they had been declared within the `AlarmClock` class definition.

The `boolean` variable `alarmTriggered` is set to `true` when the clock time reaches the alarm time. An external class in which an `AlarmClock` object is created can refer to this value to tell whether it should display an alarm or not.

Lines 8 through 14 define the first constructor for the `AlarmClock` class, within which the variables declared on lines 5 and 6 are initialized. However, the `Clock` constructor (the one without arguments) is *automatically* called by this constructor before the first statement in the `AlarmClock` constructor. To refresh your memory, that constructor was as follows:

```
Clock()
{
  timeHours = 12;
  timeMinutes = timeSeconds = 0;
}
```

This means that the three variables inherited from the `Clock` class are initialized before the `AlarmClock` variables.

Recall that we also defined a second constructor in the `Clock` class that accepted three arguments to allow the hour, minute, and second to be initialized to user-specified values:

```
Clock(int newTimeHours, int newTimeMinutes,
   int newTimeSeconds)
{
  timeHours = newTimeHours;
  timeMinutes = newTimeMinutes;
  timeSeconds = newTimeSeconds;
}
```

We can call this constructor explicitly from within an `AlarmClock` constructor by using the `super()` method. For example, if we wanted to initialize the clock to the time 13:14:15, we could define the `AlarmClock` constructor as follows:

```
AlarmClock()
{
  super(13, 14, 15);
  alarmHours = 12;
  alarmMinutes = 0;
  alarmSeconds = 15;
  alarmTriggered = false;
}
```

The `super()` method call is built-in Java syntax which always refers to the constructor of the class immediately above the current class in the inheritance hierarchy. A call to `super()` must be the *first* line of code in the derived class constructor.

Lines 16 through 23 define a second constructor for `AlarmClock`, this time allowing the user to specify the values for the hour, minute, and second at which the alarm is set. Note that this constructor still calls the argumentless constructor from `Clock`, since no explicit call to `super()` is made. If we wanted a constructor that allowed *both* the clock time and the alarm time to be set to arbitrary values, we would need a constructor with six arguments.

Lines 25 through 35 define the standard 'set' and 'get' methods for accessing the three alarm time variables (not all of these methods are shown, since they are all very similar), and the `isAlarmTriggered()` method on lines 37 through 40 retrieves the `boolean` flag saying whether or not the alarm time has been reached.

Finally, the `updateTime()` method on lines 41 through 50 illustrates an important feature of inheritance. Note that this method has exactly the same name, `updateTime()`, return type (`void`) and argument list (none) as a method in the `Clock` class. We say that the `updateTime()` method in `AlarmClock` *overrides* the corresponding method in the `Clock` class. This means that an object declared as an `AlarmClock` object will use the `updateTime()` method defined in the `AlarmClock` class, while a `Clock` object will use the `updateTime()` method defined in the `Clock` class.

The purpose of the `updateTime()` method in the `AlarmClock` class is to update the values of the hour, minute, and second representing the actual time, and in addition, to check if the alarm time has been reached. In other words, we want to do everything that is in the `updateTime()` method from the `Clock` class, and then check the alarm time. Rather than writing out all the code from the `updateTime()` method in the base class, we can use the `super` keyword again, as we see on line 43. This time, `super` takes on the role of an object, rather than a constructor, in that it can be used to refer to a method from the base class. Line 43 therefore calls the `updateTime()` method from the `Clock` class, which updates the values of `timeHours`, `timeMinutes`, and `timeSeconds`. Then lines 44 through 49 check if the updated time has reached the alarm time and, if so, set the `alarmTriggered` flag to `true`.

Let us now see how this class may be used in an external class. To keep things moderately simple, we have eliminated the menu that we used in `TestClock7` in the previous chapter, and have used the default initial time of 12:0:0. Running this program simply starts up the clock without requesting any input from the user.

```
1    import java.applet.*;
2    import java.awt.*;
3
4    public class TestAlarm1 extends Applet
5    {
6       AlarmClock clock;
7
8       public static void main(String argv[])
9       {
10         Frame alarmFrame = new Frame("Alarm clock");
11         TestAlarm1 testClock = new TestAlarm1();
12         testClock.init();
13         alarmFrame.add("Center", testClock);
14         alarmFrame.setSize(100,100);
15         alarmFrame.setVisible(true);
16         testClock.tellTime();
```

```
17    }
18
19    public void paint(Graphics g)
20    {
21       String currentTime;
22       Font timeFont = new Font("sansserif", Font.BOLD, 24);
23       g.setFont(timeFont);
24
25       currentTime = clock.getTimeHours() +
26          ":" + clock.getTimeMinutes() +
27          ":" + clock.getTimeSeconds();
28
29       if (clock.isAlarmTriggered())
30          g.setColor(Color.red);
31       else
32          g.setColor(Color.black);
33       g.drawString(currentTime, 10, 25);
34    }
35
36    void tellTime()
37    {
38       while (true) {
39          clock.updateTime();
40          try {
41             Thread.sleep(1000);
42          } catch (InterruptedException e) {
43          }
44          repaint();
45       }
46    }
47
48    public void init()
49    {
50       clock = new AlarmClock(12, 0, 15);
51    }
52 }
```

There are very few new features in this code. An AlarmClock object is declared on line 6. The main() method on lines 8 through 17 is the same as that used in the TestClock series earlier, except that the call to init() (on line 12) serves only to create the AlarmClock object by calling its constructor on line 50. We use the three-argument constructor to set the alarm to 15 seconds after the starting time of 12:0:0, so that we don't have long to wait to see if the alarm is triggered properly.

The tellTime() method on lines 36 through 46 is the same as in the TestClock classes, but note that the call to updateTime() on line 39 will call the AlarmClock version of this method, rather than the Clock version, since the clock variable in this case is an AlarmClock object.

The paint() method on lines 19 through 34 shows how the font of the text painted into the Frame can be changed. The Font class is part of the Java AWT, and line 22 creates a Font object called timeFont. The Font constructor takes three arguments: the first is a String specifying the font style ("sansserif" here – this is a sans-serif font like this). The second argument specifies that the font is in bold (emphasized) style, and the last argument is an int specifying the point size. This book is set in 10-point type, so a 24-point font is fairly large.

After creating and initializing the font, we must register it with the Graphics object g, which we do on line 23. This font will now be used for all text drawn to the screen (until another call to setFont() is made). We will learn more about fonts in Chapter 5, where we study the Java AWT in more depth.

Lines 25 through 27 retrieve the current time, as before, and store it in a String. Lines 29 through 32 check the value of the boolean flag alarmTriggered. If the alarm has gone off, we print the time in red, otherwise we print it in black. We can set the colour (note that the American spelling 'color' rather than the British 'colour' must be used in the code) of all drawing operations in a particular drawing object by using the setColor() method. There are various ways of specifying colours in Java, but the simplest is to use one of the pre-defined colours from the Color class. Here we use Color.red and Color.black. We will see more about the Color class in Chapter 8.

After setting the drawing colour, we print the time on line 33.

You can see that, apart from enhancing the font used to display the time, this code is virutally identical to that for displaying an ordinary Clock object.

Using base and derived classes

There is one more feature of inheritance that is often useful. Java syntax allows an object to be *declared* as belonging to a base class, and then *created* as an object of any class derived from that base class. For example, an object may be declared as belonging to class Clock, and initialized as an object of class AlarmClock. This seemingly bizarre behaviour will be most useful when we learn about arrays in Chapter 6, but we can illustrate the procedure (somewhat artificially) by making a few modifications to the TestAlarm1 class above. Rather than print out the entire class again, we will refer to the line numbers in the code above.

First, change the declaration on line 6 to:

```
Clock clock, myClock;
```

That is, we declare two objects, both of type Clock. The first object, clock, will be used as an alarm clock as before, but the second object, myClock, will be used as an ordinary clock, perhaps showing a time for a city in a different time zone.

The main() method remains unchanged. In the init() method, we leave line 50 as it is, even though clock was declared as a Clock object. Java allows us to initialize clock to any class derived from Clock, so it is legal to initialize it as an AlarmClock object.

We add the the following line after line 50:

```
myClock = new Clock(15, 0, 0);
```

This initializes `myClock` to an ordinary `Clock` object with a starting time of 15:0:0 (three hours ahead of `clock`).

In the `tellTime()` method after line 39 we add the line:

```
myClock.updateTime();
```

Since `clock` has been created as an `AlarmClock` object, the `updateTime()` method defined in the `AlarmClock` class will be used in line 39, while the `updateTime()` method from the `Clock` class will be used in the line inserted after line 39.

Finally, we add some code in the `paint()` method to display the time kept by `myClock`. After line 33, we add the code:

```
currentTime = myClock.getTimeHours() +
   ":" + myClock.getTimeMinutes() +
   ":" + myClock.getTimeSeconds();

g.setColor(Color.black);
g.drawString(currentTime, 10, 50);
```

This retrieves the time kept by `myClock` and prints it, always in black, below the time for `clock`.

If we stop here and attempt to compile the code, we will get an error from line 29, to the effect that `isAlarmTriggered()` is not a method in the `Clock` class. This may seem odd, in that although `clock` was declared to be a `Clock` object, it was initialized as an `AlarmClock` object, and `isAlarmTriggered()` *is* present in the `AlarmClock` class. Since the compiler seemed to find the right method for the `clock` object when the `updateTime()` method was called on line 39, why can't it find the `isAlarmTriggered()` method on line 29?

The answer is that it is not really the compiler that finds the right `updateTime()` method on line 39. The `clock` variable is attached to an `AlarmClock` object after the program is compiled (a process known as *dynamic binding*), so the choice of which `updateTime()` method to call isn't made until the program is actually run. As far as the compiler is concerned, `clock` was declared as a `Clock` object, so any methods it calls must be present in the `Clock` class. It is only when the program is run that it is found that `clock` is actually created as an `AlarmClock` object, and at that point a check is made for each method called by `clock` to see if an overridden version of that method exists in the `AlarmClock` class.

The point is that in order for the program to compile, any method called by an object declared to be of type `Clock` must be defined within the `Clock` class. So how can we make the compiler accept line 29? There are two ways of doing this.

First, we can actually define an `isAlarmTriggered()` method in the `Clock` class. The method doesn't have to do anything, but just having it there will satisfy the compiler. When the program is run, the correct `isAlarmTriggered()` method (from the `AlarmClock` class) will be called for the `clock` object, just as with the `updateTime()` method on line 39.

This isn't a very good solution, though, since it requires changing the code in the base class, which defeats the whole purpose of inheritance. We should be able to inherit a previously defined class without having to modify it.

The second solution is to replace line 29 by:

```
if (((AlarmClock)clock).isAlarmTriggered())
```

That is, we have replaced `clock` by `((AlarmClock)clock)`. This process is called *casting*, and lets the compiler know that although `clock` was declared to be of type `Clock`, at this point in the code it is being used as an `AlarmClock` object. The compiler will check that the class to which `clock` is being cast is derived from `Clock` and, if so, it will then check that the method being called is part of that derived class.

As you can see, the technique of declaring an object to point to a base class and then initializing it to point to an object of a derived class is most useful when that object calls methods that are present in both the base and derived classes, since then no casting is necessary. Java will automatically call the correct method to match whatever class was used to initialize the object.

One of the main purposes of inheritance in object-oriented design is to link together several classes that all have properties in common. These common properties are extracted from the various classes and placed in a base class which is then inherited by a number of other, more specialized classes. In fact, it is this idea that defines the correct use of inheritance: it is proper for one class to inherit another if the derived class is a specialized type of the base class. This is often referred to as an 'is a type of' relationship between classes: one class 'is a type of' the other one.

One of the most commonly used examples of inheritance is in the definition of a set of classes to represent various geometrical shapes. We might begin to design a set of classes by listing all the shapes we want to represent, such as point, line, circle, ellipse, square, rectangle, triangle, tetrahedron, cube, octahedron, and so on.

For each of these geometric figures, we can list the properties we want it to have. For example, all figures can have a colour and reference point defining their location in space. These common properties can be placed in a base class.

We can then look at the other figures and notice that they can be divided into groups depending on the number of spatial dimensions required to represent each shape. A point is zero-dimensional, a line is one-dimensional, the circle, ellipse, square, rectangle, and triangle are all two-dimensional, and the tetrahedron, cube, and octahedron are three-dimensional. We can therefore define four classes, one for each group of figures. Each of these four classes would inherit the base class, and add some features that are relevant to its number of dimensions. For example, the class representing two-dimensional figures could have variables for the area and perimeter of the figure, while the three-dimensional class could have a variable for the volume.

From this point, additional classes can be defined to represent each geometrical figure. For example, we might define a `Rectangle` class which inherits the two-dimensional figure class, a `Tetrahedron` class that inherits the three-dimensional figure class, and so on. We can even go a step further and define sub-classes of these classes to deal with special types of each figure. For example, a square is a special type of rectangle in which the lengths of all four sides are equal, so we might define a `Square` class which inherits the `Rectangle` class.

You can see that a hierarchy of classes can be constructed using inheritance, in which the common features of all the classes at each level in the hierarchy are extracted and used to define the class at the next layer up in the hierarchy. As we will see in later chapters, the Java libraries are all constructed in this way.

Packages

In many of the sample programs we have seen so far, the `.java` file opens with an `import` statement, such as `import java.awt.*`. We have mentioned in passing that `java.awt` is a *package*, but have not formally defined the Java package structure.

Once you have written a fair number of classes, you will notice that certain groups of classes refer to the same topic, such as a collection of classes all describing various forms of clocks. Java provides the `package` keyword which allows you to classify a number of related classes together into a single package. There are a few rules you must understand in order to make use of the `package`.

Suppose we wanted to create a package containing the clock classes we have studied in the book so far. We might just call this package the `clock` package. To label each of these classes as belonging to this package, we must insert the line

```
package clock;
```

as the *first* line in each source code file.

Inserting a `package` statement into a source file requires that the `.class` file that is produced from this file by the Java compiler be placed in a directory with the same name as the package name. That is, all the `.class` files containing classes belonging to the `clock` package must be stored in a directory named `clock`.

This directory must be created as a sub-directory of the directory in which the main Java program (that is, the program that `imports` the `clock` package) is found. Alternatively, if you plan on using the `package` in many different applications (which is the usual reason for creating a package in the first place), you can place the `clock` directory in some central location, and define an *environment variable* named CLASSPATH in your computer's start-up file. The format and location of the statement that defines an environment variable depends on your computer system. On a Windows-based PC, you might insert a line in your `autoexec.bat` file that looks something like this:

```
CLASSPATH=".;c:\java\mypackages;c:\java\otherstuff"
```

This line defines CLASSPATH as a list of three directories separated by semicolons. The first directory is given as a single dot, which means 'current directory', that is, the directory you happen to be in at the time. The other two directories are assumed to have been created especially for storing user-defined Java packages. To install the `clock` package, we could, for example, create a directory as a sub-directory of `c:\java\mypackages`, and store all the `.class` files belonging to the `clock` package there. The Java interpreter and compiler will start their searches for `imported` packages at the directories listed in CLASSPATH.

On a UNIX system, the precise form depends on the command shell you are using, so you should consult your system administrator.

Although a simple package name such as `clock` might be suitable if you only plan to create one or two packages for your own use, it is also possible to create hierarchies of packages. This is how the Java libraries themselves are arranged. For example, the `java.awt` package is actually a package named `awt` that is a sub-package of `java`.

If we planned on creating several packages for the various sections of this book, for example, we might define a top-level package called `book`, and then several sub-packages named `clock`, `games` (since several of the examples in the book create simple game programs), and so on. We could then insert the line

```
package book.clock;
```

at the start of all the files defining Java clocks.

A compound package name such as this must be reflected in the directory structure where the package files are stored. Class files from the `book.clock` package must be stored in a directory named `clock` which is a sub-directory of the `book` directory. The `book` directory, in turn, must be a sub-directory of one of the directories in the CLASSPATH (if CLASSPATH is defined), or of the directory where the main Java code is found.

All the Java library packages are actually compressed into a single file called `classes.zip` which will be found in the `lib` directory of your main Java installation. The Java compiler and interpreter will know about the location of this directory, so it does not need to be explicitly included in your CLASSPATH. If you have access to a compression program that can create `zip` format files, you can compress your own packages (maintaining the directory structure inside the zip file!) and then just place the zip file at the correct location in the directory structure. If you do that, however, the actual name of the zip file must appear in the CLASSPATH variable, rather than just the directory path.

Any Java class that is not assigned to a named package (through the use of a `package` statement in its source file) is assigned to a nameless 'default' package. The default package does not need to be placed in a special directory to be found, so it is useful to leave the `package` statement out of your files until they are fully written and tested.

The *visibility modifiers* `public`, `private`, and `protected` apply mainly to packages, rather than individual classes. In fact, the `package` keyword can also be used as a qualifier for classes, methods and variables, just like `public`, `private`, and `protected`. It is the default qualifier if no other qualifier is used, however, so you will rarely see `package` used in that context.

The access rights allowed by the various modifiers are shown in the table.

	public	protected	package (default)	private
Same class	yes	yes	yes	yes
Same package	yes	yes	yes	no
Different package, sub-class of current class	yes	yes	no	no
Different package, not a sub-class	yes	no	no	no

You can see that a `public` field (method or variable) is accessible everywhere. A `private` field is accessible only within the class where it is defined. The other two possibilities differ in relation to classes in other packages. If a class is in a different package, but is derived (using inheritance) from a class in the current package, then the derived class has access to `protected` fields but not `package` fields. Classes in other packages that are *not* derived from the current class have no access to either `protected` or `package` fields.

Since we wish to leave open the possibility of inheriting most of the classes in this book, we usually use the default (`package`) visibility for methods and fields. This allows all classes in the same package to have access to all parts of these classes. Although this strictly violates the principles of object-oriented design, the idea is that a group of classes that has been included in a package have all been thoroughly debugged and tested so it should be safe for them to access each other freely.

Abstract classes

When we construct a hierarchy of classes, we sometimes encounter a class which is the ancestor of a number of other classes, but which does not represent an actual object itself. For example, when we construct a hierarchy to represent the various geometric figures, the class representing two-dimensional figures does not contain enough information to actually build a two-dimensional figure. To do that, we need to go one layer deeper and choose precisely *which* figure we want to draw (a rectangle, circle, triangle, etc.). The base class itself, therefore, should not be allowed to spawn any actual objects.

In Java, a class can be defined but forbidden from giving birth to objects by declaring it to be an `abstract` class (or by declaring one of the methods inside the class to be `abstract`). An `abstract` class is essentially a template which defines some methods that all classes derived from the abstract class must implement in their own way. It is possible to declare a variable using the abstract class as the data type, but the new operator cannot be used to create an object of an abstract type. Let us see how an abstract class is defined and used.

Let us define an abstract class called Figure which contains two methods. The class will serve as the base class for other classes which represent specific two-dimensional figures.

```
public abstract class Figure
{
  public abstract double area();
  public abstract double perimeter();
}
```

Note that both the class itself and the methods it contains are declared as abstract. The first method will calculate the area of a figure, and the second will calculate the perimeter. (It is not necessary for *all* methods within an abstract class to be abstract, but if any of the methods in a class is abstract, the class itself must be declared as abstract. Any class inheriting this abstract class must either provide code to implement *all* the abstract methods declared in the base class, or else be declared as an abstract class itself.)

Now let us define a class called MyRectangle which inherits Figure, and provides its own version of the area() and perimeter() methods. (We call the class MyRectangle rather than just Rectangle since there is a Java library class called Rectangle which we will use later in the book.)

```
public class MyRectangle extends Figure
{
  double length, width;
  MyRectangle()
  {
    length = width = 0.0;
  }

  MyRectangle(double newLength, double newWidth)
  {
    length = newLength;
    width = newWidth;
  }

  public double area()
  {
    return length * width;
  }

  public double perimeter()
  {
    return 2 * length + 2 * width;
  }
}
```

ABSTRACT CLASSES 85

This class contains two `double` variables for the length and width of the rectangle, and provides code for its version of the `area()` and `perimeter()` methods.

We may use the `Figure` and `MyRectangle` classes in declarations in various ways. We can use `MyRectangle` on its own in the usual way:

```
MyRectangle rect1 = new MyRectangle(10, 20);
```

This declares and initializes `rect1` to be a `MyRectangle` object, with initial values of 10 and 20 for `length` and `width`, respectively.

Alternatively, we can say:

```
Figure fig1 = new MyRectangle(10, 20);
```

This declaration is legal, since `fig1` is declared as a pointer to a `Figure` object, and it is legal to assign the pointer to any object derived from a `Figure` object.

However, it is *not* possible to say:

```
Figure fig1 = new Figure();
```

Since `Figure` is an abstract class, it is not possible to create objects from it, so the `new Figure()` part of the statement is illegal.

In a similar way, we can define another class, `RightTriangle`, which also inherits `Figure` and represents a right-angled triangle:

```
public class RightTriangle extends Figure
{
   double side1, side2;

   RightTriangle()
   {
      side1 = side2 = 0.0;
   }

   RightTriangle(double newSide1, double newSide2)
   {
      side1 = newSide1;
      side2 = newSide2;
   }

   public double area()
   {
      return side1 * side2 / 2;
   }

   public double perimeter()
   {
      return side1 + side2 +
```

```
            Math.sqrt(side1 * side1 + side2 * side2);
      }
}
```

Here, we declare `side1` and `side2` to be the two sides containing the right angle. The area of a right-angled triangle is half the product of these two sides. If you recall your Pythagoras, you will remember that 'the square on the hypotenuse (the side opposite the right angle) is equal to the sum of the squares on the other two sides'. The `perimeter()` method uses the built-in `Math.sqrt()` method to calculate the square root of this sum of squares, and adds it to the other two sides to obtain the perimeter of the triangle.

At this point, you may be wondering why we need the `Figure` class. Although it states the existence of the `area()` and `perimeter()` methods, these methods still have to be written into each class derived from `Figure`, so why bother with `Figure` at all?

To see why an abstract base class is useful, we will introduce another class which declares a `MyRectangle` object and a `RightTriangle` object, and then displays their area and perimeter in a `Frame`. The `TestFigure1` class is as follows:

```
1   import java.applet.*;
2   import java.awt.*;
3
4   public class TestFigure1 extends Applet
5   {
6      MyRectangle rect1;
7      RightTriangle tri1;
8
9      public static void main(String argv[])
10     {
11        Frame figureFrame = new Frame("Testing figures");
12        TestFigure1 testFigure = new TestFigure1();
13        testFigure.init();
14        figureFrame.add("Center", testFigure);
15        figureFrame.setSize(400,300);
16        figureFrame.setVisible(true);
17     }
18
19     void displayInfo(Graphics g, Figure figure, int startY)
20     {
21        String figureData;
22
23        figureData = "Area = " + figure.area();
24        g.drawString(figureData, 10, startY);
25        figureData = "Perimeter = " + figure.perimeter();
26        g.drawString(figureData, 10, startY + 20);
27     }
28
29     public void paint(Graphics g)
30     {
```

```
31          Font timeFont = new Font("Helvetica", Font.BOLD, 14);
32          g.setFont(timeFont);
33
34          displayInfo(g, rect1, 20);
35          displayInfo(g, tri1, 120);
36      }
37
38
39      public void init()
40      {
41          rect1 = new MyRectangle(20, 30);
42          tri1 = new RightTriangle(20, 30);
43      }
44  }
```

After declaring `rect1` and `tri1` on lines 6 and 7, the `main()` method creates a `Frame` in the usual way. The `init()` method initializes the two figures, and then the `paint()` method sets up the `Font` and calls the `displayInfo()` method to print out information on the rectangle and triangle. Note that, although `rect1` and `tri1` are declared as objects of different types (`MyRectangle` and `RightTriangle`), they are both passed to `displayInfo()` as the `Figure` object (the second argument on line 19). Lines 23 and 25 call the correct version of `area()` and `perimeter()`, depending on the actual data type of the `Figure` object that has been passed to `displayInfo()`. We are therefore using the same method to handle objects of different data types, something we could not have done if we hadn't declared the abstract class `Figure`, and then derived other classes from it.

Interfaces

Java allows a derived class to inherit only one base class. Other object-oriented languages such as C++ allow *multiple inheritance*, which means that a derived class can inherit any number of other classes. Multiple inheritance, however, can lead to logical inconsistencies in the code if it is not used carefully, so the designers of Java decided not to allow it.

At times, however, it would be useful to be able to inherit, after a fashion, the methods of more than one class. For example, suppose that, in addition to displaying some data about various geometric figures, we also wanted to draw them. For any two-dimensional figure, there are several operations that may be related to the drawing of the figure. We can specify the position within the frame where the figure is to appear, we can set the drawing colour, we can specify whether the figure should be filled with the colour or just drawn as an outline, and we can give the command to go ahead and draw the figure. Most of these operations will require different commands for each type of figure. The drawing instructions for a rectangle, for example, will require four line segments to complete the figure, while those for a triangle will require three. However, if we could specify the various methods in a base class of some sort, we could use the same method name to implement the drawing procedure for each derived class, thus allowing the same sort of compact code as we used in the previous section for displaying the data about each object.

If we want to display the data for the object *and* draw the object on screen, we can only use an abstract base class for one of these operations, since Java does not allow multiple inheritance. However, we can implement the other operation using an *interface*.

There are really only two differences between an interface and an abstract class. The first is that, in an interface, *all* methods must be declared as abstract, while an abstract class may contain some methods that are not abstract, and are therefore inherited directly by any derived class. While the keyword `extends` is used to specify a class inheriting another class, the keyword `implements` is used to specify a class inheriting an interface. A class that implements an interface must provide definitions for *all* methods declared in the interface.

The other difference is that a class (or another interface) may `implement` any number of interfaces, so that interfaces offer a way of providing multiple inheritance.

Let us define an interface that provides some of the methods used in drawing a two-dimensional figure. The interface `DrawFigure` allows the position of the figure to be set, and allows the figure to be drawn:

```
import java.awt.*;

public interface DrawFigure
{
   public void setPosition(int x, int y);
   public void draw(Graphics g);
}
```

Note that we need not declare either the interface or its methods as `abstract`, since all methods in an interface are automatically `abstract`.

We now show how the `MyRectangle` class can inherit both the abstract `Figure` class and implement the `DrawFigure` interface.

```
1   import java.awt.*;
2
3   public class MyRectangle extends Figure implements DrawFigure
4   {
5      double length, width;
6      int upperLeftX, upperLeftY;
7
8      MyRectangle()
9      {
10        length = width = 0.0;
11     }
12
13     MyRectangle(double newLength, double newWidth)
14     {
15        length = newLength;
```

```
16          width = newWidth;
17        }
18
19        public double area()
20        {
21          return length * width;
22        }
23
24        public double perimeter()
25        {
26          return 2 * length + 2 * width;
27        }
28
29        public void setPosition(int x, int y)
30        {
31          upperLeftX = x;
32          upperLeftY = y;
33        }
34
35        public void draw(Graphics g)
36        {
37          g.drawLine(upperLeftX, upperLeftY, upperLeftX +
38            (int)width, upperLeftY);
39          g.drawLine(upperLeftX + (int)width, upperLeftY,
40            upperLeftX + (int)width,
41            upperLeftY + (int)length);
42          g.drawLine(upperLeftX + (int)width,
43            upperLeftY + (int)length,
44            upperLeftX, upperLeftY + (int)length);
45          g.drawLine(upperLeftX, upperLeftY + (int)length,
46            upperLeftX, upperLeftY);
47        }
48      }
```

On line 3, we inherit Figure using extends and inherit DrawFigure using implements. We have added a couple of variables on line 6 to store the location of the upper left corner of the rectangle.

Since we are implementing the DrawFigure interface, we must provide definitions for its two methods, setPosition() and draw().

Lines 29 through 33 just assign the position values to upperLeftX and upperLeftY. The draw() method on lines 35 through 47 using the drawLine() method of the Graphics class to draw the four sides of the rectangle. The first two arguments of drawLine() give the *x* and *y* co-ordinates of one end of the line segment, and the last two arguments give the co-ordinates of the other end of the segment. Remember that the horizontal co-ordinate is measured from the left edge of the Frame, and that the vertical co-ordinate is measured downwards from the top of the Frame. Thus the four drawLine() calls draw the edges in the order: top, right, bottom, left.

90 CONSTRUCTORS, INHERITANCE, AND INTERFACES

Lines 37 to 46 contain several cases where a variable such as `length` or `width` has the notation `(int)` in front of it. This is a *cast*, which converts one data type to another. In this case, `length` and `width` are `double`s, but the `drawLine()` method requires `int`s as its arguments. In certain cases, Java allows one data type to be 'cast' into another type. In this case, where we cast a `double` to an `int`, the conversion is done by just discarding the fractional part of the `double`. Obviously this loses some information and may not always be acceptable.

We can make similar modifications to the `RightTriangle` class to allow it to implement the `DrawFigure` interface. We could then add these two lines to the `paint()` method in `TestFigure1` above:

```
displayImage(g, rect1, 10, 60);
displayImage(g, tri1, 10, 160);
```

These lines will draw the rectangle and triangle below their respective descriptions. The `displayImage()` method is also added to the `TestFigure1` class:

```
void displayImage(Graphics g, DrawFigure drawFigure,
   int startX, int startY)
{
   drawFigure.setPosition(startX, startY);
   drawFigure.draw(g);
}
```

The second argument of `displayImage()` is a `DrawFigure` variable which accepts both `rect1` and `tri1` as legal values. Note that we have not changed any of the other code in `TestFigure1`. Since `rect1` and `tri1` are instances of classes that have inherited *both* `Figure` and `DrawFigure`, it is legal to treat them as either type of object, if the situation requires it. In that way, they can be passed as `Figure` arguments to the `displayInfo()` method, and as `DrawFigure` arguments to `displayImage()`.

Exercises

1   To see the need for initializing an object before using it, comment out the line in the `TestAlarm1` class that calls the `AlarmClock` constructor (line 50). What errors do you get when you compile and run the program?

2   Write a third constructor for the `AlarmClock` class which initializes the three time parameters inherited from `Clock` as well as the three alarm parameters. Use a call to `super()` to call the `Clock` constructor.

3   Consider the following code.

```
AlarmClock clock1, tempClock;
clock1 = new AlarmClock(7, 30, 0);
```

```
tempClock = clock1;
clock1.setTimeHours(10);
```

What value would be returned by the call `tempClock.getTimeHours()`? [Hint: remember that `clock1` and `tempClock` actually work as *pointers* to objects of type `AlarmClock`.]

4 Write a new class called `Timer` which works as a countdown timer. After its initial time has been set, a `Timer` object should count backwards until it reaches 0:00:00, at which point it should stop (you might also like to change the colour of the display at that point). Use `extends` to derive `Timer` from `Clock` so that you will have access to the set and get methods for the time. However, since `Timer` counts backwards, you will need to override the `updateTime()` method to count backwards rather than forwards. Write another class called `TestTimer` (similar to `TestAlarm1`) which declares a `Timer` object and tests it.

5 Write a new class called `Circle` which `extends` the abstract `Figure` class in the text. Provide a single variable called `radius` and two constructors (one without arguments which sets `radius` to 0.0 and one with a single argument that allows the user to initialize `radius`). Also provide definitions of the `area()` and `perimeter()` methods. Remember that the area of a circle is πr^2, and the perimeter (circumference) of a circle is $2\pi r$, where r is the radius and π is a mathematical constant (look up the Java documentation for the `Math` class in the `java.lang` package and find a `static` constant that you can use for pi). Test your `Circle` class by adding a `Circle` object to the `TestFigure1` class, and adding code to the `init()` and `paint()` methods in that class to create the circle and display its information.

6 Enhance the `Circle` class from exercise 5 by having it implement the `DrawFigure` interface. Provide a `setPosition()` method (where `upperLeftX` and `upperLeftY` now refer to the rectangle that contains the circle) and a `draw()` method (look up the `Graphics` class documentation and remember that a circle is a specialized oval) to draw the circle. Add a call to `displayImage()` in `TestFigure1` to draw the circle.

CHAPTER 5
The Java AWT and event handling

The Java AWT

We have made several references to the Java AWT, or Abstract Windowing Toolkit, in the last few chapters. You will have gathered by now that it is a large collection of classes that provide most of the graphical interface to Java programs. The AWT is a standard part of all Java installations, so its contents can be used as if they are an integral part of the language.

Actually, the AWT is only one of several packages that are provided with the standard Java Development Kit (JDK). The core package is java.lang, which contains many commonly used classes (such as the Math class that we used in the previous chapter). The java.lang package is imported into all Java source files by default, so there is no need to explicitly import it.

We have also met the java.applet package in previous chapters. We will encounter several other packages in the course of this book, but by far the most commonly used package in Java programs is the java.awt package.

The reason that we have not studied the package in depth earlier is that, in order to understand its structure, we need an understanding of inheritance. All Java packages are built hierarchically, with more general base classes giving rise to specific derived classes. These derived classes may, in most cases, be used to define objects which can be used directly in a Java program, or they may be used to derive other customized classes defined by an individual programmer.

As the Java AWT is quite large (and is even larger in Java 1.1 than it was in Java 1.0), we need to approach it in stages. At the top level, it is easiest to divide the AWT into three main areas:

- Graphics classes. These classes allow various graphical figures (lines, polygons, and so on) to be drawn, images to be inserted, fonts to be defined, colours to be set, and so on. These classes are all *non-interactive*, in the sense that they produce output on the screen, and do not respond to input from the user.
- Component classes. The elements of a graphical user interface (GUI) such as buttons, drop-down lists, menus, checkboxes and so on are provided by the component classes. One subclass of the Component class is the Container class, which provides empty containers such as frames, panels, and dialog

boxes. Many of these components *do* respond to input from the user, so in order to use them we need to understand the concept of event handling, which we study later in this chapter.
- Layout managers. Many primitive GUI environments require the programmer to specify the co-ordinates and dimensions of each component as it is inserted. Java uses a variety of *layout managers* to provide several templates into which components can be inserted. Since Java programs must cope with a variety of GUI environments on different computer systems, these layout managers use relative positioning rules rather than absolute ones.

Most of the classes in java.awt are either base classes in their own right, or else inherit other java.awt classes. The main exception to this is that all classes in all Java packages inherit the Object class from the core java.lang package. This Object class provides a root for all the inheritance chains used in all packages, and provides a few general purpose methods which usually must be overridden in the derived classes if they are to be useful. For example, the Object class defines a toString() method, which produces a String containing a description of the object in question. Derived classes should provide their own version of toString(), in order that customized information for that specific class can be generated.

The graphics classes in the AWT include classes such as Color (for defining colours used in drawing), Polygon (for defining polygonal shapes), and Font (for defining fonts used in drawing text). The main graphical class is Graphics itself, which must be used to do the actual drawing. We have already seen several examples of the use of the graphics classes in previous chapters. Since the basic technique for drawing graphics and text is much the same no matter what type of graphics is being drawn, we will not dwell on these methods further here. We will meet some of the more specialized techniques for producing graphics later in this book. In the meantime, as always, the reader is urged to browse through the Java documentation to see what classes and methods are available for producing graphics.

Before we move on, however, it is worthwhile considering how Java manages to produces graphics and GUI components in a platform-independent way. If you have used more than one type of computer (for example, a PC, a Macintosh, or a UNIX system), you will no doubt realize that programs written for one system usually do not run on the other. For example, a word processor or a game produced for a PC will simply be rejected by any other type of computer system as an unrecognizable file.

The Java compiler produces a class file from each class in a source file. This class file contains a byte code version of the Java program that is portable between different machine types. For instructions such as calculations that do not require any display on the screen, this portability is achieved by the Java Virtual Machine (JVM), which interprets the byte codes in the class file and translates them into machine code for the particular machine on which the program is running.

For graphical output, each Java class in the AWT must be rendered on screen using the GUI components of the particular machine type being used to run the program. For example, on a PC, some version of Windows (such as Windows 95, Windows 98, or Windows NT) is used to display graphical output, so the Java GUI components must be rendered using the Windows GUI. On a UNIX machine running the Motif windowing system, Motif components must be used to display Java graphical objects.

To accomplish this, there is a sub-package of `java.awt` called `java.awt.peer`, which consists of a set of interfaces that exactly mirrors the set of actual components defined in the `java.awt` package. Whenever Java is ported to a new machine type, these interfaces must be implemented so that Java components can be displayed using whatever windowing system is found on this new machine. The Java Virtual Machine then makes use of this peer code to display a component on screen.

In practice, the interfaces in `java.awt.peer` are very rarely used in writing GUI-based Java programs. One of the beauties of the Java model is that platform-independent, GUI programs can be written once on any machine and ported to all other major machine types. The mechanics of the translation between machines is handled automatically and invisibly when the program is actually run on the various machines.

We will now turn to a study of the GUI facilities in the AWT, which leads us into an examination of how *events* are generated and handled in Java.

Interacting with a program

Even if you have little experience in actually writing computer programs, you may be familiar with a wide variety of applications, such as web browsers, word processors, and games. Packages such as these usually allow you to enter data using a variety of methods. Web browsers rely most heavily on the mouse, word processors use the keyboard for entry of text, and games may allow input from both mouse and keyboard, in addition to other devices such as joysticks, trackballs, and more elaborate devices such as foot pedals, steering wheels, and simulated weapons.

How does a program interact with all these devices? At the lowest level, all of these devices generate a small electrical signal when a key or button is pressed, a trackball is moved, and so on. The signal is passed to the computer's processor, where it is detected. After that, it is up to the software to decide whether the signal is relevant to the program, and if so, to act on it.

Each such signal is called an *event*, and one of the most important components of an operating system (a computer's controlling program) is its ability to detect and act on various events. Java provides a platform-independent way of attaching *event handlers* to the various components in a GUI program. In this way, when the user generates an event (by pressing a button with the mouse, for example), a specific method can be called to generate a response to the event.

The Java event model

In order to write code that handles events, we must understand the basic idea underlying Java's treatment of events: its so-called *event model*. Before we go into details, however, a few words are needed about changes between version 1.0.2 and the various sub-versions of version 1.1.

Unfortunately, the event model is completely different in the two versions. This difference applies not only to the way the code is written, but to the environments in which the actual programs will run. Since one of the main uses of Java is in writing applets for use in web pages, this means that older editions of popular web browsers such as Netscape's Navigator and Communicator, and Microsoft's Internet Explorer, will *not* run Java applets written using later versions (1.1 upwards) of Java. At the time when this book was written (early 1998), the most recent versions of Communicator (version 4) and of Internet Explorer (also version 4) will run *some* applets written using Java 1.1, but they do not support all the features. By the time the book is published, however, newer versions of both these browsers will probably support Java 1.1 applets.

Because of space limitations in this book, and because, once newer versions of web browsers appear that support Java 1.1, older Java 1.0.2 applets will fade in significance, this book will use the Java 1.1 event model exclusively.

The Java package `java.awt.event` contains several class definitions that specify the general types of events that can be handled in Java 1.1. We will consider the most commonly used event classes here. The reader is urged to consult the Java documentation for a complete list.

The most common event classes are:

- `ActionEvent`: An `ActionEvent` is generated when a button[1] is pressed, or a choice is made from a drop-down or pop-up menu.
- `ItemEvent`: This is generated when an item in a list or set of checkboxes is selected or deselected.
- `KeyEvent`: Pressing any key on the keyboard generates this event.
- `MouseEvent`: Clicking one of the mouse buttons, moving or dragging the mouse pointer, and entering or leaving an area on the screen with the mouse all generate a `MouseEvent`.

A GUI-based Java application (or applet, in a web page) usually contains several components in addition to the main frame or window that holds the application. These components may be buttons, checkboxes, text fields, labels, and so on. Each of these components may *listen* for events from one or more of the event classes defined in `java.awt.event`. In order to listen for an event, an *event listener* must be attached to the corresponding component. Each event class has a corresponding

---

[1] By 'button' we mean a GUI component drawn onto the screen, not a physical button such as a mouse or keyboard button. Even though the GUI button is often pressed by using the mouse, the actual clicking of the mouse button generates a `MouseEvent`, which is a different type of event from an `ActionEvent`.

96 THE JAVA AWT AND EVENT HANDLING

listener (or, in the case of the `MouseEvent`, *two* listeners) associated with it. All listeners are defined as *interfaces*, not as actual classes. This means that if you want to listen for a particular type of event within a class that you have written, the class must implement the correct listener interface for the type of event that you want to handle.

If all of this sounds rather confusing, the best way to see exactly what is involved is to look at a few examples.

In our first example, we produce the window shown in Figure 5.1.

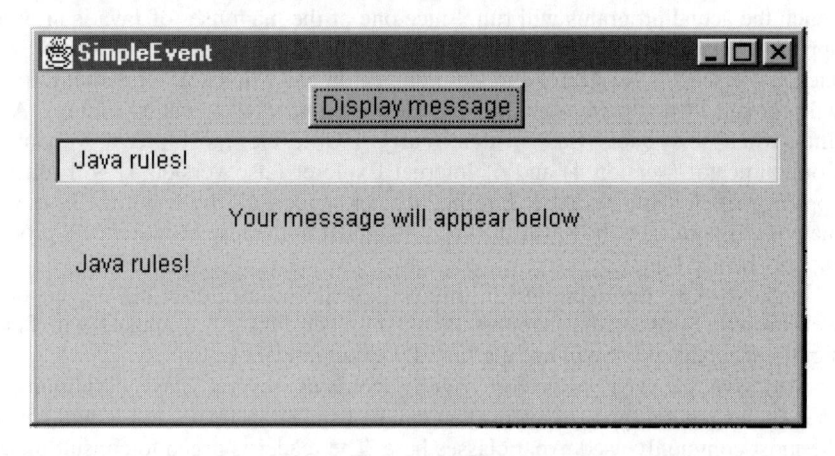

Figure 5.1 The window produced by the `SimpleEvent` program.

The display consists of a text field into which the user can type some text. When the 'Display message' button is clicked with the mouse, the text in the text field is copied into the space in the lower half of the window, as shown in the figure.

In using this program, quite a few types of event are actually generated and caught by the Java code. Most of the events, however, are handled automatically. For example, when the user selects the text field by putting the mouse cursor over it and clicking the mouse button, all of these mouse events are handled automatically – no extra code need be written by the programmer. Similarly, when the user types text into the text field, each key on the keyboard generates events which are handled automatically, with the corresponding character being displayed within the text field.

The only event that is *not* automatically handled is that generated when the 'Display message' button is pressed. We must provide the Java code which reads the text entered into the text field, and then copies this text into the lower half of the window.

The Java code that produces the window in Figure 5.1 is as follows.

```
1    import java.applet.*;
2    import java.awt.*;
3    import java.awt.event.*;
4    public class SimpleEvent extends Applet
5        implements ActionListener
```

```
 6    {
 7      String usersMessage = "";
 8      Button messageButton;
 9      TextField messageText;
10      Label messageLabel;
11
12      public static void main(String argv[])
13      {
14        Frame messageFrame = new Frame("SimpleEvent");
15        SimpleEvent testMessage = new SimpleEvent();
16        testMessage.init();
17        messageFrame.add("Center", testMessage);
18        messageFrame.setSize(400,200);
19        messageFrame.setVisible(true);
20      }
21
22      public void init()
23      {
24        messageButton = new Button("Display message");
25        messageButton.addActionListener(this);
26        messageText = new TextField(50);
27        messageLabel =
28           new Label("Your message will appear below");
29        this.add(messageButton);
30        this.add(messageText);
31        this.add(messageLabel);
32      }
33
34      public void paint(Graphics g)
35      {
36        g.drawString(usersMessage, 20, 100);
37      }
38
39      public void actionPerformed(ActionEvent event)
40      {
41        String command = event.getActionCommand();
42        if (command.equals("Display message")) {
43          usersMessage = messageText.getText();
44          repaint();
45        }
46      }
47    }
```

Lines 1 through 3 `import` the required packages. Note that in addition to `java.applet` and `java.awt`, we must also import `java.awt.event`, since we will be handling events generated by some of the AWT components.

As mentioned above, the only event we will need to handle explicitly is that generated by pressing the button. A button press produces an `ActionEvent`, and to handle an `ActionEvent`, we need to implement the `ActionListener` interface.

There are two ways we can do this – this program considers only one of the ways. We will look at the other method in the next example.

In this program, we define the `SimpleEvent` class on lines 4 and 5, saying that it `implements ActionListener`. Recall from our discussion of interfaces in Chapter 4 that when a class `implements` an interface, it must provide definitions for *all* methods contained in that interface. As we can discover by consulting the Java documentation, the `ActionListener` interface contains only one method: `actionPerformed()`. We must therefore provide a definition for this method within the `SimpleEvent` class. This is done on lines 39 to 46, but we will explain this method a bit later.

Let us return to the beginning of the class definition. On lines 7 through 10, we define the components that are used by the program. The `String usersMessage` will be used to store the user's message, as typed into the text field. The `Button` object `messageButton` is one of the AWT components, and is used for the 'Display message' button. The `TextField` object provides the text field, and the `Label` is used to display the constant text 'Your message will appear below'. All of these components are provided as part of the `java.awt` package, and may be plugged directly into your programs.

The `main()` method on lines 12 through 20 is similar to those we have seen in earlier chapters – it simply creates a `Frame` in which the program will be displayed, and initializes the program and its containing `Frame`.

The `init()` method on lines 22 to 32 initializes the components, attaches the event handler, and adds the components to the applet. Let us consider each line in this method to see how all this is done.

Line 24 initializes the `Button` by calling its constructor and passing the argument 'Display message' to this constructor. This, as you can probably guess, is the text that is displayed on the `Button` when it appears on screen.

Line 25 attaches an event handler to the `Button`. The `addActionListener()` method takes a single argument, which must be of type `ActionListener`. This means that the object passed as the argument to `addActionListener()` must implement the `ActionListener` interface, and must therefore provide an `actionPerformed()` method. The purpose of line 25 is to tell the `Button` which class contains the `actionPerformed()` method that should be run when the `Button` is pressed.

The argument of the `addActionListener()` method is an object called `this`. At first glance you might think that `this` is a variable that we have forgotten to declare (since you won't find any declaration for it anywhere in the class). In fact, it is another Java keyword with a special meaning.

Whenever the keyword `this` is used within a class method, it refers to a pointer to the particular instance of the class that called that method. In the `SimpleEvent` class, for example, the `main()` method declares an instance of `SimpleEvent` called `testMessage` (line 15). The `testMessage` object then calls `init()` (line 16), and it is within the `init()` method that reference to `this` is made (line 25). Therefore, in this case, the `this` pointer refers to the `testMessage` object. In general, it is a very handy way of retrieving a pointer to whatever object called a method, something you will need to do quite often.

In this case, we are telling the `messageButton` that the current object (that is, the current instance of `SimpleEvent`) is the object that contains the desired `actionPerformed()` method. We didn't have to do it this way. For example, we could have defined another class which implemented `ActionListener`, declared an object of that other class, and then passed *that* object as the argument to `addActionListener`. In this case, though, it makes more sense to do everything within the single class, since pressing the button affects other components within that class.

Line 26 initializes the `TextField` to be an empty field, of width 50 characters. The width of a `TextField` is actually difficult to specify in advance, since you can change the font used within the `TextField` after its creation, which of course changes the number of characters it can contain.

Lines 27 and 28 initialize the `Label` by defining its message.

Lines 29 through 31 add the three components to the applet. Notice that we do not specify the relative positions of the three components – we don't try to place the `Button` at location (10, 20) for example. We are actually relying on the default positioning provided by Java for AWT components. We will see in Chapter 7 how to use more advanced positioning methods called *layout managers* which allow us much more control over the appearance of the program. (In the meantime, you might like to experiment with the default layout by running the program and then manually resizing the window using the mouse. You may be surprised by the results.)

The `paint()` method on lines 34 through 37 simply draws the `usersMessage` text onto the window at position $x = 20$ and $y = 100$ pixels.

Finally, we consider the `actionPerformed()` method on lines 39 through 46. Note that its argument is an `ActionEvent` object (line 39). The `actionPerformed()` method is called automatically whenever the `Button` to which it was attached is pressed. The `ActionEvent` object generated by the button press is passed as the argument to the method, and various bits of information can be extracted from it within the `actionPerformed()` method.

On line 41, for example, we use the `getActionCommand()` method of the `ActionEvent` class to extract the name of the command. In the case of a `Button`, the `getActionCommand()` method returns a `String` containing the text displayed on the `Button` itself. If we had used more than one `Button`, and assigned the same `actionPerformed()` method to all the `Buttons`, we could tell which `Button` had been pressed by examining the action command string.

On line 42, we use the `equals()` method of the `String` class to compare the command from the `ActionEvent` with the text 'Display message'. If it matches, we extract the text entered by the user into the `TextField` `messageText`, using the `getText()` method. This text is stored in the class `String` variable `usersMessage`. We then call `repaint()` to update the message using the `paint()` method.

In this program, since we only had one `Button`, we didn't really need to extract the action command and compare it with the `Button`'s caption, but we have included the code so you can see how it is done.

We now summarize the principles of event handling:

- Decide which AWT components you require in your program.
- *Declare* these components as variables within the class.
- *Initialize* each component in the `init()` method (or within the constructor, if the class does not inherit the `Applet` class).
- For each component which will generate an event that requires customized code, attach the correct *listener* for the type of event you want to handle.
- Write the required method or methods for each listener, so that the required steps are carried out whenever each event is generated.

These steps may look rather involved, but once you've written a few programs that handle different types of events, the procedure will become quite familiar.

Event handling using adapters and inner classes

The `ActionListener` interface which must be implemented in order to handle an `ActionEvent`, such as that generated by pressing a `Button`, has only a single method: `actionPerformed()`. The easiest way to handle a button press is as shown in the example in the previous section. The class containing the `Button` is defined so that it `implements ActionListener`, and an `actionPerformed()` method is defined within that class to do whatever is supposed to be done when the `Button` is pressed.

Other event types, however, have associated listener interfaces that contain more than one method. In many cases, you only need one or two of these methods to handle the event in your particular program. For example, the `KeyEvent`, which is generated by pressing and releasing one of the keys on the keyboard, is caught by the `KeyListener` interface, which contains three methods: `keyPressed()`, `keyReleased()`, and `keyTyped()`. The first method is called when a key is pressed down, the second when a key is released, and the third when a key is 'typed', which means that a key press is followed by a key release.

If we wish to write a program that handles keyboard events, but only responds to, say, the event generated when a key is released, we would like to write only the `keyReleased()` method. However, if the class within which the keyboard events are to be caught `implements` the `KeyListener` interface, it must provide definitions for *all three* of the `KeyListener` interfaces, even though two of them will only be empty methods.

The problem is worse for the `MouseListener` interface, which contains five methods that respond to different mouse events.

To cope with the inconvenience of having to implement several empty methods every time we wish to use one of the listener interfaces containing more than one method, the `java.awt.event` package provides an *adapter* class for each of the listener interfaces. Each adapter class contains empty definitions for all the methods in the corresponding interface. The name of an adapter class may be obtained from the corresponding listener interface by replacing 'Listener' by 'Adapter'. For example, the adapter class corresponding to the `KeyListener` interface is called `KeyAdapter`.

To illustrate the use of an adapter class, we present a variant of the `SimpleEvent` class above. The `KeyboardEvent` class produces a window as shown in Figure 5.2.

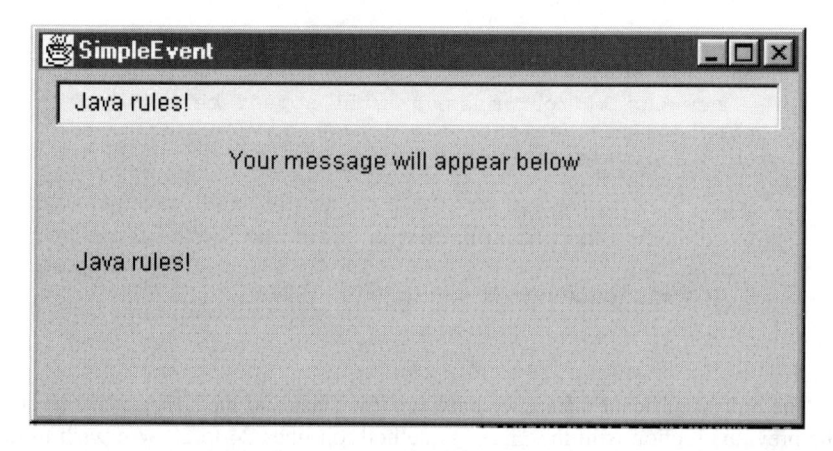

Figure 5.2 The window produced by the `KeyboardEvent` class.

The interface is the same as Figure 5.1, except that the 'Display message' button is absent. When the user types text into the text field in Figure 5.2, it is updated in the display area immediately after each key release. As you might expect, we make use of the `KeyEvent` to detect key releases. The code for Figure 5.2 follows.

```
1   import java.applet.*;
2   import java.awt.*;
3   import java.awt.event.*;
4
5   public class KeyboardEvent extends Applet
6   {
7      String usersMessage = "";
8      TextField messageText;
9      Label messageLabel;
10
11     public static void main(String argv[])
12     {
13        Frame messageFrame = new Frame("KeyboardEvent");
14        KeyboardEvent testMessage = new KeyboardEvent();
15        testMessage.init();
```

102 THE JAVA AWT AND EVENT HANDLING

```
16        messageFrame.add("Center", testMessage);
17        messageFrame.setSize(400,200);
18        messageFrame.setVisible(true);
19     }
20
21     public void init()
22     {
23        messageText = new TextField(50);
24        messageText.addKeyListener(new KeyAdapter() {
25           public void keyReleased(KeyEvent event) {
26              usersMessage = messageText.getText();
27              repaint();
28           }
29        });
30        messageLabel =
31           new Label("Your message will appear below");
32        this.add(messageText);
33        this.add(messageLabel);
34     }
35
36     public void paint(Graphics g)
37     {
38        g.drawString(usersMessage, 20, 100);
39     }
40  }
```

The only significant difference between this class and the SimpleEvent class in the previous section is in the init() method, on lines 24 to 29. We wish to detect key releases when the user is typing text into the TextField named messageText. On line 24, we use the addKeyListener() method to tell messageText where KeyEvents should be sent.

If we used the same method here as we did with the SimpleEvent example in the previous section, we would have defined the KeyboardEvent class so that it implements KeyListener. We would then need to provide definitions for the three methods that make up the KeyListener interface. Since we only want to use one of the methods (keyReleased()), it is more convenient *not* to implement the KeyListener interface, and to use the KeyAdapter class instead.

The addKeyListener() method requires a single argument, which must be an object that implements the KeyListener interface. In the SimpleEvent class above, we passed this as the argument to the addActionListener() method, since the SimpleEvent class itself implemented the ActionListener interface. Here, we are creating a new object explicitly for handling the KeyEvent. On line 24, we create a new KeyAdapter object right inside the call to addKeyListener().

What makes this example of object creation different from others we have seen is that, following the new KeyAdapter() statement, there is an opening brace followed by a definition of the keyReleased() method on lines 25 to 28.

This is an example of an *anonymous class*, or class with no name. Version 1.1 and higher of Java allow such class definitions to appear in the middle of your code, wherever they are to be used. Although we will not delve too deeply into the mechanics of anonymous classes and other types of nested classes,[1] the anonymous class is frequently used to define adapter objects to handle events.

The rules for an anonymous class that are needed to understand the code on lines 24 to 29 are as follows. Whenever an anonymous class is defined by the use of the new operator followed by the name of an existing class, such as KeyAdapter, the anonymous class automatically becomes a subclass of the existing class. That is, the anonymous class defined on line 24 inherits KeyAdapter. Following the opening brace at the end of line 24, we may add variables and methods to the anonymous class in exactly the same way as to an ordinary class. Here, we need to override only the definition of the keyReleased() method, so we provide the code for that on lines 25 through 28. The keyReleased() method is called whenever a key is released over the messageText TextField, so the code within keyReleased() will be executed every time a key is released. The code simply extracts the text currently in messageText, stores it in usersMessage, and then repaints the window. In this way, every key press is echoed to the display area in the lower half of the window.

The closing brace on line 29 matches the opening brace at the end of line 24 which begins the definition of the anonymous class. The closing parenthesis on line 29 closes the argument list of the call to the addKeyListener() method started on line 24, and the semi-colon on line 29 ends the statement begun on line 24.

The simpler Java AWT components

Having seen a couple of examples of how to use components from the Java AWT, and how to handle events produced by these components, we can now take a more systematic look at the simpler components and their associated events. You are urged to read this section with the Java documentation close at hand, so you can browse the classes and see how the documentation is arranged. You will make frequent use of the documentation when you write programs yourself.

We will not cover all the AWT components in this chapter. Some of the more advanced features, such as menus and scrollbars, will be covered in Chapter 8.

The formats for the AWT components that are capable of generating events are all very similar. A given component can generate events of one (or in a few cases, more than one) type, usually by the user pressing a key on the keyboard or clicking or moving the mouse. If the program is to respond to one of these events, a corresponding listener must be attached to the component, either by implementing

---

[1] Java 1.1.x also allows two other kinds of nested, or *inner* classes: member classes and local classes. Although these classes can be useful in certain situations, the author feels that excessive use of such classses make proper object-oriented design more difficult, so we will not consider them further in this book.

the listener interface, or defining an adapter object to handle the event. We have seen examples of both these methods in the preceding sections.

We will now survey the simpler AWT components and describe the events they may generate. Following this, we will present a more substantial example that illustrates several of the components in action.

- `Button`: A button which may be pressed by clicking on it with the mouse.
  - Event generated: `ActionEvent`, generated when the button is pressed.
  - Listener interface: `ActionListener`. Contains only one method, `actionPerformed()`, which is called whenever the `ActionEvent` for the `Button` is generated.
  - Adapter class: None, since the interface has only one method. The class containing the `Button` must implement `ActionListener`, and provide a definition for the `actionPerformed()` class.
- `Checkbox`: A small box or circle that may be selected or deselected by clicking on it with the mouse. A set of `Checkboxes` is usually used to allow the user to select one or more items from a list by clicking on the box adjacent to each item. A set of `Checkboxes` may be added to a `CheckboxGroup` object to convert them into a set of 'radio buttons'. Only one of a set of radio buttons may be selected at any time.
  - Event generated: `ItemEvent`, generated when the `Checkbox` is selected or deselected.
  - Listener interface: `ItemListener`. Contains only a single method, `itemStateChanged()`, called whenever the `Checkbox`'s state is changed.
  - Adapter class: None.
- `Choice`: A 'drop-down menu' from which the user may select one item only. The main difference in appearance between a `Choice` object and a set of radio buttons is that when not in use, the `Choice` object retracts so that only the top item in the list is visible.
  - Event generated: `ItemEvent`, generated when the user selects an item from the drop-down list.
  - Listener interface and adapter class: as for the `Checkbox`.
- `List`: A scrollable list of items, from which the user may select one or, if allowed, more than one item. The number of items visible at once in the scrollable list may be specified when the list is created.
  - Events generated: `ItemEvent`, generated when an item is selected or deselected; `ActionEvent`, generated when the user double-clicks with the mouse on one of the items.
  - Listener interfaces: `ItemListener` and `ActionListener`, described under `Checkbox` and `Button` above.
  - Adapter classes: None.

In addition to the specialized events generated by these components, there are several events that may be generated by all AWT components. As such, they are associated with the `Component` class, from which all AWT components are derived using inheritance. The following events may therefore be acted on if generated by any component.

- `ComponentEvent`: Generated whenever the component is moved, resized, hidden, or shown.
  - Listener interface: `ComponentListener`, which contains four methods: `componentMoved()`, `componentResized()`, `componentHidden()`, `componentShown()`. The corresponding method is called whenever the particular event occurs.
  - Adapter class: `ComponentAdapter`, which contains empty versions of the four methods in the `ComponentListener` interface. If only one or two of these methods is required, an anonymous class may be used to derive a class from `ComponentAdapter`, and define the required methods.
- `FocusEvent`: Generated whenever the component gains or loses *focus*. A component has the focus of the application whenever it is the active component. For example, in order to type into a `TextField`, you must first give focus to the `TextField`, which you can do by clicking on it with the mouse. When another component, such as a `Button`, is selected after typing text into the `TextField`, the `TextField` loses the focus and `Button` gains it. Each of these components will generate a `FocusEvent` whenever it gains or loses focus.
  - Listener interface: `FocusListener`, which contains two methods: `focusGained()`, `focusLost()`.
  - Adapter class: `FocusAdapter`.
- `KeyEvent`: Generated whenever a key on the keyboard is pressed. We have seen an example using a `KeyEvent` above.
  - Listener interface: `KeyListener`, which contains three methods: `keyPressed()`, `keyReleased()`, `keyTyped()`. A 'typed' key must be both pressed down and released.
  - Adapter class: `KeyAdapter`.
- `MouseEvent`: Generated whenever the mouse is moved, or whenever one of the mouse buttons is clicked. (For an example using `MouseEvent`s, see the checkers game in Chapter 8.)
  - Listener interfaces: The `MouseEvent` has two listeners, one for mouse motion events, and the other for mouse button events. The `MouseMotionListener` contains two methods: `mouseDragged()` and `mouseMoved()`. The mouse is said to be *dragged* when it is moved with one of its buttons held down. If the mouse is moved without any buttons being held, it is just *moved*. The `MouseListener` contains five methods: `mousePressed()`, `mouseReleased()`, `mouseClicked()`, `mouseEntered()`, `mouseExited()`. The first three methods refer to pressing down, releasing, or clicking (pressing and releasing) one of the mouse buttons. The last two methods respond to the mouse cursor entering

or exiting the component generating the event. For example, a 'mouse entered' event is generated when the mouse cursor crosses the boundary as it enters the area occupied by a component.
- Adapter classes: `MouseAdapter` and `MouseMotionAdapter`.

There are several other more advanced AWT components that generate other types of events, but we will consider these in Chapter 8. We will now have a look at an example using several of the basic components described above.

A Java AWT example – the game of nim

We will now consider a somewhat more involved example of a program that makes use of several components from the Java AWT. The program allows the user to play the game of *nim* against the computer.

The rules for the game of nim are quite simple. The game begins with a number of counters (such as coins or sticks) placed on the table between the two players. Play alternates between the two players, with each player allowed to take one, two or three counters at each turn. The objective is to force the other player to take the *last* counter. In other words, the player who removes the last counter loses the game.

For our program, we wish to write an interface to the game that allows the user to play against the computer by selecting the various game options from lists, checkboxes, and so on. The code below produces the interface shown in Figure 5.3.

The initial number of counters may be selected from a `Choice` object at the top of the window. Below this, a pair of `Checkboxes`, used as radio buttons, allows the user to choose whether the human player or the computer player goes first. Underneath this, one `Button` will start a new game using the choices from the first two rows, while the other `Button` ends the program.

Underneath these main controls, we find a set of three radio buttons that allow the human user to select the number of counters to remove. These radio buttons must be available *only* when it is the human's turn to move. As well, if there are only one or two counters left, then only the '1' or '2' counter buttons should be available.

Java allows components to be enabled or disabled during the running of a program. A disabled component is still visible, but is greyed out and will not respond to mouse clicks or keyboard presses (that is, it will not generate any events when the user tries to interact with it).

The bottom section of the window will display the counters remaining, using some drawing methods from the `Graphics` class. The display must be updated after each human and computer move.

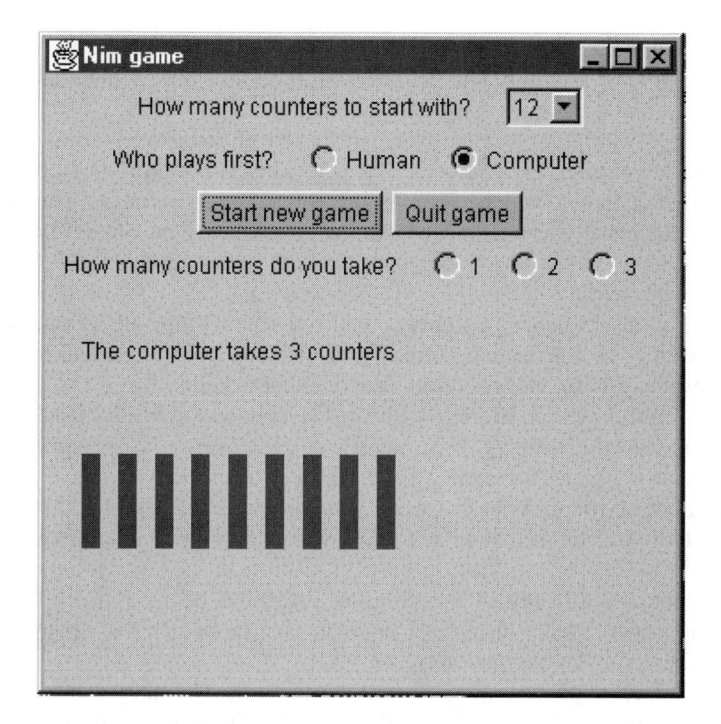

Figure 5.3 Interface for the nim game.

Above the display of the counters is printed a message stating how many counters the computer removed on its last move.

Finally, when one player removes the last counter, a separate window, as shown in Figure 5.4, pops up with a message stating who won. This window contains a Label with the message, and a Button which hides the window and returns the user to the main game window.

Before we present the code, we need to work out the strategy that the computer will use to play the game. We could make things easy on the human player and just have the computer play randomly, but there is actually a very simple strategy that will allow the computer to win almost all the time against a human player that does not know the equivalent strategy.

Figure 5.4 The 'game over' popup window in the nim game.

The goal of the game is to leave your opponent with a single counter on your last move. Therefore, if there are two counters left, you take one; if there are three left, you take two, and if there are four left, you take three.

Going one layer up in the game, you can see that if you leave your opponent with five counters, you are also guaranteed to win. This is because your opponent can take one, two or three counters, leaving you with four, three, or two counters, from which you can leave your opponent with only 1 counter. You can easily extend the argument to show that if you leave your opponent with 1, 5, 9, 13, 17, ... counters, you will always win.

Looking at this sequence of numbers, you can see that they are all one more than a multiple of 4, so the winning strategy is to leave your opponent with $4n + 1$ counters, where n is an integer greater than or equal to zero.

What do you do if you are left with $4n + 1$ counters yourself? Clearly, if your opponent knows the strategy, you have lost. However, it is possible that your opponent doesn't know the strategy and has just been lucky to leave you with a losing number of counters. In that case, you can play randomly for that one move and hope that the opponent will *not* leave you with $4n + 1$ counters on the next move.

The computer's strategy in the program presented below follows these ideas, except that, when faced with $4n + 1$ counters, the computer will always take one counter rather than playing randomly.

The code for the game is divided into two classes. The main class contains the code for the window in Figure 5.3, and associated code for playing the game. The other class contains the code for the popup window shown in Figure 5.4. We will consider the code for the main class first.

This code is the longest we have presented in this book so far, but you should not feel intimidated by it. Virtually all the programming techniques used in this example should be familiar to you from this and earlier chapters. We will discuss the main points of the code following the listing.

```
1   import java.applet.*;
2   import java.awt.*;
3   import java.awt.event.*;
4
5   public class Nim extends Applet
6   {
7     Label selectNumberLabel, playFirstLabel,
8        selectInitialLabel;
9     Button newGameButton, quitButton;
10    Choice selectInitialChoice;
11    Checkbox humanFirstBox, computerFirstBox,
12       choose1Box, choose2Box, choose3Box, dummyBox;
13    CheckboxGroup playFirstGroup, selectNumberGroup;
14    int countersLeft;
15    String computerTakes = "";
16
17    public static void main(String argv[])
18    {
```

```
19      Frame messageFrame = new Frame("Nim game");
20      Nim testMessage = new Nim();
21      testMessage.init();
22      messageFrame.add("Center", testMessage);
23      messageFrame.setSize(350,350);
24      messageFrame.setVisible(true);
25    }
26
27    public void init()
28    {
29      selectInitialLabel =
30        new Label("How many counters to start with?");
31      selectInitialChoice = new Choice();
32      selectInitialChoice.addItem("10");
33      selectInitialChoice.addItem("12");
34      selectInitialChoice.addItem("15");
35      this.add(selectInitialLabel);
36      this.add(selectInitialChoice);
37
38      playFirstLabel = new Label("Who plays first?");
39      playFirstGroup = new CheckboxGroup();
40      this.add(playFirstLabel);
41      humanFirstBox =
42        new Checkbox("Human", playFirstGroup, true);
43      computerFirstBox =
44        new Checkbox("Computer", playFirstGroup, false);
45      this.add(humanFirstBox);
46      this.add(computerFirstBox);
47
48      newGameButton = new Button("Start new game");
49      newGameButton.addActionListener(new ActionListener() {
50        public void actionPerformed(ActionEvent event) {
51            initializeNewGame();
52        }
53      });
54      this.add(newGameButton);
55
56      quitButton = new Button("Quit game");
57      quitButton.addActionListener(new ActionListener() {
58        public void actionPerformed(ActionEvent event) {
59        System.exit(0);
60        }
61      });
62      this.add(quitButton);
63
64      selectNumberLabel =
65        new Label("How many counters do you take?");
66      selectNumberGroup = new CheckboxGroup();
67      choose1Box = new Checkbox("1", selectNumberGroup,
68  false);
```

```
69        choose2Box = new Checkbox("2", selectNumberGroup,
70   false);
71        choose3Box = new Checkbox("3", selectNumberGroup,
72   false);
73        dummyBox = new Checkbox("", selectNumberGroup, true);
74
75        choose1Box.addItemListener(new ItemListener() {
76          public void itemStateChanged(ItemEvent event) {
77            doHumanMove(event);
78          }
79        });
80        choose2Box.addItemListener(new ItemListener() {
81          public void itemStateChanged(ItemEvent event) {
82            doHumanMove(event);
83          }
84        });
85        choose3Box.addItemListener(new ItemListener() {
86          public void itemStateChanged(ItemEvent event) {
87            doHumanMove(event);
88          }
89        });
90        this.add(selectNumberLabel);
91        this.add(choose1Box);
92        this.add(choose2Box);
93        this.add(choose3Box);
94        disableHumanMove();
95      }
96
97      public void paint(Graphics g)
98      {
99        int counterWidth = 10, counterHeight = 50;
100       g.setColor(Color.black);
101       g.drawString(computerTakes, 20, 150);
102       g.setColor(Color.red);
103       for (int counter = 0; counter < countersLeft; ++counter)
104         {
105            g.fillRect(20 + 2*counter*counterWidth, 200,
106              counterWidth, counterHeight);
107         }
108     }
109
110     private void initializeNewGame()
111     {
112       countersLeft = Integer.parseInt(
113         selectInitialChoice.getSelectedItem());
114       Checkbox whoFirst =
115  playFirstGroup.getSelectedCheckbox();
116       if (whoFirst.getLabel().equals("Computer")) {
117         doComputerMove();
118       } else {
119         computerTakes = "";
```

```java
      enableHumanMove();
    }
    repaint();
  }

  private void doComputerMove()
  {
    int numTaken;
    int remainder = countersLeft % 4;
    if (remainder == 1)
      numTaken = 1;
    else if (remainder == 0)
      numTaken = 3;
    else
      numTaken = remainder - 1;
    computerTakes =
      "The computer takes " + numTaken + " counter";
    if (numTaken > 1)
      computerTakes += "s";
    countersLeft -= numTaken;
    repaint();
    if (countersLeft == 0) {
      EndFrame youWinFrame = new EndFrame("You win!");
      youWinFrame.setVisible(true);
    } else {
      enableHumanMove();
    }
  }

  private void enableHumanMove()
  {
    dummyBox.setState(true);
    selectNumberLabel.setEnabled(true);
    choose1Box.setEnabled(true);
    if (countersLeft > 1)
      choose2Box.setEnabled(true);
    if (countersLeft > 2)
      choose3Box.setEnabled(true);
  }

  private void disableHumanMove()
  {
    selectNumberLabel.setEnabled(false);
    choose1Box.setEnabled(false);
    choose2Box.setEnabled(false);
    choose3Box.setEnabled(false);
  }

  private void doHumanMove(ItemEvent event)
  {
    int humanTakes =
```

```
171            Integer.parseInt(event.getItem().toString());
172         disableHumanMove();
173         countersLeft -= humanTakes;
174         if (countersLeft == 0) {
175           repaint();
176           EndFrame youLoseFrame =
177             new EndFrame("The computer wins!");
178           youLoseFrame.setVisible(true);
179         } else {
180           doComputerMove();
181         }
182       }
183   }
```

Lines 7 through 13 declare the various AWT components that we will use in the game. The `Label`s on lines 7 and 8 are used for the constant messages that appear on the window. Line 9 declares the two `Button`s that start and end the game. Line 10 declares the `Choice` object which allows the user to select the initial number of counters. The `Checkbox`es on line 11 are used for the radio buttons specifying who plays first, while the other `Checkbox`es on line 12 are used to choose the number of counters for the human player to remove. (The purpose of `dummyBox` will be explained when we show how the radio buttons are defined.)

Line 13 declares two `CheckboxGroup`s, to which the `Checkbox`es are added to form sets of radio buttons.

Line 14 declares the `int` variable which stores the number of counters remaining. Line 15 declares a `String` which is used to store the message stating how many counters the computer has selected on its latest move.

The `main()` method on lines 17 through 25 is the same form as those used in earlier examples.

The `init()` method creates and initializes all the components. The `Choice` object is created on line 31. Lines 32 to 34 add three items to the list contained with this object using the `addItem()` method. Note that `addItem()` expects a `String` as an argument, not an `int` or any other data type. If we want to interpret the list item as an `int` we will need to convert it later on (as we will see).

The first `Label` and the `Choice` object are added to the `Frame` on lines 35 and 36. We are still using Java's default method of adding components to a `Frame`, which means that they are added left-to-right on the current row until the width of the `Frame` is reached, after which a new row is started. We need to specify the dimensions of the `Frame` quite carefully in order for the display to appear as shown in Figure 5.3. You might like to experiment with the `Frame` dimensions, and with the sizes of the components themselves, to see what effect they have.

The first set of radio buttons is defined on lines 39 to 44. On line 39, we first define the `CheckboxGroup` which is to hold the two radio buttons. The `CheckboxGroup` has no actual parameters itself — it serves merely as a container into which the two `Checkbox`es are placed to convert them into radio buttons.

A `Checkbox` is defined on lines 41 and 42 by calling the `Checkbox` constructor. The first argument passed to the constructor is the label to be attached to the `Checkbox`. The second argument is the `CheckboxGroup` to which the `Checkbox` is to be added, and the final argument specifies that this box should be checked when it first appears in the window.

This particular constructor is only used when the `Checkbox` is to be added to a `CheckboxGroup`. A `Checkbox` that is to appear as a box on its own (not as one of a set of radio buttons) would use a two-argument constructor where the first argument is the label and the second states whether the box is to be checked or not.

After the second `Checkbox` is created on lines 43 and 44, the two boxes are added to the `Frame` on lines 45 and 46. Notice that the `CheckboxGroup` itself does not have to be added to the `Frame` – it is an invisible component, serving only to group the `Checkboxes` together into a set of radio buttons. It *does* have a visible effect, though, since radio buttons are drawn differently than non-radio button `Checkboxes`. Usually, radio buttons are small circles, while ordinary `Checkboxes` are small squares.

The 'Start new game' `Button` is added on lines 48 to 54. The `ActionEvent` generated by the `Button` is handled using an anonymous class, in the same way as the `KeyEvent` was handled in the `KeyboardEvent` class earlier in this chapter. In this case, the anonymous class is defined using the name of an *interface* (`ActionListener`) rather than another *class*, as was done in the `KeyboardEvent` example. When an anonymous class is defined using the name of an interface, it automatically `extends` the interface, so that definitions for all the methods in the interface must be provided within the anonymous class. In this case, `ActionListener` contains only the `actionPerformed()` method, so that is the only method we must provide.

If we only have one or two `Buttons` in the program, it is often more convenient to use an anonymous class to associate the `ActionListener` directly with the `Button`, rather than implementing the interface and providing an `actionPerformed()` method elsewhere in the class. The anonymous class has the advantage of keeping the listener's code with that of the `Button` to which it is attached, making the code easier to read (by humans).

The `ActionEvent` generated by `newGameButton` will therefore call the `initializeNewGame()` method, which we will discuss below.

The 'Quit game' `Button` is defined on lines 56 to 62. It is handled in the same was as `newGameButton`, except that the `System.exit()` method is called in response to its `ActionEvent`. This method stops the program immediately and shuts down all its windows. The argument (0) passed to `System.exit()` may or may not be used by the operating system running the Java program. Some operating systems (such as UNIX) interpret a return value from a program as a flag indicating the state the program was in when it stopped. It is traditional to return a value of 0 if the program exited without any errors. This is a system dependent feature, and has no effect on any part of the Java program itself.

114   THE JAVA AWT AND EVENT HANDLING

The radio button group which allows the human player to choose the number of counters to remove is defined on lines 64 to 91.[1] Although the human player has at most only three choices (one, two or three counters may be removed in any one turn), we have defined a fourth Checkbox called dummyBox. The reason for this is that Java requires that, in any set of radio buttons, one of the buttons must always be checked. When the human is about to make a move, however, we do not want any of the three choices to be checked, since the human must make a free choice. We therefore define the fourth Checkbox which is *not* displayed on screen (it is not added to the Frame after the other three Checkboxes are added on lines 88 to 90). By checking dummyBox, we clear the three visible Checkboxes and allow the human to make a free choice.

On lines 72 to 86, we have attached event handlers to the three visible Checkboxes. A Checkbox generates an ItemEvent whenever its state is changed. We can therefore wait until the human selects one of the three choices, and then process the human's move as soon as the choice is made. This has the advantage that the user does not need to click a separate button after making the choice of how many counters to remove – selecting the radio button simultaneously makes the choice *and* triggers the code to make the move. (This also has the disadvantage that the human cannot change his/her mind after making a choice.)

The ItemListener interface contains only a single method, so we use an anonymous class to implement the interface and handle the ItemEvent. We call the doHumanMove() method, and pass the actual ItemEvent object event to this method, since we need to be able to tell which of the three choices the human has made (note that all three radio buttons are handled by the same doHumanMove() method).

Finally, line 91 calls the disableHumanMove() method, which greys out the human move radio buttons at the start of the program. The human cannot make a move until the game has been started, so we force the user to start the game first, before accepting a move.

When the program is run, only the main() and init() methods will be executed. At this point, the window shown in Figure 5.3 will be displayed (without any graphics in the lower part of the window), and the program will wait for the user to make some choices. The rest of the program therefore consists of the various event handler methods that are called in response to the user's actions.

The initializeNewGame() method, on lines 107 to 119, is called when the 'Start new game' Button is pressed. The job of this method is to initialize the number of counters, and determine who is to play first. On line 110, the getSelectedItem() method extracts the item that was selected from the selectInitialChoice object. This is returned as a String, but we need to store it as an int in the countersLeft variable. The parseInt() method of the Integer class (one of the classes in the java.lang package, which is imported by

---

[1] This set of three buttons could be implemented more efficiently using an array, but we do not cover arrays until Chapter 6.

default into all Java programs) accepts a `String` containing an integer value and converts it to an `int`.

On line 111, we determine which of the two radio buttons in the `playFirstGroup` group has been selected, using the `getSelectedCheckbox()` method of the `CheckboxGroup` class. This method returns a `Checkbox` object, and *not* the label associated with this box. We therefore must use the `getLabel()` method of the `Checkbox` class (on line 112) to extract the label, which is returned as a `String`. The `equals()` method of the `String` class compares that `String` with the constant `String` 'Computer'. If a match occurs, the computer is to play first, and the `doComputerMove()` method is called to start the game off. Otherwise, the `computerTakes` message on screen is cleared, and the three radio buttons allowing the human to make a move are enabled.

The `doComputerMove()` method on lines 121 to 143 implements the strategy for winning the game that we described above. Recall that the `%` operator calculates the remainder when its first operand is divided by its second, so we first find the remainder when `countersLeft` is divided by 4 (line 124). If this is 1, the computer is in a losing position, so it just takes one counter in the hope that the human opponent doesn't understand the winning strategy (lines 125 and 126). Otherwise, it takes the required number of counters to leave the human opponent with $4n + 1$ counters, and therefore puts itself into a winning position (lines 127 to 130).

The `computerTakes` label is updated on lines 131 to 134, the `countersLeft` variable is updated on line 135, and the display is repainted on line 136.

The `paint()` method (lines 94 to 105) draws the `computerTakes` message on the screen, and also paints in the remaining counters. The `fillRect()` method of the `Graphics` class draws a filled rectangle. Its four arguments are: x and y co-ordinates of the upper left corner, width, and height. We have hard-coded in the co-ordinates for the locations of the message string and the counters (not in general a good programming practice) because we are using Java's default method for placing the other components on screen, and the graphics must be positioned relative to these components so they don't overwrite each other. When we see how to use more advanced positioning methods (in Chapter 7), we will be able to place the various components in a more portable manner.

Finally, on line 137 a check is made to see if the computer took the last counter, and the game is over. If so, the popup window is created and displayed (lines 138 and 139). Otherwise, the human is given a move on line 141.

The two methods `enableHumanMove()` and `disableHumanMove()` on lines 145 to 162 use the `setEnabled()` method of the `Component` class to turn the radio buttons off and on, according to whether it is the human's move, and taking note of how many counters are left.

The final method, `doHumanMove()`, on lines 164 to 178, is called when the human selects one of the radio buttons in the `selectNumberGroup` `CheckboxGroup`. To discover which of the three boxes was chosen, we extract the item from the event using the `getItem()` method on line 167. This method returns a generic `Object`, but we can extract the name of the item using the `toString()`

method, which returns the label associated with the Checkbox. This label is in turn converted to an int using the parseInt() method.

Since the human has just made a move, we disable the radio buttons on line 168, and adjust the number of counters left on line 169. As in doComputerMove(), we then check to see if the game is over and, if so, display the popup window. Otherwise, we let the computer have its move (line 176).

You can see that the code for an AWT-based program splits into two main sections: the init() method, where the components are created and initialized, and a collection of event handling methods that respond to the user's interaction with the various components. After the init() method is processed, the order in which the various methods are called depends entirely on the actions of the user.

Finally, we will examine the EndFrame class, which provides the popup window that appears at the end of the game. Its code follows.

```
1   import java.awt.*;
2   import java.awt.event.*;
3
4   public class EndFrame extends Frame
5   {
6      Button closeFrameButton;
7      Label endGameLabel;
8
9      public EndFrame(String newEndGameMessage)
10     {
11        super("Game over");
12        setBackground(Color.blue);
13        closeFrameButton = new Button("Return to main window");
14        closeFrameButton.addActionListener(new ActionListener() {
15          public void actionPerformed(ActionEvent event) {
16            setVisible(false);
17          }
18        });
19        endGameLabel = new Label(newEndGameMessage);
20        endGameLabel.setFont(new Font("Helvetica",
21           Font.BOLD, 14));
22        endGameLabel.setForeground(Color.yellow);
23
24        Panel buttonPanel = new Panel();
25        buttonPanel.add("Center", endGameLabel);
26        buttonPanel.add("Center", closeFrameButton);
27        this.add("Center", buttonPanel);
28        this.setSize(200, 100);
29     }
30  }
```

The EndFrame class is an illustration of how a Frame can be used to display a separate window from the main application. Up to now, we have only used a Frame to create a container for the main application inside the main() method.

Note that `EndFrame` extends the `Frame` class (line 4). The class contains only one method: its constructor. The `String` passed to the constructor contains the message to be displayed above the `Button`. On line 11, the constructor of the superclass (`Frame`) is called to give the popup window a title in its title bar. Next, the background colour is set to blue. The `closeFrameButton` is created on line 13, and an event handler added on lines 14 to 18. Pressing the `Button` simply hides the window by calling the `setVisible()` method with a `false` argument – it does not delete it. If you glance back at the code in the main `Nim` class, however, you will see that every time the popup window is displayed, it is created anew (lines 138 and 172–73). Java's automatic garbage collection facility will delete any old, unused copy of `EndFrame` that happens to be around, so the programmer does not need to do it explicitly in the code.

The `Label` is created to contain `newEndGameMessage`, and its foreground colour is set to yellow.

On lines 24 to 27, the `Label` and `Button` are added to a `Panel`, which is in turn added to the `Frame` itself. A `Panel` is basically a container into which components can be placed to group them together. In more complex layouts, several `Panel`s can be arranged on top of a `Frame` (or even other `Panel`s), in much the same way as you can mount several small items on a larger piece of card, which can in turn be mounted onto a large display board.

The reason we have used a `Panel` here is that components added directly to a `Frame` will resize themselves to fill the `Frame`. If we omitted the `Panel`, the `Button` would fill the `Frame` and obliterate the `Label` underneath it. Adding the two components to a `Panel` and then adding the `Panel` to the `Frame` causes the components to retain their proper size, with the `Panel` becoming the object that fills the `Frame`.

We will study `Panel`s in more detail in Chapter 7, where we introduce Java's layout managers.

Exercises

1 Write an applet containing a `Choice` component into which you should load a few `String`s of your choice. The applet should also contain a `Button` which, when pressed, causes the current item displayed in the `Choice` component to be read, and the `String` drawn onto the background of the `Frame` using the `drawString()` method.

2 Study the Java documentation of the `List` component, and then modify the applet from exercise 1 by replacing the `Choice` with a `List`. Give the list a display window of four items, and add at least five `String`s to the `List` so that scrolling is enabled. As before, pressing the `Button` should display the selected item.

3   Modify the applet from exercise 2 to allow multiple selections from the `List` and display all selections (concatenated into a single `String`) when the `Button` is pushed.

4   Modify the nim game from the text so that the three radio buttons used for selecting the number of counters are replaced by `Buttons`. The same enabling and disabling rules should be applied to the `Buttons`.

5   Further modify the nim game by replacing the `Choice` box with a `TextField` into which the user can type the number of initial counters. By doing this, you are allowing a source of error to creep in, as the user may enter a non-numerical string, or may enter a number that is too large or too small (e.g. negative). Try to work out how you might allow for this in the program.

6   Modify the `EndFrame` class by adding a `Button` which will hide the `EndFrame` window and start a new game in the main window automatically (that is, without having to press the 'Start new game' button on the main window). In order to do this, you will need some way of calling a method in the `Nim` class from within the `EndFrame` class. This can be done by adding a `Nim` variable to the `EndFrame` class, and initializing this variable by requiring that a `Nim` object be passed to the `EndFrame` constructor. When an `EndFrame` object is created in the `Nim` class (on lines 138 and 172 in the `Nim` code), pass a `this` pointer to the `EndFrame` constructor along with the `String` it is to display. Then, inside the `EndFrame` class, pressing the `Button` can use this pointer to call methods in the `Nim` class.

7   Write an applet which will allow several geometric shapes to be displayed in various colours and sizes. You may wish to use the code at the end of Chapter 4 to implement the drawing.

   Provide three radio buttons that allow the user to select one of 'Rectangle,' 'Right Triangle,' or 'Circle.' One of these radio buttons should be selected at all times, so there is no need to provide a dummy button as we did in the game of nim.

   Provide three `TextFields`, with associated `Labels` saying 'Length,' 'Width,' and 'Radius.' If the user selects either the 'Rectangle' or 'Right Triangle' button, the 'Length' and 'Width' fields (and associated labels) should be enabled, with the 'Radius' field being disabled. If the user selects 'Circle,' reverse the enablings of the `TextFields`. The user should be able to enter the dimensions of the figure into the corresponding `TextField`.

   Provide a `Choice` box containing a list of colours. The user selects the colour to be used to draw the figure.

   Finally, provide two `Buttons`, labelled 'Draw' and 'Quit'. Pressing the 'Draw' button should draw the selected figure with the dimensions and colour chosen. The 'Quit' button should exit the program.

   Although most of the programming techniques you need have been used in this chapter, you may need to do a bit of reading in the Java documentation. For example, try drawing *filled* figures rather than just outlines.

CHAPTER 6
Arrays and strings

Arrays and their properties

Up to now, all the variables we have used in the example programs have been declared as single entities. We have single primitive data types, such as `ints` and `floats`, and single objects, such as `AlarmClock` objects and various components from the Java AWT. In all these cases, only a single instance of each of these objects was required, so declaring a single variable was perfectly adequate.

In many cases, however, it would be convenient to declare a set of variables, all of the same data type. For example, in the game of nim program in Chapter 5, we needed three radio buttons which allowed the user to select the number of counters to remove. These three buttons all had the same basic function – to allow the human player to remove counters – but the only difference between them was the number of counters (one, two, or three) that the player wished to remove.

In the program in Chapter 5, we declared three separate variables to represent these three radio buttons, and gave each variable a different name. It would be easier if we could define a *single* name (such as `removeCounters`) for all three buttons, and then specify to which button we are referring by adding an index number to the variable name, such as `removeCounters[1]` to refer to the first button.

This is just what is provided by the *array* data type in Java. An array is a data type which we have not yet encountered in any of the sample programs. In many respects, arrays have the same properties as other objects in Java, but there are enough features unique to arrays that it is probably safer to think of them as the third main data type (in addition to primitive and reference data types).

To get a feel for how arrays are declared, created, and used in a Java program, it is best to start with a simple example. Let us suppose that you keep weather records for your home town. Most hobby shops sell simple weather monitoring equipment such as an outdoor thermometer that stores the maximum and minimum temperature in a 24-hour period. If you record the maximum and minimum temperature each day for, say, a full month, you may wish to store the data on a computer and calculate a few elementary statistics. Common weather data that is often published in newspapers at the end of each month includes things like the average temperature, the number of days on which the temperature dropped below freezing or rose above 20 degrees Celsius, and so on.

120 ARRAYS AND STRINGS

We will present a small Java program which stores one temperature reading per day (taken at noon) for a 10-day period and calculates the average temperature and the number of days where the temperature was below freezing (0 degrees Celsius). We will not include any graphical interface in the program in order that you may concentrate on the code using arrays. The program simply prints out the average and number of days in the command window.

```
1   public class Temperatures
2   {
3     public static void main(String argv[])
4     {
5       Temperatures testTemperatures = new Temperatures();
6     }
7
8     Temperatures()
9     {
10      double[] noonTemps = {5.6, 2.3, 10.9, -1.3, -3.4,
11         0.0, 7.8, -6.0, -0.7, 1.8};
12      double average = calcAverage(noonTemps);
13      int freezeDays = calcFreezeDays(noonTemps);
14      System.out.println("Average = " + average);
15      System.out.println("Number of freezing days = " +
16         freezeDays);
17    }
18
19    double calcAverage(double[] temps)
20    {
21      double sumTemps = 0.0;
22
23      for (int index = 0; index < temps.length; ++index) {
24        sumTemps += temps[index];
25      }
26      if (temps.length > 0)
27        return sumTemps / temps.length;
28      return 0.0;
29    }
30
31    int calcFreezeDays(double[] temps)
32    {
33      int freezeCount = 0;
34
35      for (int index = 0; index < temps.length; ++index) {
36        if (temps[index] <= 0.0)
37          ++freezeCount;
38      }
39      return freezeCount;
40    }
41  }
```

Since the `Temperatures` class does not run as an applet and makes no use of any of the AWT components, we need not import any of the Java packages at the start of the program. We just define the class directly on line 1. The `main()` method is particularly simple, since the only output produced by the program is text printed to the command window. The `main()` method therefore just creates a `Temperatures` object by calling the constructor on line 5.

Within the constructor we find the first mention of an array. The general idea is to store the 10 temperatures within an array of 10 `double`s, called `noonTemps`. The syntax for declaring and initializing an array is shown on lines 10 and 11. The first part of the statement on line 10 is:

```
double[] noonTemps
```

This looks like an ordinary variable declaration except for the brackets `[]` after the data type `double`. These brackets indicate that the variable `noonTemps` is to be an *array* of `double`s and not just a single `double` variable. The *length* of the array (that is, the number of items contained in the array) is not specified by this declaration – that must be determined later, and can be done in two ways.

The remainder of the statement on lines 10 and 11 shows one of the ways in which the length of the array can be specified, and by which the array elements can be initialized. (We'll consider the second method a bit later.) The values to be stored in the array are specified as a list of values separated by commas, and enclosed in braces. If you count up the number of items, you will find there are 10.

How do we refer to individual elements within the `noonTemps` array? The notation is fairly straightforward, but contains one little feature that is hard to get used to at first. The *first* element of an array is specified by adding the notation `[0]` to the array name. That is, the first element of `noonTemps` is written `noonTemps[0]`, and, after the initialization on lines 10 and 11, contains the value 5.6. The second element is written `noonTemps[1]`, and so on. This method of indexing array elements is known as *zero-based arrays*.

The reason for this seemingly perverse method of indexing arrays is largely historical. Most of Java's low-level syntax is copied from the earlier C and C++ languages, and arrays in C and C++ are zero-based as well. There are good reasons for this in C, since arrays are treated somewhat differently in C than they are in Java, but in the interests of conformity with C syntax, the designers of Java have copied this array notation into Java as well.

Once you remember the method for referring to array elements, you can use an array element in much the same way as any other variable of the same type. For example, you can use an array element as part of an expression, as in:

```
double twiceTemp = 2 * noonTemps[3];
```

New values can be assigned to array elements, as in:

```
double newValue = 7.7;
noonTemps[4] = newValue / 2.0;
```

Lines 12 and 13 show that an array can be passed to a method just like any other object. Also like objects, arrays are passed by *reference* and not by value. The `calcAverage()` method called on line 12 is defined on lines 19 to 29. The method expects a `double[]` (that is, an array of `doubles`) as an argument, and returns a `double` value, which is to be the average of the values in the array.

Within the method, we see one of the great advantages of using an array to store a set of related data. The standard method of calculating the average of a set of values is to add all the values up and then divide the total by the number of values. If we had stored the 10 temperatures in 10 different variables, each with a different name, we would need an expression like

```
(t1 + t2 + t3 + t4 + t5 + t6 + t7 + t8 + t9 + t10) / 10
```

Besides being cumbersome, this expression works only if we wish to find the average of precisely 10 values. We would need a different expression for each different number of values.

The code in the `calcAverage()` method shows how arrays can be used to calculate an average using a `for` loop. We define a local variable called `sumTemps` in which the sum of the temperature data is built up. We initialize it to 0.0 on line 21. Then, in the `for` loop on lines 23 to 25, we begin with the first element in the array (which, remember, has index 0, not 1!), and add up all the temperatures up to the last one stored in the array. All arrays have a built-in field called `length` which contains the number of elements currently stored in the array. The `temps.length` value is used on line 23 as the stopping condition of the `for` loop.

Line 23 illustrates one other thing that is often hard to get used to when you first use arrays. Since an array containing, say, 10 elements *begins* with index 0, the tenth and last element of the array has index 9. In other words, if an array `temps` contains `temps.length` elements, these are stored between indexes 0 and `temps.length` - 1. This is the reason the stopping condition within the `for` loop on line 23 is `index < temps.length` and not `index <= temps.length`.

If you forget where the upper or lower limit of an array is, and inadvertently try to access an index that is less than 0 or greater than or equal to the `length` of the array, Java will inform you that you are doing this by producing an error message in the command window. The message will contain the phrase 'ArrayIndexOutOfBoundsException', along with a lot of other information, but if you get that message, you'll know you've over- or under-stepped the bounds of an array.

After adding up all the temperatures stored in the `temps` array, line 26 tests the value of `temps.length` to ensure that it is greater than 0 (that is, it makes sure there was at least one element in the array). If so, an average may be calculated by dividing `sumTemps` by the number of elements in the array, which is what we do on line 27. If the array contains no elements, we return 0.0 as the default value on line 28. This is not an ideal solution to the problem of how to handle a zero-length array, since it is also possible that the average value for a set of temperatures could come out to be zero. Ideally, we would like the `calcAverage()` method to recognize that division by zero is an error, and flag the error condition in a way that makes it obvious that an error has occurred. We will see how to do this in Chapter 10 where we study exceptions.

The `calcFreezeDays()` method should now be fairly easy to understand. We declare `freezeCount` as the variable that will count the number of days with a temperature at or below freezing. We then loop through the array and compare each element of `temps` with 0.0, adding 1 to `freezeCount` if the temperature is a freezing temperature.

This simple example has shown the following.

- An array is declared using the square bracket notation, as in `double[] noonTemps`.
- One way an array may be initialized is by setting the newly declared array equal to a set of elements enclosed within braces, as on lines 10 and 11.
- The number of elements in an array may be found using the `length` property.
- Arrays are passed by reference to methods.
- The *first* element of an array is located at index 0.
- The *last* element of an array with size `length` is located at index `length - 1`.

We close this section with a second example that illustrates the second method of initializing an array after it is declared. The class `RandTemps`, shown below, is similar to `Temperatures` above, except that instead of specifying the contents of the array as a list, we merely specify the *size* of the array, and then generate some 'random' temperature values to load into the array elements. After generating these random elements, we calculate the average temperature and the number of freezing days in the same way as before. The code for the first part of the class follows. The class also contains the `calcAverage()` and `calcFreezeDays()` methods from the `Temperatures` class, but these are unchanged.

```
1   public class RandTemps
2   {
3       static double MAX_TEMP = 10.0;
4       static double MIN_TEMP = -10.0;
5
6       public static void main(String argv[])
7       {
8           RandTemps testRandTemps = new RandTemps();
9       }
10
11      RandTemps()
12      {
13          double[] noonTemps = new double[10];
14          for (int index = 0; index < noonTemps.length; ++index)
15              noonTemps[index] = Math.random() *
```

```
16                (MAX_TEMP - MIN_TEMP) + MIN_TEMP;
17      double average = calcAverage(noonTemps);
18      int freezeDays = calcFreezeDays(noonTemps);
19      System.out.println("Average = " + average);
20      System.out.println("Number of freezing days = " +
21        freezeDays);
22    }
23
24    // Other methods copied from Temperatures
25  }
```

Lines 3 and 4 illustrate a new programming technique: the use of the `static` keyword to declare a *class-wide* parameter for a given class. The keyword `static` before the declaration of a parameter or method (such as `main()`) within a class indicates that the parameter or method is attached to the class itself, and not to any particular instance of that class. That is, the `MAX_TEMP` parameter is defined to have the constant value of 10.0, and is a property of the `RandTemps` class itself, not of any particular instance of it. As such, it may be referred to from outside the `RandTemps` class as `RandTemps.MAX_TEMP` (or from within the `RandTemps` class simply as `MAX_TEMP`).

It is good programming practice to define `static` parameters to represent parameters within a class, rather than simply writing in the bare numbers. This is for two main reasons. First, it improves the readability of the program, since it is much more obvious what the term `MAX_TEMP` on line 16 refers to than if it had been written simply as 10.0. Second, it makes the value of this parameter much easier to change, if so desired. By declaring a `static` parameter at the start of the class, we need only change its definition in one place, rather than hunting through the code for every place where that parameter occurs.

A method can be declared as `static` as well. Static methods, like static variables, are methods associated with the class itself and not with any particular instance of the class. The `Math` class in `java.lang` contains many `static` methods for calculating various mathematical functions. For example, the `sqrt()` method is a `static` method in the `Math` class that calculates the square root of its argument. You can use this method with a statement such as `Math.sqrt(2.0)`. You do not need to declare a `Math` variable first, and then use that variable to call the `sqrt()` method – you can just call the method directly by prefixing its name with the name of the class which contains it.

The second method of initializing an array is illustrated on line 13. Here we declare the `noonTemps` array in the usual way (`double[] noonTemps`). In the second half of the statement, however, we use the `new` operator to find and allocate space for 10 `doubles`. The location of this space is assigned to `noonTemps` by the `=` operator. By default, Java initializes each of these `doubles` to the value of 0.0.

Finally, lines 14 to 16 show how 'random' values can be generated and stored in these array elements. We have enclosed the word 'random' in quotes since these numbers are not truly random. They are produced by the `random()` method, which is part of the `Math` class (in turn, part of the `java.lang` package, which is imported into all programs by default, and is therefore always available). This is a `static` method of the `Math` class, and may therefore be referred to using the notation `Math.random()` (that is, we do not need to declare an object of the `Math` class to be able to access the `random()` method, since declaring the method to be static makes it a method associated with the class itself and not with any specific instance of it).

The `random()` method actually uses a deterministic algorithm to calculate a series of `double` numbers uniformly distributed between 0.0 and 1.0. These numbers *appear* random (and pass most of the statistical tests for randomness) but, because they are generated using a deterministic formula, they are called *pseudo-random* numbers.

Since the `random()` method produces numbers between 0.0 and 1.0, we must scale these numbers if we want random numbers in another range. In this program, we would like random temperatures between `MIN_TEMP` and `MAX_TEMP`. We therefore scale the interval used by `random()` to have a range of (`MAX_TEMP` - `MIN_TEMP`). If we stopped here, however, the lower range of the interval would still be 0.0, and the upper range would be (`MAX_TEMP` - `MIN_TEMP`), or 20.0 in our case. To shift the range to the right location, we must add `MIN_TEMP` to the result. Lines 15 and 16 will therefore produce random numbers in the range `MIN_TEMP` to `MAX_TEMP`.

The remainder of the constructor is identical to the constructor in the `Temperatures` class. If you run the `RandTemps` program several times, however, you should notice that you get different results on each run, since different random temperatures are being generated for the `noonTemps` array.

Arrays of objects

The arrays we considered in the previous section were arrays of primitive data types such as `doubles` or `ints`. For such arrays, constructing the array is a two-stage process. First, we declare the variable to be an array of a particular data type. Then, we initialize the array, either by setting it equal to a list of data enclosed within braces, or by using the `new` operator to allocate space for the array, and then storing some data in each array element.

Java allows arrays of *any* data type – primitive or reference. If we wish to create an array of a reference data type, however, construction of the array becomes a *three*-stage process.

The first two stages are similar to the stages for creating an array of a primitive data type. We must first declare the array variable, then specify the size of the array using the `new` operator. The second step, however, only allocates an array of *pointers* to a set of objects of the required type. In order to complete the process, we must create an object to attach to each pointer.

126 ARRAYS AND STRINGS

To illustrate the process, suppose we wish to create an array of Buttons, where a Button is the Java AWT component introduced in Chapter 5. Since a Button is a reference data type, the procedure for creating the array is as follows.

```
Button[] buttonArray;
buttonArray = new Button[5];
for (int index = 0; index < 5; ++index)
   buttonArray[index] = new Button("Button " + index);
```

The first line declares the array variable buttonArray. The second line allocates five pointers to Button objects and assigns these pointers to buttonArray. At this stage, all five of these pointers are null, so if we attempted to, say, attach an ActionListener to buttonArray[2], we would get a null pointer error, since although buttonArray[2] exists, it does not yet have a Button to point to.

To complete the construction of the array, we must create a Button for each array element to point to, which is what is done in the for loop. Each Button is created using the new operator, and assigned a label giving its index in the array.

Note the difference between the two uses of the new operator in this code extract. Its first use is to allocate an array of five pointers to Buttons – in this case, *square* brackets are used after the data type Button. In the second case, the new operator is used to create an individual Button, and *parentheses* (round brackets) are used after the data type Button. Using square brackets means that an array is being created, while using parentheses means that a constructor is being called, and an actual instance of a Button is being created.

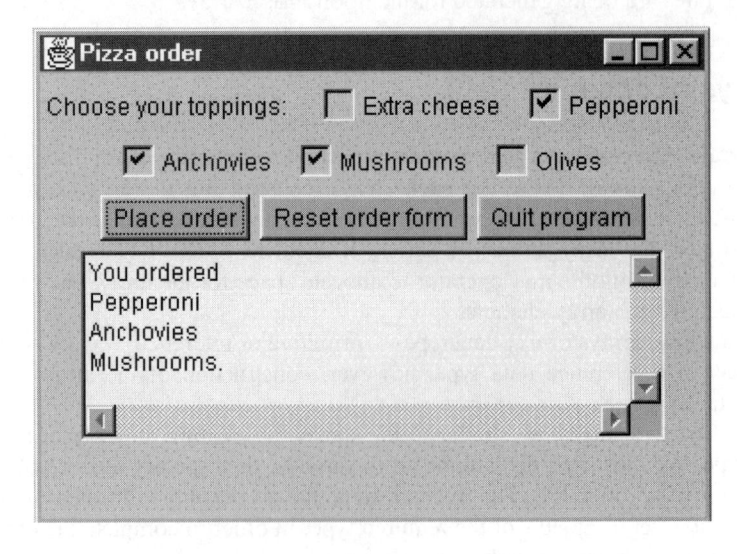

Figure 6.1 The interface for the Pizza applet.

To illustrate an array of reference types in practice, we present a simple AWT-based program that might be part of a form used to order a pizza. The window is shown in Figure 6.1.

The window contains five Checkboxes (used as ordinary checkboxes this time, not as radio buttons) which allow the user to select none or more toppings for the pizza. Pressing the 'Place order' button prints out the list of toppings selected in the text area at the bottom (as shown in the figure). The 'Reset order form' button clears all the checkboxes, and prints the message 'Awaiting your order.' in the text area. 'Quit program' stops the program and closes the window.

The program uses an array of Checkboxes to store the topping choices. It also illustrates the use of Checkboxes that are not contained within a CheckboxGroup, and introduces the TextArea component – a multi-line text field.

```
1   import java.applet.*;
2   import java.awt.*;
3   import java.awt.event.*;
4
5   public class Pizza extends Applet
6   {
7     Label pizzaLabel;
8     Button orderButton, resetButton, quitButton;
9     TextArea orderDetails;
10    Checkbox[] topping;
11    static int NUM_TOPPINGS = 5;
12
13    public static void main(String argv[])
14    {
15      Frame messageFrame = new Frame("Pizza order");
16      Pizza testMessage = new Pizza();
17      testMessage.init();
18      messageFrame.add("Center", testMessage);
19      messageFrame.setSize(350,250);
20      messageFrame.setVisible(true);
21    }
22
23    public void init()
24    {
25      pizzaLabel = new Label("Choose your toppings:");
26      topping = new Checkbox[NUM_TOPPINGS];
27      topping[0] = new Checkbox("Extra cheese", false);
28      topping[1] = new Checkbox("Pepperoni", false);
29      topping[2] = new Checkbox("Anchovies", false);
30      topping[3] = new Checkbox("Mushrooms", false);
31      topping[4] = new Checkbox("Olives", false);
32
33      orderButton = new Button("Place order");
34      orderButton.addActionListener(new ActionListener() {
35        public void actionPerformed(ActionEvent event) {
36          processOrder();
37        }
```

```
38        });
39        resetButton = new Button("Reset order form");
40        resetButton.addActionListener(new ActionListener() {
41          public void actionPerformed(ActionEvent event) {
42            resetForm();
43          }
44        });
45        quitButton = new Button("Quit program");
46        quitButton.addActionListener(new ActionListener() {
47          public void actionPerformed(ActionEvent event) {
48            System.exit(0);
49          }
50        });
51        orderDetails =
52          new TextArea("Awaiting your order.", 5, 40);
53        add(pizzaLabel);
54        for (int index = 0; index < NUM_TOPPINGS; ++index)
55          add(topping[index]);
56        add(orderButton);
57        add(resetButton);
58        add(quitButton);
59        add(orderDetails);
60      }
61
62      void processOrder()
63      {
64        String order = "You ordered ";
65        boolean toppingsOrdered = false;
66
67        for (int index = 0; index < NUM_TOPPINGS; ++index) {
68          if (topping[index].getState()) {
69            toppingsOrdered = true;
70            order += "\n" + topping[index].getLabel();
71          }
72        }
73        if (!toppingsOrdered)
74          order += "no toppings";
75        order += ".";
76        orderDetails.setText(order);
77      }
78
79      void resetForm()
80      {
81        for (int index = 0; index < NUM_TOPPINGS; ++index) {
82          topping[index].setState(false);
83        }
84        orderDetails.setText("Awaiting your order.");
85      }
86    }
```

The various components are declared on lines 7 to 10. Line 10 declares the array of `Checkbox`es that will store the toppings from which the user may choose. The `static` parameter on line 11 is the total number of toppings available.

The `main()` method contains nothing that we have not seen before. The `init()` method creates all the components and adds them to the window in the usual way. The array of pointers to `Checkbox` objects is created on line 26. Then each `Checkbox` is created separately on lines 27 to 31, using a call to the `Checkbox` constructor that takes only two arguments: the caption for the `Checkbox` and the initial state of the `Checkbox`. Here, the captions are the names of the toppings available, and all `Checkbox`es should initially be unselected.

The three `Button`s are created and have `ActionListener`s attached to them on lines 33 to 50. There is nothing new here.

The `TextArea` component is created on lines 51 and 52. A `TextArea` is just a `TextField` with more than one row of text. The constructor called on line 52 has three arguments: the initial text to be displayed, the number of rows and the number of columns. Here, we set up `orderDetails` to have 5 rows and 40 columns.

The remainder of the `init()` method adds the components to the window. Notice that since the `Checkbox`es are stored in an array, we can use a loop on lines 54 and 55 to add all of them, rather than having to write out a separate `add()` call for each one.

The `processOrder()` method on lines 62 to 77 is called when the `orderButton` is pressed. It builds up a text `String` which contains a list of the toppings that were selected. If no toppings were selected, the message 'You ordered no toppings.' is displayed. The `boolean` variable `toppingsOrdered` is set to `true` if any of the `Checkbox`es have been selected.

The loop on lines 67 to 72 examines each `Checkbox` to see if it is has been selected, using the `getState()` method of the `Checkbox` class. If one of them has, the name of the topping is obtained using the `getLabel()` method, and this name is appended to the `order` string. (We will study the `String` data type in more detail later in this chapter.) Before each topping name is added to `order`, a 'newline' character (`\n`) is inserted to put each topping on a separate line. On lines 73 and 74, the `toppingsOrdered` flag is tested to see if any toppings have been selected. If not, the correct message is constructed.

Finally, the text within the `TextArea` is set to the `order` string. If the text contains too many lines to fit in the `TextArea`, vertical scrollbars are automatically activated in the `TextArea` to allow the user to scroll through the text.

The `resetForm()` method (lines 79 through 85) is called when the 'Reset form' `Button` is pressed, and uses the `setState()` method to clear all the `Checkbox`es.

You can see from this example that any data type may be used in an array, and that individual array elements of a particular data type act in the same way as a single variable of that data type. In particular, methods of that data type may be called, as on line 82, by simply giving the array element's name (`topping[index]`) followed by the dot operator, followed by the method to be called (`.setState(false)`).

Strings

We have used the `String` data type quite often in the last few chapters without giving any details about its use. We could get away with this because `String` may be used in the obvious way – to store text strings. However, the `String` class in Java has a great many methods associated with it, some of which provide quite powerful string-handling functions. Since manipulating text is a common programming task, we should examine some of these methods in more detail. As always, the reader is advised to browse the Java documentation to see the full range of `String` methods available.

As we've just mentioned, the `String` class in Java is used to store a string of text.[1] We have already seen some of the common operations that may be performed on `String`s in some of the example programs from this and previous chapters. We will review these common features here and then proceed to some of the more exotic abilities of the `String` class.

A `String` may be created in much the same way as any other object:

```
String myString = new String("Hello there.");
```

This statement calls the `String` constructor and passes the constant text 'Hello there.' to the constructor. The `myString` variable is declared and initialized to this constant text.

It is more usual, however, to initialize a `String` by simply setting it equal to the constant text after the declaration, as in:

```
String myString = "Hello there.";
```

This statement has the same effect as the earlier one, in which the constructor is called explicitly, and is easier to write and understand. This is the only Java class that can be initialized to new data without an explicit call to the constructor.

The `String` is also unusual in that it allows the use of a couple of operators: the + operator and the += operator. Two `String`s may be joined together (or *concatenated*) by using the + operator:

```
String str1 = "the first bit", str2 = " and the second bit";
String joinedString = str1 + str2;
```

The `joinedString` variable now contains the text 'the first bit and the second bit'.

The += operator joins its second operand onto the end of its first operand, as in:

```
String str1 = "the first bit", str2 = " and the second bit";
str1 += str2;
```

---

[1] If you have programmed in C or C++, it is especially important to realize that the `String` in Java is not the same as an array of `char`.

This results in `str1` containing the same text as `joinedString` did above.

The primitive data types `int`, `float`, `char`, and so on are all automatically converted to `Strings` when they form one operand of the + operator, provided that the other operand is already a `String`. For example:

```
String resultStr = "The result is ";
int num1 = 12;
String finalStr = resultStr + num1;
```

The `finalStr` variable contains the text 'The result is 12'. However, using the same variables, the statement:

```
String finalStr = num1 + 3 + " is the result.";
```

produces the text '15 is the result.' because the first + operator has two `int` operands, so it adds them together rather than converting them to `Strings` and concatenating them. The second + operator has an `int` as its left operand and a `String` as its right operand, so it *will* convert the `int` to a `String` and then join it to the right operand.

The `String` class contains a large number of methods that allow the programmer to inspect or alter a `String` object in various ways. For example, the number of characters in a `String` can be obtained using the `length()` method, as in:

```
int strLength = finalStr.length();
```

Notice that `length()` is a *method* (that is, it requires the parentheses), unlike the `length` property for an array, which is an `int` in its own right.

The `substring()` method returns a portion of the `String` that calls it. It comes in two forms: one with a single `int` argument and the other with two `int` arguments. In the first case, `substring()` returns that portion of the original `String` starting at the index given by the argument, and extending to the end of the `String`. The index is *zero-based* just like an array, so that the first character has index number 0. For example:

```
String testString = "abcdefghij";
String partString = testString.substring(1);
```

The `partString` variable contains the text 'bcdefghij'.

The second form of `substring()` returns the substring consisting of text with index numbers starting with the first argument and going up to, but not including, the second argument.

There are many other methods available for various operations on `Strings`, but we will turn now to ways of dealing with the individual characters in a `String`.

Unicode, bytes, and chars

Readers with prior programming experience may have used languages such as C in which characters are stored using the *ASCII code*. The ASCII (an acronym for American Standard Code for Information Interchange) code provides a method whereby all the characters on a standard computer keyboard can be stored numerically in the computer's memory. The simplest form of ASCII contains 128 codes (from 0 to 127) which are assigned to the symbols on the keyboard. For example, the digits 0 through 9 are assigned ASCII codes 48 through 57, upper-case letters A through Z are assigned codes 65 through 90 and so on. The various punctuation symbols also have their own ASCII codes. An extension of ASCII to 256 codes allowed another 128 characters to be defined. This upper set of 128 characters varied from one implementation to another, but it was often used to store special graphics characters or mathematical symbols.

Using the ASCII code, a string of text may be stored as an array of numbers, with one number for each character. Since computer memory is divided up into bytes, where each byte contains 8 bits, a single byte may store one of 256 different ASCII codes. An array of characters could therefore be stored as an array of bytes in memory.

As the use of computers became more widespread, there arose a need for a method to store textual information in a wide variety of languages, many of which use different alphabets from the standard 26-letter alphabet used in English. For this reason, the Unicode encoding system (a trademark of the Unicode Consortium) was developed. Unicode characters are stored in two-byte (16-bit) blocks, allowing up to 65,536 different symbols to be defined. In its latest release (version 2.0), Unicode contains 38,885 codes for symbols covering the main written languages of the world, along with other symbols used in various professions.

Java uses Unicode to store character data, and is in principle able to deal with text from almost any language that is currently stored on a computer. However, it is highly unlikely that you would be able to bring up a document in, say, Korean on your desktop PC, since the display of all these characters requires that you have the font for that language installed. It is therefore not a good idea to blindly assume that all your potential users will have available all the fonts needed to display all the Unicode characters. The Unicode system only provides an encoding system whereby all these different symbols may be stored – it does *not* provide a method by which they can be *viewed* or *printed out*.

Although the Unicode system is obviously a lot more powerful than the original ASCII code, it does make conversions between Java `String`s and individual `char`s more complicated than in a language like C. It is often convenient to be able to deal with individual characters within a `String` however, so we will show an example of how this may be done.

The `String` class provides several methods that convert a `String` to and from arrays of `byte`s or `char`s. Recall from Chapter 3 that a `byte` is a primitive data type in Java, and is equivalent to an `int` except that it is stored using only a single byte.

The Java `char` data type will store a single Unicode character, and is therefore two bytes in size.

The lowest 128 codes (excluding the first 32 codes which have machine-dependent meanings) in Unicode are the same as the ASCII code. Since a Unicode character consists of two bytes, the 'upper' byte will contain nothing but zeroes for an ASCII character, while the 'lower' byte will be identical to the ASCII code for that character.

Recognizing this fact, Java provides several constructors and conversion methods which allow Java `Strings` to be constructed from and converted to arrays of `bytes`. This is useful if we wish to use the actual values of the characters within a `String` for a calculation or index.

For example, the `getBytes()` method returns an array of `bytes` containing the ASCII codes of the characters in the `String`.

Java also provides methods to convert between a `String` and an array of `chars`. Dealing with an array of `chars` can be much easier than using utility methods such as `substring()` to attempt to access individual characters within a `String`.

We will see some of these conversions in action in the example later in this section.

String tokenizers

Another common task that is performed on a `String` is that of *tokenizing* it. For example, some text typed in by the user may need to be split into individual words, with each word being interpreted as part of a command. This is a common feature of older so-called 'adventure games,' in which the player played the part of an adventurer exploring a fantasy world. The adventurer's actions are controlled by typing in simple commands such as 'take sword,' 'kill dragon,' or 'give gold to merchant.' In order for the computer to interpret these commands, each line of text must first be broken up into its constituent words, and then the words must be interpreted to produce the required action.

To accomplish the first step, a command such as 'give gold to merchant' must be split into a series of *tokens*, where each token is a single word. This is done in practice by looking for the *delimiters*, or separator characters (blanks in this case) between the words. The first blank occurs between 'give' and 'gold,' so 'give' would be identified as the first token in the command.

This sort of operation occurs often enough for Java to provide a special class called a `StringTokenizer` to deal with it. The `StringTokenizer` class is part of the `java.util` package, so you must include the line

```
import java.util.*;
```

at the start of any class that uses it. A `StringTokenizer` object is created by attaching it to the `String` which is to be tokenized. After that, the tokenizer splits off tokens and returns them as required.

For example, we might use the following code to split the 'give gold to merchant' command into tokens.

```
String command = "give gold to merchant";
StringTokenizer commandToken = new StringTokenizer(command);
while (commandToken.hasMoreTokens())
   System.out.println(commandToken.nextToken());
```

The first line creates the command string, and the second line creates a `String-Tokenizer` and attaches it to `command`. By default, if we use the one-argument constructor for a `StringTokenizer`, the delimiter characters are taken to be *white space*, that is, blanks, tabs, and new line characters. A two-argument constructor exists which allows the programmer to specify which characters are to be used as delimiters.

The `while` loop will split off and print the tokens one at a time. The `hasMoreTokens()` method return a `boolean` value stating whether or not `commandToken` has any more tokens remaining. If so, the `nextToken()` method is used to extract the next token, which is printed. A `StringTokenizer` maintains a marker within its associated string so that it steps through the string on each successive call to `nextToken()`.

A String example – counting letters and word sizes

As an example of how some of the features above can be used in practice, we will examine a program that allows the user to enter some text into a `TextArea`, and then calculates some statistics, such as the number of times each letter of the alphabet was used, and the number of words of various lengths. The interface is shown in Figure 6.2.

The user types the text (or uses cut and paste to copy it from another window) into the top `TextArea`. Pressing the 'Analyze text' `Button` tells the program to calculate the letter frequencies in the entered text, and count the number of words of each length. These are displayed in the bottom two `TextAreas`, as shown in the figure. We see from the letter count box that the letter 'a' was used 15 times, 'b' twice, and so on. From the 'word sizes' box, we see that there is one one-letter word, three six-letter words, two seven-letter words, and so on.

The 'Clear text' `Button` removes the text from all three `TextAreas`, and the 'Quit program' `Button` exits the program.

In order to calculate the letter counts, the text is converted into a `byte` array, and then a loop is used to examine the Unicode value of each letter in the text. Since the letters 'a' through 'z' have consecutive Unicode values, we can map them directly into an array of `ints` which we use to count the number of times each letter occurs. We can do this by subtracting the Unicode value for 'a' from the Unicode value for each letter, which will map 'a' into array location 0, 'b' into 1, and so on.

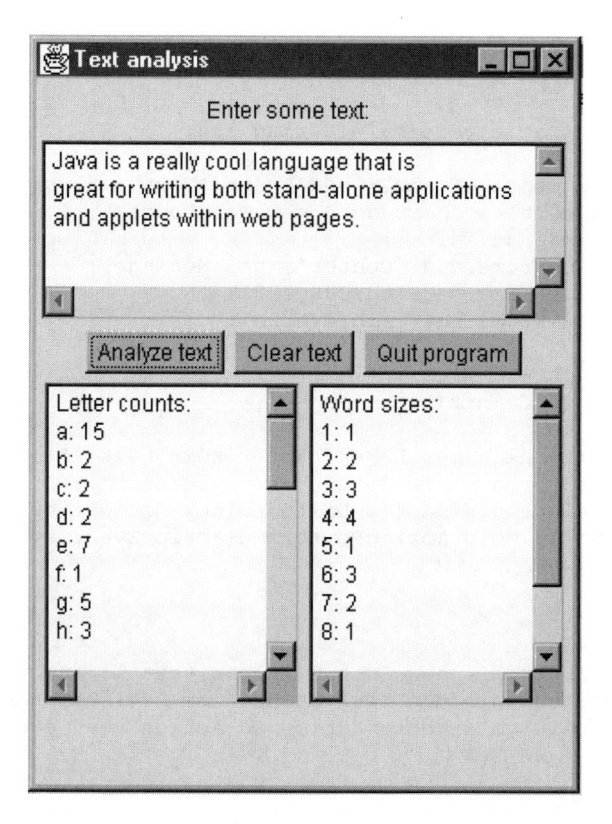

A STRING EXAMPLE – COUNTING LETTERS AND WORD SIZES

Figure 6.2 The interface for the `WordCount` applet.

To count the number of occurrences of words of a given length, we create a `StringTokenizer` and attach it to the `String` obtained from the user's text.

Each word is then extracted as a token and stored as a separate `String`. The `length()` method can then be used to measure the length of the word. We use another array of `int`s to keep track of the counts, with the word length used as the index of the array.

The code is as follows.

```
1   import java.applet.*;
2   import java.awt.*;
3   import java.awt.event.*;
4   import java.util.*;
5
6   public class WordCount extends Applet
7   {
8      Label enterLabel;
9      Button countButton, clearButton, quitButton;
10     TextArea usersText, letterCounts, wordSizes;
```

```
11      static int MAX_LETTERS = 26;
12      static int MAX_WORD_LENGTH = 10;
13
14      public static void main(String argv[])
15      {
16        Frame messageFrame = new Frame("Text analysis");
17        WordCount testMessage = new WordCount();
18        testMessage.init();
19        messageFrame.add("Center", testMessage);
20        messageFrame.setSize(300,400);
21        messageFrame.setVisible(true);
22      }
23
24      public void init()
25      {
26        enterLabel = new Label("Enter some text: ");
27        countButton = new Button("Analyze text");
28        countButton.addActionListener(new ActionListener() {
29          public void actionPerformed(ActionEvent event) {
30            analyzeText();
31          }
32        });
33
34        clearButton = new Button("Clear text");
35        clearButton.addActionListener(new ActionListener() {
36          public void actionPerformed(ActionEvent event) {
37            clearText();
38          }
39        });
40
41        quitButton = new Button("Quit program");
42        quitButton.addActionListener(new ActionListener() {
43          public void actionPerformed(ActionEvent event) {
44            System.exit(0);
45          }
46        });
47
48        usersText = new TextArea(5, 38);
49        letterCounts = new TextArea(10, 17);
50        wordSizes = new TextArea(10, 17);
51        add(enterLabel);
52        add(usersText);
53        add(countButton);
54        add(clearButton);
55        add(quitButton);
56        add(letterCounts);
57        add(wordSizes);
58      }
59
60      void analyzeText()
61      {
```

A STRING EXAMPLE – COUNTING LETTERS AND WORD SIZES

```
62      String message = usersText.getText();
63
64      letterCounts.setText(countLetters(message));
65      wordSizes.setText(measureWords(message));
66    }
67
68    String countLetters(String message)
69    {
70      int[] charCount = new int[MAX_LETTERS];
71      String lowercaseMessage = message.toLowerCase();
72      byte[] messageChars = lowercaseMessage.getBytes();
73
74      String lower_a = "a";
75      byte[] lower_a_code = lower_a.getBytes();
76
77      for (int index = 0; index < messageChars.length;
78  ++index)
79        {
80          int countIndex = messageChars[index] -
81  lower_a_code[0];
82          if (countIndex >= 0 && countIndex < MAX_LETTERS)
83            charCount[countIndex]++;
84        }
85
86      StringBuffer countMessage =
87        new StringBuffer("Letter counts:\n");
88      byte[] letterCode = new byte[1];
89      letterCode[0] = lower_a_code[0];
90      for (int letter = 0; letter < MAX_LETTERS; ++letter) {
91        String letterString = new String(letterCode);
92        countMessage.append(letterString + ": " +
93          charCount[letter] + "\n");
94        letterCode[0]++;
95      }
96      return countMessage.toString();
97    }
98
99    String measureWords(String message)
100   {
101     StringTokenizer messageToken =
102       new StringTokenizer(message);
103     int[] wordLength = new int[MAX_WORD_LENGTH + 1];
104
105     while (messageToken.hasMoreTokens()) {
106       String nextWord = messageToken.nextToken();
107       int wordSize = nextWord.length();
108       if (wordSize <= MAX_WORD_LENGTH)
109         wordLength[wordSize - 1]++;
110       else
111         wordLength[MAX_WORD_LENGTH]++;
112     }
```

```
113
114        StringBuffer lengthMessage =
115           new StringBuffer("Word sizes:\n");
116        for (int size = 0; size < MAX_WORD_LENGTH; ++size) {
117           lengthMessage.append(size + 1 + ": " +
118           wordLength[size] + "\n");
119        }
120        lengthMessage.append("> " + MAX_WORD_LENGTH + ": " +
121           wordLength[MAX_WORD_LENGTH]);
122
123        return lengthMessage.toString();
124     }
125
126     void clearText()
127     {
128        usersText.setText("");
129        letterCounts.setText("");
130        wordSizes.setText("");
131     }
132  }
```

Remember to import the java.util package (line 4) which we will need for the StringTokenizer class.

No new AWT components are used in this program. We have a Label (line 8) for the 'Enter some text' caption at the top, the three Buttons (line 9), and the three TextAreas (line 10). We define a couple of parameters (lines 11 and 12) which are used to manage the arrays that store the letter and word data. The main() method is similar to those used in previous programs.

The init() method (lines 24 to 58) initializes the components and attaches listeners to the three Buttons. The three TextAreas are then initialized and all the components are added to the frame.

The analyzeText() method (lines 60 to 66) is called when the 'Analyze text' Button is pressed. It extracts the text from the usersText TextArea. Line 64 then calls countLetters() to do the letter counts. This method returns a String which contains the output to be displayed in the letterCounts box, so the setText() method is used to display it. Similarly, the measureWords() method calculates the number of words for each length and returns a String which is displayed in the wordSizes box.

The countLetters() method on lines 68 to 95 works out the frequency of each letter. The charCount array on line 70 is to be used to store the counts. Since Java automatically initializes all primitive data types to zero, there is no need to initialize the individual elements of this array to zero before using it.

Since we just want a count of the numbers of each letter that were used, we don't want to distinguish between upper- and lower-case letters. On line 71, therefore, we use the toLowerCase() method of the String class to convert message to lower-case only. Then, on line 72, we convert lowercaseMessage to a byte array using the getBytes() method. This extracts the lower byte from each Unicode value, so

A STRING EXAMPLE – COUNTING LETTERS AND WORD SIZES 139

if all the characters in the text are from a standard Western keyboard, we will obtain the ASCII code for each character.

We want to use the ASCII code as an index for the `charCount` array, but since the ASCII code for the letter 'a' is not zero (it is 97), we need to subtract this value from the ASCII code for each letter before we can use it as an array index. Rather than hard-wire the code for 'a' into the program, we use lines 74 and 75 to construct a `String` containing only the single character 'a', and then convert this one-element `String` into a `byte` array. The first element of this array (`lower_a_code[0]`) will then contain the value that must be subtracted from each ASCII code.

The loop on lines 77 to 82 scans through the array `messageChars`. The index of the current character is obtained on line 79, by subtracting the code for 'a' from `messageChars[index]`. If the result lies between 0 and `MAX_LETTERS`, the current character is a letter between 'a' and 'z', so we increment the corresponding counter on line 81.

Once we have finished the counting, we need to construct the `String` that will be displayed in the `letterCounts` box. This is done on lines 84 through 93. On line 84, we use a `StringBuffer` object instead of a `String` to begin building this `String`. The `String` data structure does not allow its contents to be modified once the initial `String` has been created. This means that all `String` operations that *appear* to modify the `String`, such as concatenating another `String` onto the end, actually cause a copy of the original `String`, incorporating the changes, to be made and returned as a result of the operation.

If we make a lot of changes to a `String`, repeated copying can be inefficient. The `StringBuffer` class *does* allow changes to be made after the initial object is created, and can therefore be more efficient for building a `String` from a series of concatenations. For a program as short as this one, there will be no noticeable difference, but it is wise to be aware of the method in case you need to modify `String`s frequently.

A `StringBuffer` object is created the same way as a `String` (lines 84 and 85), except that a constructor must be used (you can't just set a `StringBuffer` object equal to a `String` constant). To append a `String` to an existing `StringBuffer`, the `append()` method must be used (it is not legal to use the + operator for a `StringBuffer`), as shown on lines 90 and 91. When the `StringBuffer` is complete, it must be converted back to a `String` using the `toString()` method (line 94).

The actual text that is placed into `countMessage` consists of one line for each letter giving the letter itself followed by the count for that letter. We define a one-element `byte` array on line 86, and initialize it on line 87 with the ASCII code for 'a'. Using a `byte` to represent the letter rather than a `char` allows us to increment the `byte` value within a loop to generate successive letters. This is possible because a `byte` is just a short form of the `int` data type. Arithmetic operations are allowed on `byte`s, but not on `char`s.

Inside the loop, we create `letterString` from the `byte` array on line 89. This produces the actual letter as a `String`, so that it may be appended onto countMessage. Lines 90 and 91 append letterString followed by a colon (:), followed by the actual number of times that letter appears (charCount[letter]), followed by a newline character (\n). Then the byte code is incremented on line 92.

The measureWords() method on lines 97 to 122 uses a StringTokenizer to step through the text and split off each word as a separate token. The wordLength array on line 101 is declared to hold one more than MAX_WORD_LENGTH elements, since the final element will be used to store the count for words longer than MAX_WORD_LENGTH.

The loop starting on line 103 continues as long as more tokens exist within messageToken. The next token is extracted and stored in nextWord (line 104) and its length is determined (line 105). If the word's length is less than MAX_WORD_LENGTH, we increment the corresponding counter. Note that we actually store the count for words of length wordSize in array element number wordSize − 1, so that the count for words on length 1 is stored in wordLength[0], and so on. We do this simply because arrays all start at index 0 and, since there will be no words of length 0, we can use all the elements in the array by shifting the storage down by one space.

Finally, we use another StringBuffer to construct the message displaying the counts for words of various lengths, and return this as a String.

You can see from this example that Java provides a powerful array of tools for dealing with Strings, even at the individual character level.

Exercises

1. Write a Java class containing an array of ints of size 12. Ask the user to input an int value (use the readInt() method from Chapter 2) and then calculate and store the multiplication table of that int (that is, multiply the int by the numbers from 1 to 12) and store these values in the array. The output of the program should be the multiplication table, followed by the sum and average of all the numbers in the array.

2. Modify the program from exercise 1 by first asking the user to input the size of the array (that is, the number of products to calculate in the multiplication table), followed by the number whose multiplication table is to be calculated. Using the number that was input for the array's size, use the new operator to create an array of the correct size. The output from the program should be the same as in exercise 1.

3. Write a small Java class named StudentMarks with a String variable called studentName and an int variable called mark. Provide appropriate constructors and interface methods for this class.

   Now write a second class named StudentRecords. This class should contain an array of five StudentMarks objects, along with the main() method and any other methods you require. Create and initialize this array, and store some names for your five students in the `studentName` variable of each `StudentMarks` object.

When the program is run, the user should be prompted with each student's name and asked for a mark for that student. When all five students' marks have been entered, the program should print out each student's name and mark, one per line, as a check that the data was entered properly. It should also print out the average mark, and the maximum and minimum marks.

4 Modify the program in exercise 3 by making the `mark` variable in the `StudentsMarks` class an *array* of three `int`s, rather than just a single `int`. When the program is run, the user should now be prompted with each student's name as before, but this time, three marks are required for each student.

The output of the program should consist of, for each student, the name, the three marks for that student, and the average of the three marks for that student. In addition, at the end of the output, the average, maximum, and minimum for each of the three marks should be given.

5 You may have noticed that the `main()` method has a single argument that is an array of `Strings` (usually referred to as `argv[]`). This array contains any *command-line arguments* that are typed on the command line when the `java` command is given to start a program. For example, suppose we run a Java program named `TestArgs` with the command

```
java TestArgs arg0 17 testing
```

The three terms `arg0`, `17`, and `testing` are the command-line arguments (they are extra information that is added after the main command that runs the program). These three terms would be loaded as `Strings` into the `argv[]` array in `main()` when the program starts.

Write a simple Java program consisting only of a `main()` method that prints out the command-line arguments, if any, with one argument per line.

6 Modify the `RandTemps` class in the text so that its constructor requires an `int` argument which is used to specify the size of the `noonTemps` array. Provide this value as a command-line argument, so that the command

```
java RandTemps 20
```

creates an array of size 20. Check the value input by the user to make sure it is valid (not negative).

7 Write a simple interface to an adventure game along the following lines. Build an applet with a `TextField` into which the user types a command, and a `Button` labelled 'Do command'. Commands should consist of two words, with the first being a verb and the second a noun, such as 'take sword' or 'kill dragon'. If the command is 'recognized' as a valid verb-noun pair, the message "You <verb> the <noun>" should be printed in the window, where <verb> and <noun> are the two words in the command.

To recognize a command, construct two arrays of `Strings` called `verbList` and `nounList`. Initialize these arrays to contain the verbs and nouns you wish to be recognized – three or four words in each list should do. When the user enters a two-word command, retrieve it from the `TextField` and use a `StringTokenizer` to split the command up into separate words. Compare the first word (using the `equals()` method) with the verbs in `verbList` and the second word with the nouns in `nounList`. If a match is found for both words, print out the message, otherwise, print out 'Command not recognized'. You should provide a few reasonable error checks, such as ensuring that the user has entered two words.

8 A simple text encryption method (sometimes called a *cryptogram*) consists of a letter substitution code. To construct the code, each of the 26 letters in the alphabet is substituted by another letter. For example, the phrase 'THE LITTLE WHITE DOG' may be encoded as 'AFX GQAAGX PFQAX ZJB' where T has been replaced by A, H by F, and so on.

Write a Java applet which allows the user to encrypt and decrypt messages using a substitution code. The interface should consist of a `TextField` into which the message is entered, and two `Buttons` labelled 'Encrypt' and 'Decrypt'. Pushing the 'Encrypt' `Button` will translate the message from ordinary English to the encrypted version, and 'Decrypt' does the reverse.

To do this, you will need to use a method similar to that in the letter-counting program in the text. The message to be encrypted or decrypted must be split up into individual letters, and the corresponding letter in the code must be found to construct the alternative message.

To build the code in the first place, you can work out the substitution table on paper and hard-code it into the program. (Alternatively, if you are mathematically inclined, you might like to work out an algorithm in which the substitution code is generated randomly by the computer. If you do this, you need to ensure that each letter in the original alphabet translates to a different letter in the code.)

CHAPTER 7
Layout managers

Arranging components on the screen

The graphical interface examples we have seen in the preceding chapters have all relied on a judicious choice of window size to make the components appear in a pleasing arrangement. As you may have discovered if you ran some of these programs, resizing the window after the application appears can cause the various components to move around, destroying any illusion that the layout was carefully planned. Clearly it would be better if there were some way we could specify the layout of the various components and depend on the layout to maintain its form if the window is resized.

In most GUI languages, the absolute position of each component must be specified by giving its pixel co-ordinates at the time it is created. Most modern GUI programming environments will have some sort of graphical editor which allows components to be placed on the screen using the mouse, so that the programmer doesn't have to measure the exact position and enter the numbers by hand. However, the principle is the same: once a component is placed on the screen in the editor, the co-ordinates are written into some pre-generated code provided by the editor.

In Java, things are done a bit differently. The main reason for this is that Java was designed to be more or less platform independent. It should be possible to write a Java program on one type of computer and run it on any other type of computer that supports Java. Since different computers use different methods of representing graphical components on screen, it is dangerous to rely on absolute positions for objects when drawing them on various computers.

For this reason, Java provides several *layout manager* classes, which are basically classes containing a set of rules that govern how components can be placed inside a container. The placing of components inside frames or panels is done *relatively* rather than absolutely. That is, rather than saying 'place this button 20 pixels from the left edge and 40 pixels from the top,' we say something like 'place this button to the right of the text area and below the label'. It is the job of the layout manager to take all these relative positioning instructions and generate a layout in which all the components are displayed in the right places *on any computer*.

The Java AWT contains a generic Container class which serves as a base class from which several specific types of container are derived. The Frame is one such container, and the Panel is another. As their name implies, Containers are designed mainly to hold other components. A `Container` object may have a layout manager attached to it in order to provide some rules as to how components are added to the `Container`.

The FlowLayout manager

We have actually been using a layout manager for all our GUI examples, although you may have been unaware of it. If we don't specify a specific layout manager for a `Container`, Java provides a `FlowLayout` as the default manager. A `FlowLayout` arranges components in much the same way as words are organized on the page of a book. The first component to be added is placed in the upper left corner. The next component is placed to the immediate right of the first one, and so on until adding a component would cause it to extend beyond the right boundary of the `Container`. At this stage, the next component is placed back on the left, immediately under the first row.

You can now see why resizing the `Container` will cause the components to move around. If you make the `Container` wider, more components will fit on each row, so the layout manager moves components to earlier rows to pack them as closely as possible.

Even though the `FlowLayout` does not need to be explicitly attached to a `Container`, it is the simplest layout manager available, so it is the easiest one on which to demonstrate the principles of using layouts.

We present a simple program which declares a few AWT components, then explicitly creates a `FlowLayout` object, attaches it to the enclosing `Frame`, and adds the components to the `Frame`. Note that the `add()` method used to add components to a `Container` is a method from the `Container` class, not the `FlowLayout` class – we are adding components to the `Container`, and the layout manager attached to that container has the job of saying where each component should go, using instructions that may be provided in the `add()` method.

The program also illustrates how to change the only three attributes that can be set in a `FlowLayout`: the alignment of the components, and the sizes of the horizontal and vertical gaps between components. The code follows.

```
1   import java.applet.*;
2   import java.awt.*;
3   import java.awt.event.*;
4
5   public class SimpleFlow extends Applet
6   {
7      Choice alignChoice, horizGapChoice, vertGapChoice;
8      Button quitButton;
9      FlowLayout layout;
10
11     public static void main(String argv[])
12     {
```

```
13      Frame messageFrame = new Frame("Simple FlowLayout");
14      SimpleFlow testMessage = new SimpleFlow();
15      testMessage.init();
16      messageFrame.add("Center", testMessage);
17      messageFrame.setSize(350, 150);
18      messageFrame.setVisible(true);
19    }
20
21    public void init()
22    {
23      layout = new FlowLayout();
24      this.setLayout(layout);
25      alignChoice = new Choice();
26      alignChoice.add("Left");
27      alignChoice.add("Centre");
28      alignChoice.add("Right");
29      alignChoice.addItemListener(new ItemListener() {
30        public void itemStateChanged(ItemEvent event) {
31          setAlignment(event);
32        }
33      });
34      add(new Label("Alignment: "));
35      add(alignChoice);
36
37      horizGapChoice = new Choice();
38      horizGapChoice.add("0");
39      horizGapChoice.add("5");
40      horizGapChoice.add("10");
41      horizGapChoice.add("15");
42      horizGapChoice.addItemListener(new ItemListener() {
43        public void itemStateChanged(ItemEvent event) {
44          setHorizGap(event);
45        }
46      });
47      add(new Label("Horizontal gap: "));
48      add(horizGapChoice);
49
50      vertGapChoice = new Choice();
51      vertGapChoice.add("0");
52      vertGapChoice.add("5");
53      vertGapChoice.add("10");
54      vertGapChoice.add("15");
55      vertGapChoice.addItemListener(new ItemListener() {
56        public void itemStateChanged(ItemEvent event) {
57          setVertGap(event);
58        }
59      });
60      add(new Label("Vertical gap: "));
61      add(vertGapChoice);
62
63      quitButton = new Button("Quit");
```

```
64      quitButton.addActionListener(new ActionListener() {
65        public void actionPerformed(ActionEvent event) {
66          System.exit(0);
67        }
68      });
69      add(quitButton);
70    }
71
72    void setAlignment(ItemEvent event)
73    {
74      String align = event.getItem().toString();
75      if (align.equals("Left"))
76        layout.setAlignment(FlowLayout.LEFT);
77      else if (align.equals("Centre"))
78        layout.setAlignment(FlowLayout.CENTER);
79      else
80        layout.setAlignment(FlowLayout.RIGHT);
81      layout.layoutContainer(this);
82    }
83
84    void setHorizGap(ItemEvent event)
85    {
86      String gap = event.getItem().toString();
87      int gapValue = Integer.parseInt(gap);
88      layout.setHgap(gapValue);
89      layout.layoutContainer(this);
90    }
91
92    void setVertGap(ItemEvent event)
93    {
94      String gap = event.getItem().toString();
95      int gapValue = Integer.parseInt(gap);
96      layout.setVgap(gapValue);
97      layout.layoutContainer(this);
98    }
99  }
```

We declare three `Choice` objects (line 7) which allow the user to select an alignment (left, centre, or right) and several values for the horizontal and vertical gaps between the components. We also declare a `FlowLayout` object (line 9) which will be attached to the main window, and will be used to lay out the components.

We initialize the `FlowLayout` on line 23 by calling its argumentless constructor. There are two other constructors for `FlowLayout` which allow the alignment and gap sizes to be set at creation time, but we will modify these dynamically when the program is running. On line 24, we attach `layout` to the main window using the `setLayout()` method.

The remainder of the `init()` method initializes the `Choice` objects and `quitButton`, and attaches event handlers to them. Attaching an event handler to each `Choice` object means that the corresponding method will be called each time the user makes a selection from one of them.

When the window first appears, the default appearance of a `FlowLayout` is to centre the components within each row, and insert a 5-pixel gap between components in both the horizontal and vertical directions.

The `setAlignment()` method (lines 72 to 82) is called when the user wishes to change the alignment of the layout. The label of the selection is extracted on line 74 and the `setAlignment()` method of the `FlowLayout` class is called to set the alignment to the chosen value. In order to make the new alignment take effect, the `layoutContainer()` method must be called (line 81). Its argument is the `Container` object which is to be reconfigured. In this case, the object is the main window itself, so we pass a `this` argument to the method. You can think of `layoutContainer()` as a sort of 'repaint' method for a layout manager – it is called to update the display so that any changes to the layout are made visible.

The `setHorizGap()` and `setVertGap()` methods respond to the user changing the distances between components. They use the `setHgap()` and `setVgap()` methods of `FlowLayout` to set the new values, and then call `layoutContainer()` to implement the changes.

In Figure 7.1 we see the program after the user has selected right alignment, a horizontal gap of 5 pixels, and a vertical gap of 10 pixels.

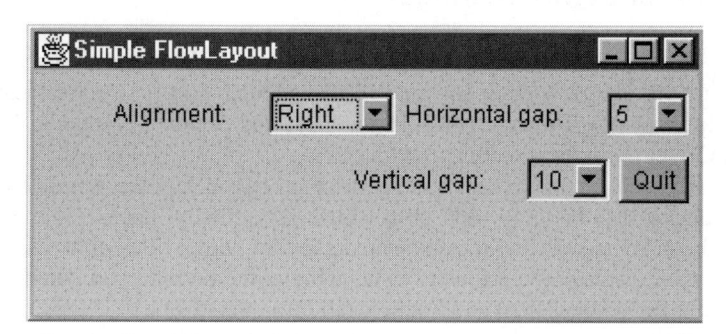

Figure 7.1 The interface to the `SimpleFlow` applet.

The GridLayout manager

Java has several ready-made layout managers in its AWT package.[1] After `FlowLayout`, probably the easiest manager to use is `GridLayout`.

As its name implies, `GridLayout` provides a rectangular grid of cells into which components can be placed. Components are added in a left-to-right, top-to-bottom

---

[1] It is also possible to design and write your own layout managers, but that is beyond the scope of this book.

order (the same as with `FlowLayout`), but are also resized so that all components are the same size. It is not possible to define a grid of, say, four rows and five columns, and then place components into specific cells – components are added to row 1 until it is full, then to row 2 and so on. The net effect is a chessboard pattern, with all components neatly lined up in rows and columns, regardless of the type or original size of the component.

A `GridLayout` may be created by calling the two-argument constructor to specify the number of rows and columns, as in:

```
GridLayout layout = new GridLayout(4,5);
```

This creates a grid with four rows and five columns. The only other attributes that may be specified are the horizontal and vertical gaps between components. This is handled in the same way as with the `FlowLayout` above.

Once a `GridLayout` has been attached to a container, components are added to it using the `add()` method, just as with the `FlowLayout`.

We will see the `GridLayout` in action in the tic-tac-toe example later in this chapter.

The BorderLayout manager

The `BorderLayout` class allows up to five components to be arranged within a container: one on each edge and one in the middle. The four edge locations are named after compass points: North, East, West and South. The middle location is named Center (with the American spelling!).

This arrangement may seem quite restrictive, but in fact the `BorderLayout` is one of the most commonly used layout managers. Firstly, not all of the locations need to be occupied, so that if you wanted a layout with a title bar across the top, a larger central display, and a footer or status bar at the bottom, you could do this by using only the North, Center and South locations in the layout.

Secondly, the `BorderLayout` does not restrict its components to being the same size. Larger components are allocated more space, while smaller components get less space.

Finally, in many cases, a component will stretch to fill up the full space available for its location. This feature is a mixed blessing – sometimes it is what you want to do, other times it can just be annoying. Fortunately, there is a way to disable the stretching, although it is bit awkward.

Since the final appearance of a `BorderLayout` container is determined by the order in which the five areas are filled, it is important to understand that North and South stretch right across the top and bottom, respectively, of the final figure. West, Center and East then fill up the space between North and South, with any missing components being filled in by the others stretching to close up the gap. A `BorderLayout` container looks similar to Figure 7.2.

```
          ┌─────────────────────────────────┐
          │            North                │
          ├────────┬───────────────┬────────┤
          │  West  │    Center     │  East  │
          ├────────┴───────────────┴────────┤
          │            South                │
          └─────────────────────────────────┘
```

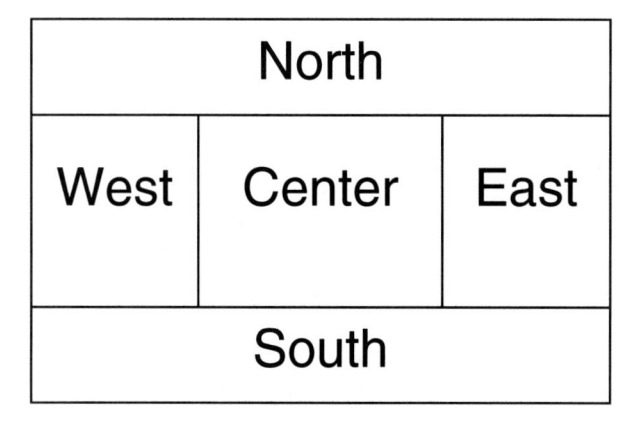

Figure 7.2 The sections of a `BorderLayout`.

After attaching a `BorderLayout` object to a container, a component may be added to one of the locations using the `add()` method, but *two* arguments (the location and the component to be added) must be passed to the method. For example:

```
Button myButton = new Button("Hi there.");
TextField myText = new Text("A text field.");
setLayout(new BorderLayout());
add("North", myButton);
add("South", myText);
```

This code creates a `Button` and a `TextField`, attaches a `BorderLayout` to the current window, and then adds the `Button` to the 'North' location, and the `TextField` to the 'South' location. Note that the location parameter that is passed to the `add()` method must be a `String`, so it must either be a constant like 'North', enclosed in quotes, or a `String` variable with one of the five locations stored in it.

The CardLayout manager

The `CardLayout` manager isn't a layout manager in the normal sense of the term, since it doesn't actually position components relative to each other within a container. Rather, it allows two or more components to be stacked in a pile, just like a stack of cards. The `show()` method from the `CardLayout` class then allows one of these 'cards' to be moved to the top of the stack, making it visible.

To use a `CardLayout`, declare and create it as a separate object, since you will need to refer to the `CardLayout` object explicitly elsewhere in your program if you want to change the card that is visible. Then attach it to the container using `setLayout()` in the usual way. When you add components to the container, use the add() method with two arguments. As with the `BorderLayout`, the first argument is a `String` and the second is the component being added. However, the `String` in this case is a *name* that can be used to refer to the component later on, when you want to make it visible. For example:

```
CardLayout myCard = new CardLayout();
setLayout(myCard);
Button myButton = new Button("My Button");
TextArea myTextArea = new TextArea(5, 10);
add("TheButton", myButton);
add("TheTextArea", myTextArea);
```

A `CardLayout` is created and attached to the current window. Then a `Button` and a `TextArea` are created and added to the container. The name 'TheButton' is assigned to `myButton` and 'TheTextArea' to `myTextArea`.

To make one of the cards visible, we use the `show()` method:

```
myCard.show(this, "TheButton");
```

Note that it is the `CardLayout` object `myCard` that calls the show method, and *not* the container object to which the layout has been assigned. The first argument of `show()` refers to the container object, and the second argument is the name of the component which is to be displayed. Here we request that 'TheButton' be displayed.

The first argument here is `this`, since the `CardLayout` has been attached to the top level window. As we will see in the example below, it is more usual for a layout manager to be attached to a separate container such as a `Panel`. It is this object which would then be passed to the `show()` method.

Panels

So far, the only container we have used is the `Frame` class, which we define in all of our `main()` methods. The `Frame` is used to simulate a browser when the program is run as an application. For more complex layouts, however, it is more convenient to build up the final window in stages. For example, suppose you are building the interface to a pocket calculator. Even the simplest calculator will have quite a few controls and display areas, such as the number keys (from 0 to 9), function keys such as +, -, x, /, =, and so on, keys for clearing the current entry, storing and clearing memory, clearing everything, and of course the numerical display for producing the answer.

If you were writing a calculator applet in Java, you would find it very difficult to produce a layout for all these buttons and other components if you tried to place all the buttons directly into the master `Frame`. A much better approach is to divide the overall display up into several sub-areas or panels, within each of which the display is much simpler. For example, the number buttons from 1 through 9 fit neatly into a three by three grid, so a `GridLayout` can be used for them. This group of 9 buttons can be combined with the 0 button by using a `BorderLayout`, placing the 9-button group above the single 0 button. The function buttons are usually arranged in a single column, so another `GridLayout` can be used for them. By combining `GridLayouts` or `FlowLayouts` with `BorderLayouts`, even quite complex layouts can be built up hierarchically without too much bother.

The process is rather like making a poster board that you might use when giving a presentation to an audience. Starting with a large piece of cardboard, you can paste smaller boards onto the large board, with each smaller board containing several of the items you want to display. It is easier to rearrange the overall poster by moving the smaller panels about than by trying to rearrange all the separate components.

The `Panel` class in the Java AWT provides this ability. A `Panel` may have a layout manager attached to it using the `setLayout()` method, and may have components (or other `Panels`) added to it using the appropriate form of the `add()` method. `Panels` themselves are usually invisible (although they can have their background colour set), and serve mainly as convenience containers allowing subsets of components to be arranged and placed within a larger layout.

Example – a tic-tac-toe game

We will examine a larger example that illustrates all four layout managers working together. We also make considerable use of `Panels`.

The `TicTacToe` class allows two humans to play a game of tic-tac-toe (or noughts and crosses as it is sometimes called). When started, the program appears as shown in Figure 7.3. There is a title at the top, a central panel telling the user to press the 'New game' button to start the game, and three buttons at the bottom.

Pressing the 'New game' button produces the playing area, which consists of a three by three grid of buttons which the players press to take their turns.

Figure 7.4 shows the display after the 'X' player has won a game.

The 'Scores' button displays the number of wins for each player, and the number of draws. This display replaces the playing area in the centre of the window.

Although the layout of the applet is not overly complicated, it is still much easier to break up the display into several panels and use several layout managers to combine these panels, creating the overall window.

At the top level, a `BorderLayout` is used to arrange the three main areas of the window. The label at the top occupies the 'North' location, the various displays in the middle occupy the 'Center', and the row of buttons at the bottom occupy 'South'.

The title at the top is a single AWT component (a `Label` with customized font and colours). The middle region uses a `CardLayout` to display one of three panels: the initial instruction panel, the grid of buttons for playing the game, and the scores. Each of these panels is constructed using a `GridLayout` to arrange the components. Finally, the row of buttons at the bottom is produced using another `GridLayout`.

Figure 7.3. The tic-tac-toe game at the start.

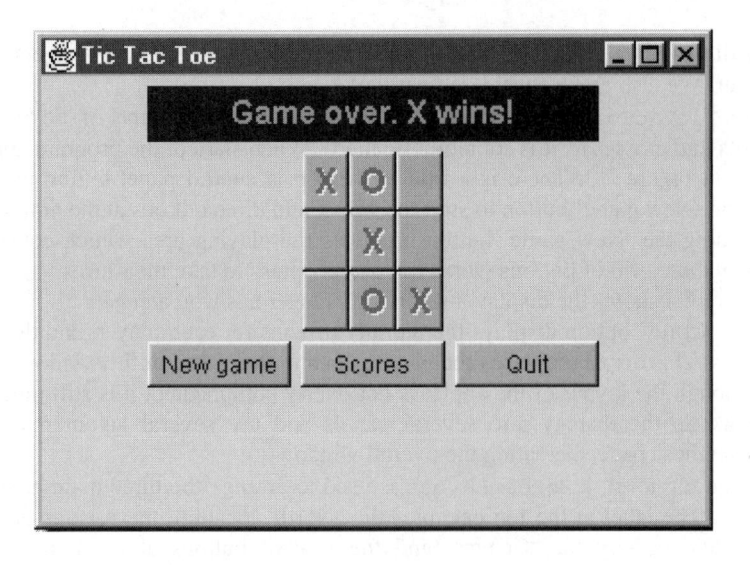

Figure 7.4 The tic-tac-toe game after a player has won.

Apart from the use of layout managers, most of the techniques used in the code should be familiar from earlier chapters. The code is quite long, but is presented in its entirety so you can see how a program making extensive use of layout managers fits together. We will discuss some of the features in more detail following the listing.

EXAMPLE – A TIC-TAC-TOE GAME

```
1   import java.applet.*;
2   import java.awt.*;
3   import java.awt.event.*;
4
5   public class TicTacToe extends Applet
6   {
7     static int GRIDSIZE = 3;
8     static final int NOT_OVER = 0;
9     static final int WIN = 1;
10    static final int DRAW = 2;
11    Button square[][], newGameButton, quitButton, scoreButton;
12    Label ticTacToeLabel, scores[];
13    Panel centrePanel, welcomePanel, scoresPanel;
14    CardLayout centreLayout;
15    String XOturn;
16    int Xwins, Owins, draws;
17
18    public static void main(String argv[])
19    {
20      Frame messageFrame = new Frame("Tic Tac Toe");
21      TicTacToe testMessage = new TicTacToe();
22      testMessage.init();
23      messageFrame.add("Center", testMessage);
24      messageFrame.setSize(350,250);
25      messageFrame.setVisible(true);
26      messageFrame.addWindowListener(new WindowAdapter() {
27        public void windowClosing(WindowEvent event) {
28           System.exit(0);
29        }
30      });
31    }
32
33    public void init()
34    {
35      XOturn = "X";
36      Xwins = Owins = draws = 0;
37      setBackground(Color.yellow);
38      Panel gamePanel = new Panel();
39      gamePanel.setLayout(new BorderLayout());
40      initializeLabels();
41      centreLayout = new CardLayout();
42      centrePanel = new Panel(centreLayout);
43      Panel squaresPanel = new Panel();
44      squaresPanel.add(initializeGrid());
45      centrePanel.add("GameGrid", squaresPanel);
46      centrePanel.add("Welcome", welcomePanel);
47      centrePanel.add("Scores", scoresPanel);
48      centreLayout.show(centrePanel, "Welcome");
49
50      gamePanel.add("North", ticTacToeLabel);
51      gamePanel.add("Center", centrePanel);
52      gamePanel.add("South", initializeButtons());
```

```
53        add(gamePanel);
54     }
55
56     Panel initializeGrid()
57     {
58        square = new Button[GRIDSIZE][GRIDSIZE];
59        Panel squarePanel = new Panel();
60        squarePanel.setLayout(new GridLayout(GRIDSIZE,GRIDSIZE));
61        for (int row = 0; row < GRIDSIZE; ++row)
62          for (int col = 0; col < GRIDSIZE; ++col) {
63             square[row][col] = new Button("   ");
64             square[row][col].setFont(new Font("Helvetica",
65                Font.BOLD, 18));
66             square[row][col].
67                 addActionListener(new ActionListener() {
68                public void actionPerformed(ActionEvent event) {
69                   squareChosen(event);
70                }
71             });
72             squarePanel.add(square[row][col]);
73          }
74        return squarePanel;
75     }
76
77     Panel initializeButtons()
78     {
79        Panel buttonPanel = new Panel();
80        GridLayout buttonLayout = new GridLayout(1,3,5,0);
81        buttonPanel.setLayout(buttonLayout);
82        newGameButton = new Button("New game");
83        newGameButton.addActionListener(new ActionListener() {
84           public void actionPerformed(ActionEvent event) {
85              enableSquares();
86           }
87        });
88        buttonPanel.add(newGameButton);
89
90        scoreButton = new Button("Scores");
91        scoreButton.addActionListener(new ActionListener() {
92           public void actionPerformed(ActionEvent event) {
93              showScores();
94           }
95        });
96        buttonPanel.add(scoreButton);
97
98        quitButton = new Button("Quit");
99        quitButton.addActionListener(new ActionListener() {
100          public void actionPerformed(ActionEvent event) {
101             System.exit(0);
102          }
103       });
104       buttonPanel.add(quitButton);
```

```java
105        return buttonPanel;
106      }
107
108      void initializeLabels()
109      {
110        ticTacToeLabel = new Label("Java Tic Tac Toe",
111          Label.CENTER);
112        ticTacToeLabel.setBackground(Color.blue);
113        ticTacToeLabel.setForeground(Color.cyan);
114        ticTacToeLabel.setFont(new Font("Helvetica",
115          Font.BOLD, 16));
116
117        welcomePanel = new Panel(new GridLayout(3,1));
118        Label[] welcome = new Label[3];
119        welcome[0] = new Label("Press", Label.CENTER);
120        welcome[1] = new Label("New game", Label.CENTER);
121        welcome[2] = new Label("to start", Label.CENTER);
122        for (int num = 0; num < 3; ++num) {
123          welcome[num].setBackground(new Color(128,0,0));
124          welcome[num].setForeground(new Color(255,100,100));
125          welcome[num].setFont(new Font("Helvetica",
126            Font.BOLD, 14));
127          welcomePanel.add(welcome[num]);
128        }
129
130        scoresPanel = new Panel(new GridLayout(3,1));
131        scores = new Label[3];
132        scores[0] = new Label("X wins: " + Xwins);
133        scores[1] = new Label("O wins: " + Owins);
134        scores[2] = new Label("Draws: " + draws);
135        for (int num = 0; num < 3; ++num) {
136          scores[num].setBackground(new Color(0, 128, 0));
137          scores[num].setForeground(new Color(100,255,100));
138          scores[num].setFont(new Font("Helvetica",
139            Font.BOLD, 14));
140          scoresPanel.add(scores[num]);
141        }
142      }
143
144      void showScores()
145      {
146        scores[0].setText("X wins: " + Xwins);
147        scores[1].setText("O wins: " + Owins);
148        scores[2].setText("Draws: " + draws);
149        centreLayout.show(centrePanel, "Scores");
150        ticTacToeLabel.setText("Java Tic Tac Toe");
151      }
152
153      void enableSquares()
154      {
155        XOturn = "X";
156        for (int row = 0; row < GRIDSIZE; ++row)
```

```
        for (int col = 0; col < GRIDSIZE; ++col) {
           square[row][col].setLabel("  ");
           square[row][col].setEnabled(true);
        }
     centreLayout.show(centrePanel, "GameGrid");
     ticTacToeLabel.setText("Java Tic Tac Toe");
  }

  void disableSquares()
  {
     for (int row = 0; row < GRIDSIZE; ++row)
        for (int col = 0; col < GRIDSIZE; ++col) {
           square[row][col].setEnabled(false);
        }
  }

  void squareChosen(ActionEvent event)
  {
     for (int row = 0; row < GRIDSIZE; ++row)
        for (int col = 0; col < GRIDSIZE; ++col) {
           if (event.getSource() == square[row][col]) {
              square[row][col].setLabel(XOturn);
              square[row][col].setEnabled(false);
              int gameState = checkGameOver();
              switch (gameState) {
              case NOT_OVER:
                 XOturn = XOturn.equals("X") ? "O" : "X";
                 break;
              case DRAW:
                 ticTacToeLabel.setText(
                    "Game over. It's a draw!");
                 draws++;
                 break;
              case WIN:
                 ticTacToeLabel.setText("Game over. " + XOturn +
                    " wins!");
                 if (XOturn.equals("X"))
                    Xwins++;
                 else
                    Owins++;
                 disableSquares();
                 break;
              }
           }
        }
  }

  int checkGameOver()
  {
     int row, col;

     boolean match = true;
```

```
        // Check rows
        for (row = 0; row < GRIDSIZE; ++row) {
          for (col = 0; col < GRIDSIZE; ++col) {
            if (!square[row][col].getLabel().equals(XOturn))
              match = false;
          }
          if (match)
            return WIN;
          match = true;
        }

        // Check columns
        for (col = 0; col < GRIDSIZE; ++col) {
          for (row = 0; row < GRIDSIZE; ++row) {
            if (!square[row][col].getLabel().equals(XOturn))
              match = false;
          }
          if (match)
            return WIN;
          match = true;
        }

        // Check diagonals
        for (row = 0; row < GRIDSIZE; ++row) {
          if (!square[row][row].getLabel().equals(XOturn))
            match = false;
        }
        if (match)
          return WIN;
        match = true;

        for (row = 0; row < GRIDSIZE; ++row) {
          if (!square[row][GRIDSIZE-row-1].getLabel().
              equals(XOturn))
            match = false;
        }
        if (match)
          return WIN;

        // Check for blank square
        for (row = 0; row < GRIDSIZE; ++row)
          for (col = 0; col < GRIDSIZE; ++col)
            if (square[row][col].getLabel().equals(" "))
              return NOT_OVER;
        return DRAW;
    }
}
```

We declare the various components on lines 11 to 14. Note that we are using a *two-dimensional array* to store the Buttons used for the playing grid (line 11). An ordinary *one-dimensional* array can be thought of as storing a set of elements as blocks arranged in a straight line, with the first block given the index number 0, and successive blocks given consecutive index numbers. A two-dimensional array, declared by putting `[][]` after the variable name, as shown on line 11, may be thought of as storing its elements in a rectangular grid. To find an element in the grid, we need two index numbers: the row and the column. The element in the upper left corner has row number 0 and column number 0, the next element over in the first row is in row 0, column 1, and so on.

If the array variable is called `square` (as on line 11), we refer to the various elements as `square[0][0]`, `square[0][1]`, and so on, where the first index refers to the row number and the second to the column number. Apart from having two index numbers, a two-dimensional array element may be used just like a one-dimensional array element, or indeed like any other variable of the same data type.

The `String XOturn` on line 15 will be used to store the letter 'X' or 'O' depending on whose turn it is. The three `int`s on line 16 will be used to keep track of the number of wins and draws.

The `main()` method on lines 18 to 31 is much the same as the other `main()` methods we have used so far. However, we have added an extra feature on lines 26 to 30. A `WindowAdapter` has been attached to the main `messageFrame` that holds the program. The `WindowAdapter` class implements the `WindowListener` interface, which listens for events generated by a window object. In this case, we listen for the `windowClosing` event, which occurs when the user shuts down the window by using the small 'x' button at the upper right of the window (if you are running in Microsoft Windows 95 or Windows NT), or shuts down the window using the equivalent procedure on another platform (such as UNIX or Macintosh). When the user attempts to close the program this way, the `System.exit()` method is called to shut down the program. Without this listener, nothing happens when the user attempts to shut down the window.

The `init()` method, starting on line 33, initializes all the variables and components. The 'X' player is set to play first on line 35, and the score counters are set to zero on line 36. The background colour of the master window is set to yellow on line 37 (the author has a penchant for bright colours – some readers may prefer to change this!).

Line 38 creates the `Panel gamePanel`, which will be used at the top level to arrange the final version of the window. It is assigned a `BorderLayout` (line 39).

The `initializeLabels()` method is then called (line 40) to set up the various `Label` components. As we will see when we consider this method below, its main task is to set up the `Panel`s for displaying the initial message (`welcomePanel`) and the scores (`scoresPanel`). These two `Panel`s, together with the `squaresPanel`, will be added to the `CardLayout` in the central section of the applet. Then, depending on which action the user is currently doing, one of these three `Panel`s will be displayed.

Line 41 creates the `CardLayout` that is used to display the central section of the applet. Line 42 creates a new `Panel` and attaches `centreLayout` to it.

Line 43 creates the `Panel` that is to hold the grid of `Button`s used in playing the game. On line 44, the `initializeGrid()` method is called to set up the array of `Button`s, This method returns a `Panel` as its result, and this `Panel` is added to `squaresPanel`. This requires a bit of explanation, as you may wonder why, if `initializeGrid()` returns a `Panel` already, we need to enclose it with yet *another* `Panel`.

The reason is that the `Panel` returned by `initializeGrid()` has a `GridLayout` as its layout manager. The `GridLayout` stretches its components to fit the surrounding container. If we added this `Panel` directly to the master layout without enclosing it inside another `Panel`, the size of the grid would change to fill all the space available to it. If you compare Figure 7.3, which shows the opening screen, with Figure 7.4, which shows the actual size occupied by the grid during play, you will see that, had we not enclosed the grid within a second `Panel`, the array of `Button`s would stretch horizontally to fill the entire area occupied by the 'Press New game to start' `Panel` in Figure 7.3.

You may still be wondering why enclosing the grid within a second `Panel` stops it from stretching. After all, why doesn't this second `Panel` just stretch as well? The reason is that the second `Panel` is assigned a `FlowLayout` by default (note that we do not explicitly assign a layout manager to `squaresPanel` after creating it on line 43), and `FlowLayout` does *not* stretch to fill up the available space. Therefore, the second `Panel` sizes itself to match the natural size and shape of the grid of `Button`s, and once it has done that, it will not change shape when added to other layouts. The result is the display seen in Figure 7.4.

Lines 45 to 47 add the three `Panel`s to the `CardLayout` in `centrePanel`, and line 48 displays the 'Welcome' `Panel` on startup. Finally, lines 50 to 52 add the title `Label`, the `centrePanel`, and the row of `Button`s to the `BorderLayout` in `gamePanel`, and `gamePanel` itself is added to the master applet.

Again, we *could* have simply assigned a `BorderLayout` to the top-level `Frame`, rather than defining an extra `Panel` such as `gamePanel`. However, if we had added the three components directly to the `Frame`, rather than adding them to `gamePanel` and then adding `gamePanel` to the `Frame`, the components would stretch to fit the `Frame`. This isn't a problem provided that the size of the `Frame` is set up properly when the applet is initialized, but if the `Frame` is resized by the user after being opened, the components stretch themselves to fit the `Frame`, which can destroy the appearance of the applet. By assigning the `BorderLayout` to `gamePanel`, and then adding `gamePanel` to the overall `Frame` (which has a `FlowLayout` by default), the components within the `gamePanel` will not resize themselves when the `Frame` is resized. You should try these different options by changing the `TicTacToe` code and seeing what happens.

The `initializeGrid()` method (lines 56 to 75) initializes the two-dimensional array `square` (line 58), and then adds these `Button`s to a `Panel` to which a `GridLayout` has been attached. An `ActionListener` is attached to each `Button`, with the `squareChosen()` method called each time one of the `Button`s is pressed.

There are a couple of points worth noting about the `initializeGrid()` method. First, by using the `GRIDSIZE` constant rather than just the number 3, we allow a grid of any size to be used in the program, merely by changing the value of `GRIDSIZE` back on line 7.

Second, we have used a *nested loop* (starting on line 61) to process the array of `Buttons`. The outer `for` loop (line 61) cycles through the rows of the two-dimensional array, while the inner loop (line 62) cycles through the columns. The outer loop begins the process by setting `row` to 0. Then, while `row` is held at this value, the inner loop takes `col` from 0 to `GRIDSIZE` - 1. Once the inner loop is finished, control returns to the outer loop, and `row` is incremented to 1. The inner loop is then repeated, so that all elements on row 1 are processed. This continues until `row` is `GRIDSIZE` - 1.

The `initializeGrid()` method also illustrates the use of a `GridLayout`. A `Panel` is created on line 59, and assigned a `GridLayout` on line 60. After each `Button` is initialized and customized, it is added to the layout on line 72. The `Panel` itself is returned as the result of the function on line 74.

The `initializeButtons()` method (lines 77 to 106) uses another `GridLayout` to store the three `Buttons` that appear at the bottom of the applet. An `ActionListener` is attached to each `Button`.

The `initializeLabels()` method (lines 108 to 142) sets up the title `Label` at the top of the applet, and also prepares the `Labels` that appear in the welcome panel and the scores panel. These two panels each have three lines of text, so a `GridLayout` is used to position these three lines in a vertical grid. The background and foreground colours are set up, and the fonts initialized.

The `showScores()` method (lines 144 to 151) updates the text in the three scores `Labels`, and calls the `show()` method for the `CardLayout centreLayout` to display the 'Scores' panel.

The `enableSquares()` method (lines 153 to 163) restores the game playing area to its initial state, ready for a new game. Since each `Button` is disabled after it is pressed during play (see below), and the label of each `Button` is changed to show an 'X' or an 'O' as appropriate, the label of each `Button` is restored to a blank, and all `Buttons` are enabled. The 'GameGrid' panel is shown in `centreLayout`, and the title `Label` is restored.

The `disableSquares()` method (lines 165 to 171) is called when one of the players wins, to prevent any further `Buttons` being pressed.

The `squareChosen()` method (lines 173 to 202) is called whenever one of the game area `Buttons` is pressed. The nested `for` loop starting on line 175 extracts the source object from `event` using the `getSource()` method (line 177) and compares it with each `Button` in turn until the identity of the pressed `Button` is found. The `Button` then has its label set to the current player (line 178) and is disabled (line 179).

After each move, a check is made to see if the game is over (line 180). The `checkGameOver()` method can return three results. The game may not be over (neither player has won yet, and there are still `Buttons` that have not yet been chosen). In this case, `XOturn` is swapped to the other player (line 183) and play continues. Secondly, the game may have ended in a draw (neither player has won, but there are no unpressed `Button`s remaining). In this case, the title `Label` displays the message (line 186) and the `draws` counter is incremented (line 188).

Finally, the last move may have been a win for the current player. In this case the appropriate message is displayed (line 191) and the correct counter is incremented (lines 193 to 196). All remaining `Button`s are then disabled (line 197) to prevent further play after a win.

The remaining method, `checkGameOver()`, is called after each move. Its purpose is to examine the game board to see if either player has won, or if the game has ended in a draw. To check for a win, the method uses the fact that it can only be the current player (as given by `XOturn`) that could have won on the last move, so it examines all rows, columns and diagonals to see if it can find a complete line of `Button`s, all of whose captions are equal to `XOturn`. The details of the method are left as an exercise for the reader, and should provide valuable experience in understanding two-dimensional arrays.

The GridBagLayout manager

The final layout manager that is part of the Java AWT is the `GridBagLayout`. As its name implies, the `GridBagLayout` is similar to the `GridLayout` in that it allows components to be positioned on a rectangular grid. However, it offers considerably more control over the appearance and placement of the various components.

A `GridBagLayout` must work in conjunction with a `GridBagConstraints` object. The latter object allows various parameters to be set for each component before it is added to the layout itself. To use a `GridBagLayout` to lay out components within a container, the following steps must be followed.

First, declare and initialize the `GridBagLayout` and `GridBagConstraints` objects. Attach the `GridBagLayout` object to the container in the usual way, using the `setLayout()` method.

Initialize the `GridBagConstraints` object by setting its parameters (we'll see what parameters are available in a moment). This is done by setting each parameter directly with an assignment statement – there are no interface functions provided.[1] These steps need be done only once, before the first component is added to the container.

Then, for *each component* that you wish to add, you must set any parameters in the `GridBagConstraints` object that are to apply to that component alone, and call the `setConstraints()` method (part of the `GridBagLayout` class) to

---

[1] If you think this goes against proper object-oriented design, you are, in the author's opinion, correct. In fact, in a proper design, the constraints object should be part of the `GridBagLayout` class itself, and not a separate class.

associate the constraints with that component. Finally, use the add() method in the usual way to add the component to the container.

The easiest way to see how this works in practice is to examine an example. In the following code, we provide an interface to the nim game from Chapter 5 using the GridBagLayout to lay out the components, rather than relying on the default FlowLayout as we did then. The interface produced is essentially the same as that shown in Figure 5.3, except for a few minor variations in spacing.

The code that follows is not the complete applet for the nim game – rather we have provided a replacement for the init() method from the program in Chapter 5. No other alterations are required in the original program.

```
// Add the following two lines to the class declarations
GridBagLayout layout;
GridBagConstraints constraints;
// Replace the old init() method with the following
// two methods

void setupGridBag()
{
   layout = new GridBagLayout();
   constraints = new GridBagConstraints();
   constraints.anchor = GridBagConstraints.CENTER;
   constraints.fill = GridBagConstraints.NONE;
   constraints.insets = new Insets(5,5,5,5);
   constraints.ipadx = 0;
   constraints.ipady = 0;
   constraints.weightx = 1;
   constraints.weighty = 1;
   constraints.gridwidth = 1;
   constraints.gridheight = 1;
}

public void init()
{
   setupGridBag();
   Panel masterPanel = new Panel();
   masterPanel.setLayout(layout);
   selectInitialLabel =
      new Label("How many counters to start with?");
   selectInitialChoice = new Choice();
   selectInitialChoice.addItem("10");
   selectInitialChoice.addItem("12");
   selectInitialChoice.addItem("15");
   constraints.gridx = 0;
   constraints.gridy = 0;
   layout.setConstraints(selectInitialLabel, constraints);
   masterPanel.add(selectInitialLabel);
   constraints.gridx = 1;
   layout.setConstraints(selectInitialChoice, constraints);
   masterPanel.add(selectInitialChoice);
```

```java
        playFirstLabel = new Label("Who plays first?");
        playFirstGroup = new CheckboxGroup();
        constraints.gridx = 0;
        constraints.gridy = 1;
        layout.setConstraints(playFirstLabel, constraints);
        masterPanel.add(playFirstLabel);

        humanFirstBox =
          new Checkbox("Human", playFirstGroup, true);
        computerFirstBox =
          new Checkbox("Computer", playFirstGroup, false);
        Panel firstPanel = new Panel(new GridLayout(1,2));
        firstPanel.add(humanFirstBox);
        firstPanel.add(computerFirstBox);
        constraints.gridx = 1;
        layout.setConstraints(firstPanel, constraints);
        masterPanel.add(firstPanel);

        newGameButton = new Button("Start new game");
        newGameButton.addActionListener(new ActionListener() {
          public void actionPerformed(ActionEvent event) {
            initializeNewGame();
          }
        });
        constraints.gridx = 0;
        constraints.gridy = 2;
        layout.setConstraints(newGameButton, constraints);
        masterPanel.add(newGameButton);

        quitButton = new Button("Quit game");
        quitButton.addActionListener(new ActionListener() {
          public void actionPerformed(ActionEvent event) {
            System.exit(0);
          }
        });
        constraints.gridx = 1;
        layout.setConstraints(quitButton, constraints);
        masterPanel.add(quitButton);

        selectNumberLabel =
          new Label("How many counters do you take?");
        selectNumberGroup = new CheckboxGroup();
        choose1Box = new Checkbox("1", selectNumberGroup,
    false);
        choose2Box = new Checkbox("2", selectNumberGroup,
    false);
        choose3Box = new Checkbox("3", selectNumberGroup,
    false);
        dummyBox = new Checkbox("", selectNumberGroup, true);
```

164 LAYOUT MANAGERS

```
91        choose1Box.addItemListener(new ItemListener() {
92          public void itemStateChanged(ItemEvent event) {
93            doHumanMove(event);
94          }
95        });
96        choose2Box.addItemListener(new ItemListener() {
97          public void itemStateChanged(ItemEvent event) {
98            doHumanMove(event);
99          }
100       });
101       choose3Box.addItemListener(new ItemListener() {
102         public void itemStateChanged(ItemEvent event) {
103           doHumanMove(event);
104         }
105       });
106
107       constraints.gridx = 0;
108       constraints.gridy = 3;
109       layout.setConstraints(selectNumberLabel, constraints);
110       masterPanel.add(selectNumberLabel);
111       Panel takePanel = new Panel(new GridLayout(1,3));
112       takePanel.add(choose1Box);
113       takePanel.add(choose2Box);
114       takePanel.add(choose3Box);
115       constraints.gridx = 1;
116       layout.setConstraints(takePanel, constraints);
117       masterPanel.add(takePanel);
118
119       setLayout(new FlowLayout(FlowLayout.LEFT));
120       add(masterPanel);
121       disableHumanMove();
122     }
```

We add the two declarations shown on lines 2 and 3 to the class variables at the beginning of the class. The remainder of the code replaces the init() method in the old Nim class in Chapter 5.

Start by looking at the init() method on line 22. We first call the setupGridBag() method, whose code is given on lines 7 through 20. Here, we have initialized layout and constraints, and then provided initial values for all the parameters that may be set in a GridBagConstraints object. We did not need to do this for most of the parameters, since we simply set them to their default values, but we've listed them all here so you can see what is available. The meanings of the various parameters are as follows.

- anchor – specifies how the component is to be arranged within its grid cell. All possible values are static constants from the GridBagConstraints class, so all constants should be prefixed by 'GridBagConstraints.'. Possible values are CENTER, NORTH, NORTHWEST, NORTHEAST,

EAST, SOUTH, SOUTHWEST, SOUTHEAST, and WEST. The default is CENTER.

- `fill` – each component can be made to stretch to fill its cell either horizontally or vertically, or both, or neither. The possible values are NONE, BOTH, HORIZONTAL, and VERTICAL. The default is NONE.
- `insets` – each component can have a number of pixels of padding inserting on each of its four edges. An `Insets` object is used to provide the padding, as shown on line 13. The arguments to the `Insets` constructor are the number of pixels of padding on the top, left, bottom, and right, in that order. The default is for no insets.
- `ipadx` and `ipady` – these parameters only have an effect if the `fill` parameter is switched off in the corresponding direction. An `ipadx` value increases the size of the component by that many pixels *on each side* in the horizontal direction, and `ipady` has a similar effect in the vertical direction. The default is zero padding.
- `gridx` and `gridy` – these give the column number and row number, respectively, of the upper left corner of the component. As with arrays in Java, numbering for columns and rows begins at 0. Note that each component can be placed at the required position, unlike the `GridLayout` where components are added left to right, top to bottom.
- `gridwidth` and `gridheight` – these give the number of columns and rows, respectively, spanned by the component. The default value in both cases is 1.
- `weightx` and `weighty` – these values only have an effect if the container to which the layout is attached is resized. The purpose of these parameters is to specify how each component will stretch to fill up the space when its container is resized. The effect is somewhat complex, so is best illustrated with an example. Consider `weightx`, which governs stretching horizontally. Suppose we have a layout with three rows and four columns. The `weightx` values for the four components in row 0 are (0, 1, 3, 5) and in row 1 are (0, 2, 1, 4). In row 2, all `weightx` values are 0. Now suppose the container is resized horizontally. Find the *maximum* `weightx` value in each column (for the example here, this gives (0, 2, 3, 5)). Add up these values (obtaining 10 here). The fraction of extra width allocated to each column (or subtracted from each column if the container is made smaller) is obtained by dividing that column's maximum `weightx` value by the sum. In our example, column 0 doesn't change at all, since its maximum `weightx` value is 0. Column 1 increases in width by 20% of the total size increase, column 2 by 30% and column 3 by 50%. Changes in height are worked out similarly, using `weighty`.

As you can see, the `GridBagLayout` offers a lot more control over its components than the other layout managers. However, the effects of a complex `GridBagLayout` specification are sometimes hard to predict, so it is still best to use simpler layout managers to build up a complex layout in simple stages, and perhaps use a `GridBagLayout` to organize the layout at the top level.

This is the approach we have taken in our nim example here. On line 25 we define `masterPanel` to hold the overall layout, and attach the `GridBagLayout` layout to it on line 26.

The `Label` and `Choice` components are to appear on the first row, so we set the (gridx, gridy) co-ordinates to (0,0) and (1,0) respectively for these two components (lines 33, 34 and 37). Notice that once a parameter (such as gridy) is set, it remains in effect until it is changed by another assignment statement. For this reason, we do not need to specify gridy again when setting the constraints for the `Choice` component – it retains its value from line 34.

The constraints for the `Label` are set on line 35. Note that the `setConstraints()` method takes two arguments: the first is the component to which the constraints are to be applied, and the second is the `GridBagConstraints` object itself. No reference is made at this stage to either the `GridBagLayout` object or to the container. The `Label` is added to `masterPanel` on line 36 in the usual way.

The 'Who plays first' `Label` is accompanied by two radio buttons, all appearing on row 1. We define gridx and gridy to be 0 and 1 on lines 43 and 44, and add the `Label`. The two radio buttons, however, look better if they are arranged in a `Panel` of their own using a simple `GridLayout` with one row and two columns. We define `firstPanel` on line 52, and add the two radio buttons to it on lines 53 and 54. Then we specify gridx to be 1 on line 55 and add `firstPanel` as a single component to the `GridBagLayout` at row 1, column 1.

The 'Start new game' and 'Quit' `Buttons` are added to row 2, columns 0 and 1.

Then we add the 'How many counters...' `Label` and its associated `Checkboxes`. As with the radio buttons above, the `Checkboxes` look better if we add them to a `Panel` of their own, using a `GridLayout` with one row and three columns (lines 108 to 111). The `Panel` is then added as a unit to the `GridBagLayout`.

Finally, we add `masterPanel` to the overall `Frame` on line 117.

The advantage of using a `GridBagLayout` to set up the nim game interface is that its configuration remains unchanged when the enclosing `Frame` is resized, as you can see when you run the program. To get a feel for how the various constraint parameters behave, it is a good idea to copy this program and change some of the parameters to see what happens. You may find some of the effects hard to predict, so you may prefer to use the simpler layout managers for most of your layouts, and reserve the `GridBagLayout` for large scale organization.

Exercises

1   Refer back to Figure 6.1 showing the interface to the pizza ordering applet. Use layout managers and `Panels` to arrange the components so that the layout does not change when the window is resized. Put the 'Choose your toppings' `Label`

at the top on its own, the first two Checkboxes on the next line, and the remaining three Checkboxes on the next line. All these lines should be centred. Use GridLayouts to arrange each row within a Panel. Arrange the three Buttons in a similar fashion. Then by judicious use of Panels and a BorderLayout, complete the layout. Finally, enclose the completed layout in a Panel (to prevent the components from stretching in the finished applet) and add this to the overall Frame.

2   Design a second layout for the pizza program which contains the confirmation of the order (the information that is currently printed in the TextArea). Construct the confirmation text from a series of Labels arranged within a Panel. Add a Button allowing the user to return to the first layout to change their order or place a new order. Remove the TextArea from the original layout.

When the program starts, display the first layout, and when the user clicks on the Order button, use a CardLayout to switch to confirmation layout.

3   Design a layout for a pocket calculator. You should include the 10 number buttons (0 through 9), five function buttons (multiply, divide, add, subtract, equals), a 'Clear' button, and a TextField to display the entered numbers and answers. Make use of the various layout managers (except for the GridBagLayout) and Panels to arrange the components. Ensure that the final layout does not change its form when the enclosing frame is resized. (Don't bother adding code to actually make the calculator work unless you are feeling ambitious – the purpose of this exercise is to set up the layout only.)

4   Redesign the TicTacToe layout using the GridBagLayout. On the welcome screen, place the 'Java Tic Tac Toe' on the first row, the Panel containing the 'Press new game to start' message on the second row, and the three Buttons on the third row. Use a grid with three rows and three columns, and use gridwidth to make the first two rows extend over all three columns.

On the main game layout, use a GridLayout to arrange the nine Buttons as before, but use a GridBagLayout to handle the overall layout.

CHAPTER 8
Graphics and animation

The graphics context

In a few of the example programs given in earlier chapters, we made limited use of Java's graphics features. In the game of nim in Chapter 5, we drew the counters as filled rectangles, and in several other programs we have drawn text into an applet.

In all of these cases, we made use of a mysterious class called Graphics, and promised that all would be explained in due course. The time has now come to make good the promise.

The Graphics class provides an interface between the programmer and a feature known as the *graphics context*. To see what a graphics context is and why it is necessary, think about what actually happens when you call one of the Graphics methods to, say, draw a line.

The drawLine() method in the Graphics class takes four arguments: the x and y co-ordinates of the starting point, and of the end point. These co-ordinates are given in terms of *pixels*. A pixel (an abbreviation of 'picture element') is really a *hardware* term – it refers to display units on the monitor or printer.[1] Since different computers will have different monitors and printers attached to them, a drawing command must be adapted so that it appears correctly on all these different devices. Whenever a display unit such as a monitor or printer is installed on your computer system, a program called a *device driver* must be installed along with it. The device driver's job is to translate display commands received from the computer itself so that the device which it is driving can understand them and produce the correct display.

The job of the graphics context in Java is to relay drawing instructions to the device driver. All graphical commands must be handled by the graphics context (as represented by the Graphics class) so that they can be sent to the appropriate device driver. In one sense, Graphics works a bit like a layout manager – just as components are added to a layout manager, so graphical components are added to a Graphics object.

The main difference between adding components to a layout manager and adding graphics objects to a graphics context is that GUI components are instances of Java classes from the java.awt package, while graphics objects, such as lines, text

---

[1] Printing is supported in Java 1.1 and 1.2, but not in Java 1.0.

strings, and so on, are *not* instances of a class. Drawing a line, for example, requires calling a method which draws the line, not creating a `Line` object and adding it to the graphics context.

The `Graphics` class is an abstract class. Recall from Chapter 4 that an abstract class in Java is a class that provides declarations of data fields and methods, but not definitions for the methods. Abstract classes may only be used as base classes for other classes derived from them, and these derived classes must provide definitions for all methods that are declared in the abstract base class.

The `Graphics` class provides declarations for all the methods that allow drawing of graphics objects. The fact that the `Graphics` class is abstract may worry you somewhat – does this mean that you have to provide your own method definitions for doing all the drawing operations? The answer, fortunately, is 'no' – the `Graphics` class works in a special way.

To see why the `Graphics` class is implemented in this seemingly perverse way, we need to remember that one of the goals of the designers of Java was to write a language which is truly portable across different computer platforms. This means that a Java program, including all its graphics, may be written on any type of machine (for example, a Windows-based PC, a UNIX workstation, or a Macintosh) and, *without any further modification*, be runnable on any other type of computer which supports Java.

If you have ever done any graphics programming in languages other than Java, you will know just how challenging this goal is. For example, a program written in, say, C or C++ that runs on a Microsoft Windows machine will not run on any other type of machine. Converting Windows programs to run on, say, UNIX/X Windows machines (or vice versa) is a very time-consuming task, and often a fully compatible port is never achieved.

The portability of Java is achieved by providing built-in conversions for all graphics, so that a command to draw a line is executed at runtime by reading the byte code in the `.class` file produced by the Java compiler and interpreting the byte commands in that file in terms of whatever graphics system is supported by the machine on which the program is running. That is, the work in creating the graphics is done by the platform-specific Java implementation.

All of this explains why the `Graphics` class is implemented as an abstract class. Each different computer system on which the Java applet will run provides its own, platform-dependent version of the `Graphics` class, which is derived from the abstract class, and provides all the platform-specific definitions of all the methods. (So you don't need to write your own versions of all the methods!)

Having said all that, you must be warned that the 'total portability' feature of Java isn't quite all it's cracked up to be. You will probably find that an applet written on one computer doesn't look quite the same on another, or even with two different browsers on the same computer. Fonts and colours often do not port very well between machines. If you are planning on writing an applet which is to be used on a wide variety of platforms (for example, an applet that will be placed on a web page that is available around the world), it is a good idea to be fairly conservative in your use of exotic fonts or non-standard colours.

In practice, you won't need to worry about how the `Graphics` class is doing its job, since all the mechanics of its operations are hidden from the programmer. All you need to remember is that all drawing operations must be done by calling methods in the `Graphics` class.

The paint(), update(), and repaint() methods

Java's `Applet` class contains three methods that are common in programs using graphics.

The `paint()` method, as its name implies, paints the applet with whatever graphics commands it contains. It is called whenever an applet starts up, in order to paint the graphics into the applet for its first appearance on screen. The default version of `paint()`, of course, doesn't draw anything, so if you want graphics to appear in your applet, you need to provide an overridden version of `paint()`. The examples in previous chapters all had a `paint()` method containing a few customized graphics commands.

The default version of the `update()` method for a component clears the drawing area, resets the drawing colour to the foreground colour of the component, and then calls the `paint()` method. By 'clears', we mean that it paints the drawing area with its own background colour, wiping out any graphics that had been drawn on it. Thus the `update()` method provides a way of changing the graphics in an applet after the applet has started running. If `update()` is called for a container object such as a `Frame`, the `update()` method for any components contained within that container are also called.

The default version of the `repaint()` method just calls the `update()` method. An obvious question, therefore, is why do we have two methods which both essentially just update the applet? The answer is that the `update()` method requires the graphics context (in the form of a `Graphics` object) as an argument, while the `repaint()` method requires no arguments. Calling `repaint()` is therefore the easier of the two ways to update the applet, and is the preferred method in practice.

In summary, if we want any graphics to appear in an applet, we *must* override the `paint()` method, since that is ultimately where all the drawing is done. The default versions of `update()` and `repaint()` are adequate for most purposes, and it is more usual to update the graphics in an applet by calling `repaint()`.

Colours

Java offers a simple way to control the colour of a feature drawn using a `Graphics` object. The `Color` class is provided for the handling of colours.[1] There are two ways

---

[1] Readers outside the USA are cautioned that the American spelling of 'color' must be used – trying to refer to a `Colour` class will cause compiler errors. Since this book was written by an expatriate

to specify colours in Java – one of the `static` pre-defined colours provided in the `Color` class may be used, or a colour may be specified using its RGB (red-green-blue) value.

If you are unfamiliar with the RGB theory of colour, have a close look at the picture tube on your television set (assuming, of course, that it is a *colour* TV!) or computer screen. If you use a magnifying glass, you will see that the screen is covered with small dots arranged in triplets, where each triplet contains a red, green, and blue dot. All colours that you see on a TV or computer screen are composed by mixing these three so-called *primary* colours in varying intensities.[1] Depending on the capability of your TV or computer screen, anything from around 16 up to millions of different colours may be produced by using varying intensities of the red, green, and blue pixels. The Java `Color` class allows 256 different intensities (ranging from 0 to 255) for each of the R, G, and B pixels, for a total of 256^3 = 16,777,216 different colours.

First, let us consider the pre-defined `static` colours provided in the `Color` class (Table 8.1).

Table 8.1 `Color` constants

`Color` constant	RGB value
`white`	255, 255, 255
`black`	0, 0, 0
`red`	255, 0, 0
`green`	0, 255, 0
`blue`	0, 0, 255
`yellow`	255, 255, 0
`magenta` (purple)	255, 0, 255
`cyan` (light blue)	0, 255, 255
`gray`	128, 128, 128
`lightGray`	192, 192, 192
`darkGray`	64, 64, 64
`orange`	255, 200, 0
`pink`	255, 175, 175

Non-American readers are again cautioned that the American spelling of 'gray' (not the British 'grey') must be used. The RGB values for these basic colours should give you a good starting point for creating your own shades, by varying the colour that is closest to the one you want.

We now show a simple example that displays some text, a line and a rectangle, each in a different colour.

Canadian living in Britain, the British spelling of 'colour' will be used whenever we are not talking explicitly about the `Color` class.

[1] If you are an artist, you may know that the three primary colours used in painting are red, yellow (not green), and blue. When a colour is created by reflection of light (as in a painting) the RYB system is used; when by projection of light (as in a TV) the RGB system is used.

```
1   import java.applet.*;
2   import java.awt.*;
3   import java.awt.event.*;
4
5   public class SimpleGraphics extends Applet
6   {
7     public static void main(String argv[])
8     {
9       Frame messageFrame =
10        new Frame("Simple graphics example");
11      SimpleGraphics testMessage = new SimpleGraphics();
12      testMessage.init();
13      messageFrame.add("Center", testMessage);
14      messageFrame.setSize(450,350);
15      messageFrame.setVisible(true);
16      messageFrame.addWindowListener(new WindowAdapter() {
17        public void windowClosing(WindowEvent event) {
18          System.exit(0);
19        }
20      });
21    }
22
23    public void paint(Graphics g)
24    {
25      g.setColor(Color.red);
26      g.drawString("This is a simple example.", 20, 100);
27      g.setColor(new Color(243, 10, 145));
28      g.drawLine(20, 110, 175, 110);
29      g.setColor(new Color((float)0.0, (float)1.0,
30        (float)0.7));
31      g.drawRect(15, 80, 175, 50);
32    }
33  }
```

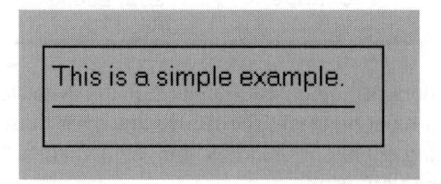

Figure 8.1 Output of the SimpleGraphics applet.

The program produces the output shown in Figure 8.1. The paint() method (line 23) takes a single Graphics argument. This method is not usually called explicitly by the programmer, however – it is called automatically by Java itself whenever the window needs repainting. This can happen in response to a repaint() call from within the program, or when the window that has been covered or minimized is redisplayed. In either case, the Graphics object describing the current graphics context is obtained automatically and sent to the `paint()` method when it is called.

We use the `setColor()` method of the `Graphics` class to set the colour for all drawing operations that follow it, up until the next `setColor()` operation. The `setColor()` method requires a `Color` object as its argument, but there are three ways this `Color` can be specified.

The first call to `setColor()` (line 25) uses one of the `static` colours provided in the `Color` class to set the colour to 'red', so that the text string is drawn in red. The second call to `setColor()` creates a new `Color` object using one of the `Color` constructors (line 27). This constructor expects three `int` arguments, each of which must be in the range from 0 to 255. The RGB values specified here (243, 10, 145) produce a dull purple colour.

The final call to `setColor()` (line 29) takes three `float` arguments. In this case, each `float` must lie in the range from 0.0 to 1.0. A value of 0.0 means that that colour component should be absent, while a value of 1.0 means that that component should be present to its maximum extent (equivalent to a value of 255 if we were using an `int` to specify the colour). Using `float`s to construct a colour is often more convenient, since you can specify each of the red, green, and blue components as a fraction of its maximum intensity. The values given in the example (0.0, 1.0, 0.7) indicate an absence of red, full intensity for green, and 70% intensity for blue, which produces a turquoise colour. Note that, if you specify a colour using constants, as we have here, you must explicitly cast the constants to be `float`s since a bare constant such as 0.7 is interpreted by the Java compiler as a `double`.

There are other colour-related methods in both the `Color` class and the `Graphics` class, so the user is, as usual, advised to consult the Java documentation for more details.

Fonts

As with colours, Java makes it quite simple to specify the font in which text will be drawn to the screen. Fonts are specified using the `Font` class.

If you have used a word processor or desktop publishing system, you will no doubt be familiar with many different fonts. In principle, a Java applet is capable of displaying any font available on your computer, but when you are designing applets, you should keep in mind that many computers will not have as many fonts installed as you may have. It is therefore a good idea to restrict the fonts you use to those that are guaranteed to be present in all Java installations.[1]

In Java 1.0, the main fonts were Dialog, TimesRoman, Helvetica, and Courier. All of these fonts are still present in Java 1.1, but except for Dialog, their use is discouraged. The reason for this is that Java aims to support *internationalization*,

---

[1] The procedure for adding extra fonts involves editing the file `font.properties`, to be found in the lib directory of your Java installation. It is recommended that you leave this job to your systems administrator if you are using a corporate computer.

that is, programs that are easy to convert from one (human) language to another. The TimesRoman, Helvetica and Courier fonts are defined only in the Latin alphabet, and their use would obviously make it more difficult to convert a document into another language (such as Japanese). For this reason, Java 1.1 has introduced more generic names to replace these three fonts. They are:

- `Serif`: This is a proportionally spaced (meaning that the horizontal space allocated to each letter varies), serifed font (a *serif* is a small line attached to the end of a stroke in a character – the main font used to write this book is a serifed font). For the Latin alphabet, it is equivalent to TimesRoman.
- `Monospaced`: A constant spacing font (one where each character takes up the same horizontal space) which resembles many typewriter fonts. `This sentence is written in Monospaced`. It is equivalent to Courier.
- `SansSerif`: A proportionally spaced, sans-serif ('without serifs') font. **This sentence is written in SansSerif**. It is equivalent to Helvetica (sometimes known as Arial).
- `Dialog` and `DialogInput`: The font used in dialog boxes.

In addition to these basic font styles, each font can also be drawn in plain or **bold**, and normal, *italic*, or ***bold italic*** style. Fonts may also be drawn in a wide variety of sizes, or *points*, to use the technical term for the size of a font.

In order to set the font for a text string, an object of the `Font` class must be declared and passed to the `setFont()` method of the `Graphics` class. The `Font` constructor requires three arguments: a `String` containing the name of the font, an `int` specifying the font's style (plain, bold, etc.), and a final `int` giving the font's point size.

A simple program demonstrating the use of the `Font` class is as follows.

```
1   import java.applet.Applet;
2   import java.awt.*;
3   import java.awt.event.*;
4
5   public class FontDemo extends Applet
6   {
7     public static void main(String argv[])
8     {
9       Frame messageFrame = new Frame("Fonts demo");
10      FontDemo testMessage = new FontDemo();
11      testMessage.init();
12      messageFrame.add("Center", testMessage);
13      messageFrame.setSize(600,500);
14      messageFrame.setVisible(true);
15      messageFrame.addWindowListener(new WindowAdapter() {
16        public void windowClosing(WindowEvent event) {
17          System.exit(0);
18        }
19      });
```

```
20      }
21
22      public void paint(Graphics g)
23      {
24          g.setFont(new Font("Serif", Font.BOLD, 14));
25          g.drawString("This is Serif, BOLD, 14 pt.",
26            20, 100);
27          g.setFont(new Font("SansSerif", Font.ITALIC, 14));
28          g.drawString("This is SansSerif, ITALIC, 14 pt.",
29            20, 150);
30          g.setFont(new Font("Monospaced", Font.PLAIN, 14));
31          g.drawString("This is Monospaced, PLAIN, 14 pt.",
32            20, 200);
33          g.setFont(new Font("Dialog", Font.BOLD, 14));
34          g.drawString("This is Dialog, BOLD, 14 pt.", 20, 250);
35          g.setFont(new Font("DialogInput", Font.BOLD, 36));
36          g.drawString("DialogInput, BOLD, 36 pt.", 20, 300);
37          g.setFont(new Font("Serif",
38            Font.BOLD + Font.ITALIC, 20));
39          g.drawString("This is Serif, BOLD + ITALIC,
40            20 pt.", 20, 350);
41      }
42  }
```

This produces the output shown in Figure 8.2. Note that the font style is specified by using one of the static values from the Font class. For example, to specify a bold style, the second argument of the Font constructor is Font.BOLD. Combining two or three styles is possible by simply adding together the corresponding values. For example, the last line drawn by the applet combines the bold and italic styles for a Serif font.

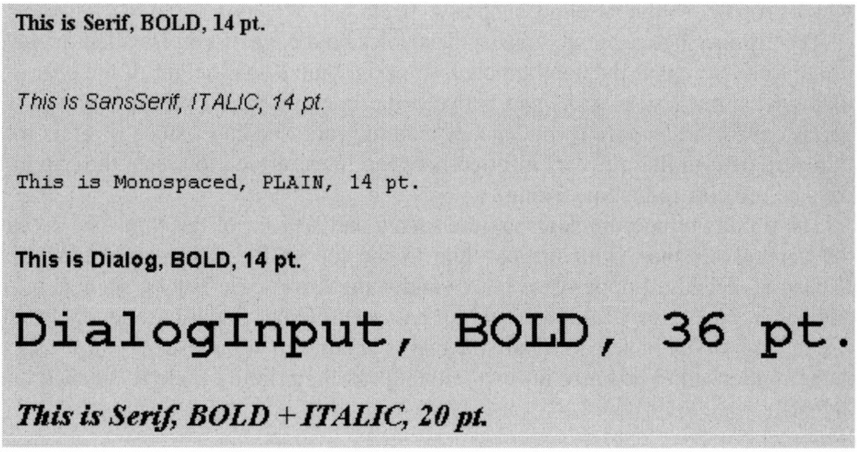

This is Serif, BOLD, 14 pt.

This is SansSerif, ITALIC, 14 pt.

This is Monospaced, PLAIN, 14 pt.

This is Dialog, BOLD, 14 pt.

DialogInput, BOLD, 36 pt.

This is Serif, BOLD + ITALIC, 20 pt.

Figure 8.2 Output of the FontDemo applet.

The font size is specified, in points, by the third argument to the `Font` constructor. As a rough guide to point sizes, most books and newspapers are printed in 10 or 12 point type. Anything smaller than 10 point is usually hard to read and should not be used excessively, although small text has its place for things like superscripts, subscripts, and other labels. It is also important to remember that specifying a particular point size for a font does *not* guarantee that the text will appear the same size on all computer screens. Even on machines running on the same platform, screens with different resolutions will display applets at different sizes. Viewing an applet on two different platforms (for example, a Windows-based PC and a UNIX workstation) may produce quite different text sizes for the same font size, even relative to other graphics objects (such as lines and rectangles) within the same applet.

Font metrics

When drawing text on an applet, it is often necessary to position the text relative to other graphics objects fairly precisely. Java offers a reasonable degree of control over the positioning of text with the methods in the `FontMetrics` class. In order to understand these methods, we need to learn a bit of printing terminology (see Figure 8.3).

Figure 8.3 shows two lines of text. Recall that the *x* and *y* co-ordinates required in the `drawString()` method of the `Graphics` class specify the starting point for the *baseline* of the text string to be drawn. If you cast your mind back to primary school when you were learning how to print the letters of the alphabet, you probably practiced your printing using a lined notebook. You were taught that most letters 'sat on the line', but some letters (such as 'g', 'p', 'y', and so on) had bits that extended below the line. From Figure 8.3, we see that the baseline is the horizontal line which marks the bottom of most of the letters in the Roman alphabet (except for those which drop below the baseline, such as g, p, etc.).

The distance between two adjacent baselines on a page of text is called the *height* of the font. Note that the height includes not only the actual height of the characters themselves, but also a small gap between the lines where no printing occurs. This gap is called the *leading* (pronounced 'ledding', not 'leeding', since it refers to the thin strip of lead that printers inserted between lines of type to create the gap in the days before electronic typesetting).

The final two measurements are the *ascent* and *descent* of the font. The ascent is the vertical distance from the baseline to the top of the tallest character. In the Roman alphabet, all upper-case letters and some lower-case letters, such as b, d, f, and so on, have a vertical size equal to the ascent. Other lower-case letters, such as a, c, e, and so on, have a vertical size that is smaller than the ascent, but no special name is attached to this size in Java (although in the printing trade it is called the *x-height*).

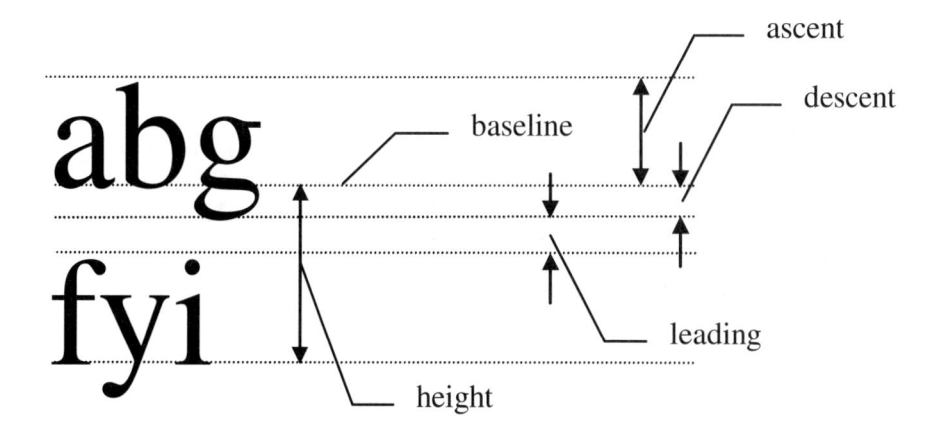

Figure 8.3 Printing terminology.

The descent of a font is the vertical distance from the baseline to the bottom of the characters that extend below the baseline, such as g, j, p, q, and y.

Java's `FontMetrics` class allows the height, leading, ascent, and descent to be found for a `Font` object. This information is useful when graphics objects must be placed precisely relative to some text. For example, if we want to underline some text, we might wish the underline to appear exactly at the location of the descent of the font.

The following `paint()` method shows an example of the use of the `FontMetrics` class, together with a few other useful methods dealing with fonts. To run this method, simply replace the `paint()` method in the `FontDemo` class above with this method.

```
1   public void paint(Graphics g)
2   {
3     g.setFont(new Font("Serif", Font.BOLD, 14));
4     Font currentFont = g.getFont();
5     FontMetrics currentFontMetrics =
6        g.getFontMetrics(currentFont);
7     int ascent = currentFontMetrics.getAscent();
8     int descent = currentFontMetrics.getDescent();
9     int leading = currentFontMetrics.getLeading();
10    int height = currentFontMetrics.getHeight();
11    String fonts[] = GraphicsEnvironment.
12       getLocalGraphicsEnvironment().
13       getAvailableFontFamilyNames();
14
15    // In Java 1.1 use:
```

```
16        // String fonts[] =
17        //    Toolkit.getDefaultToolkit().getFontList();
18
19        g.drawString("Font loaded:", 10, 25);
20        g.drawRect(5, 25 - ascent - leading,
21           currentFontMetrics.stringWidth("Fonts loaded:") +
22           10, height);
23        g.drawString(currentFont.toString(), 10, 50);
24        g.drawString("Ascent: " + ascent, 10, 75);
25        g.drawString("Descent: " + descent, 10, 100);
26        g.drawString("Leading: " + leading, 10, 125);
27        g.drawString("Height: " + height, 10, 150);
28
29        g.drawString("Fonts available:", 10, 175);
30        g.drawRect(5, 175 - ascent - leading,
31           currentFontMetrics.stringWidth("Fonts
32           available:") + 10, height);
33
34        for (int fontNum = 0; fontNum < fonts.length;
35           ++fontNum)
36           g.drawString(fonts[fontNum], 10, 200 +
37           fontNum*25);
38     }
39  }
```

The program produces some information on the font currently in use, and then lists the fonts currently available. The information is used to draw a neat box around two of the labels.

After setting the font to be serif, bold, and 14 point (line 3), we use the getFont() method of the Graphics class to obtain a Font object containing this font (line 4). We could, of course, have achieved the same result by saving the result of the call to the Font constructor in the Font object currentFont, but we wanted to show the use of the getFont() method.

On lines 5 and 6, a FontMetrics object is created and initialized to the properties of currentFont by using the getFontMetrics() method of the Graphics class. The currentFontMetrics object is then used to obtain the ascent, descent, leading, and height of the font (lines 7 to 10), using the corresponding methods from the FontMetrics class.

Lines 11 through 13 retrieve the names of the font families available on the local machine. This is a new feature introduced in Java 1.2 (also called 'Java 2'). A full explanation of the GraphicsEnvironment class is beyond the scope of this book. All you need to remember about the statement starting on line 11 is that it creates an array of Strings and stores the list of available fonts in that array.

If you are using Java 1.1, you will need to comment out the code on lines 11 to 13 and use the code shown on lines 16 and 17 instead. These lines use a class we haven't mentioned so far: the Toolkit class. In most cases, you will not use the Toolkit class directly, since it is the abstract base class of the Java AWT, and most of its functions are implemented automatically for you by the Java installation on your machine. In this way, it works in much the same way as the `Graphics` class. However, in this case, we use the `getFontList()` method of the `Toolkit` class to obtain a list of the available fonts in the current Java installation. This may be useful, for example, if you use an exotic font in your applet and want to check to see if that font is available on another system. If it is, you can proceed to use it, otherwise you may wish to load one of the ordinary fonts. The `getFontList()` method returns an array of `Strings` that contains a list of the font names.

After obtaining all the information, we proceed to draw it to the screen. The first string to be drawn is the label 'Font loaded:'. To highlight this label, we wish to draw a box around it. Rather than trying to guess what co-ordinates to use for the enclosing rectangle, we can calculate them directly by using the information from `currentFontMetrics`. The upper left corner of the rectangle will be 5 pixels to the left of the starting point, and at the top of the leading strip above the string. Since the string was drawn starting at a *y* co-ordinate of 25, this is the level of the baseline. To find the correct place for the top edge of the rectangle, we need to move upwards from the baseline by a number of pixels equal to the ascent plus the leading. Since the *y* co-ordinate is measured from top to bottom, this means that we must *subtract* that amount from the *y* co-ordinate for the baseline.

To calculate the width of the rectangle, we can make use of the `stringWidth()` method of the `FontMetrics` class. This method requires a `String` argument, and returns the width, in pixels, of that `String` when it is drawn in the current font. We add 10 pixels to this value to give the box a border of 5 pixels at each side. Finally, the height of the rectangle is just the height of the font, since that will draw the lower edge of the rectangle at a *y* co-ordinate of baseline + descent.

The current font is written out using the `toString()` method. This method is provided in the `Object` class, which is the base class for *all* Java classes. Any Java object therefore has a `String` representation which may be drawn to the screen.

The remainder of the applet uses the same techniques to write out the rest of the information. As usual, the reader is referred to the Java documentation to find out more information on other methods available in the `FontMetrics` class.

Scrollbars

In many interfaces, the size of the window on the screen is not large enough to display the entire document or layout that is contained in the program. For example, a word processor may be editing a document that is several pages long, and the screen is only large enough to show one page at a time. One way of allowing the user to view parts of a large document is by adding *scrollbars* to the window.

Scrollbars are implemented differently on different types of computer, but usually have several common features. Since I am writing this book on a PC running Windows 95, I will discuss the scrollbars on a PC platform, but users of UNIX and Macintosh machines should easily be able to see the correspondence to their own machines. Figure 8.4 shows a typical horizontal scrollbar.

Figure 8.4 A horizontal scrollbar (on a PC).

There are three areas within a scrollbar, each with its own action. The buttons at each end of the scrollbar (with the small arrows in them) may be clicked with the mouse to move the document a small amount in either direction. Clicking in the empty spaces between the end buttons and the central button has a similar effect, but usually moves the document by a larger amount. Finally, *dragging* the central button with the mouse moves the document accordingly. The relative size and position of the central button should also correspond to the amount and location of the visible portion of the document relative to the entire document.

In Java 1.0, adding scrollbars to a container was not a pleasant experience. Layouts and containers had to be carefully arranged, a large amount of code had to be written to synchronize the scrollbars with the containers, and on top of all that, some of the scrollbar features didn't work properly.

In Java 1.1, the new ScrollPane class does away with most of these problems. The ScrollPane is a container class which accepts only a single component, and does not allow a layout manager to be attached (the setLayout() method inherited from the Container class has been overridden to do nothing). This is not as restrictive as it sounds, however, since all the components and layouts can be added to a Panel, and the Panel can then be added to the ScrollPane, which treats the Panel as its single component.

Apart from the absence of a layout manager, a ScrollPane may be used like any other container object. In particular, it can be added to other layouts to provide a scrollbar for one component within a larger layout. Like the Frame, it has no natural size when it is created, so you must call the setSize() method before using it.

The default behaviour of the ScrollPane is to provide both horizontal and vertical scrollbars on an 'as needed' basis. That is, if the component it contains is larger in either the horizontal or vertical direction than the enclosing ScrollPane, the corresponding scrollbar will be provided. Otherwise, no scrollbar in that direction will be drawn. You can override this behaviour and require that a scrollbar be always present or always absent.

The ScrollPane works out the size and position of the central button by calculating the size of its child component. In most cases, where the component is a Panel that has sized itself to neatly surround the components that it contains, this presents no problem. However, occasionally you may want the scrolling area to extend over a larger area than that provided by the Panel added to the ScrollPane. In such a case, you must define a *preferred size* for the child component, which the ScrollPane will then use to determine the total scrolling area.

To see how this is done, we will add a ScrollPane to the NimBag class from Chapter 7, where we used a GridBagLayout to lay out the controls in the game of nim. Let us first just add a `ScrollPane` *without* defining any preferred size for the game area and see what happens.

Referring back to the `NimBag` class from Chapter 7, replace the `main()` method in that class by the following.

```
1   public static void main(String argv[])
2   {
3     Frame messageFrame = new Frame("Nim game");
4     NimBag testMessage = new NimBag();
5     testMessage.init();
6     ScrollPane scroller = new ScrollPane();
7     scroller.setSize(350,250);
8     scroller.add(testMessage);
9     messageFrame.setSize(350,250);
10    messageFrame.add(scroller);
11    messageFrame.setVisible(true);
12    messageFrame.addWindowListener(new WindowAdapter() {
13      public void windowClosing(WindowEvent event) {
14          System.exit(0);
15      }
16    });
17  }
```

We define a `ScrollPane` object on line 6, set its size on line 7, and add the `NimBag` applet to it on line 8. We set the enclosing `Frame`'s size to be the same as the `ScrollPane` (we don't have to do this – it can be larger or smaller) on line 9 and add the `ScrollPane` to the `Frame` on line 10. Everything else in the `NimBag` class is the same as in Chapter 7. The result is shown in Figure 8.5.

You can see that the `ScrollPane` has inserted a horizontal scrollbar, but not a vertical one, even though most of the diagram showing the number of counters left is chopped off at the bottom. Why? The reason is that the `Panel` defined within the `NimBag` class only encloses the components that were added to it, which means that the `Panel` only extends as far as the set of three 'How many counters do you take?' radio buttons. The `Panel` has no way of knowing that you intend to draw some counters in the space below these controls, so it does not increase its vertical size to account for this.

To fix this problem, we need to define a preferred size for the `NimBag` applet. We can do this by overriding the `getPreferredSize()` method. This method returns an object of the `Dimension` class, which consists of two `int`s: a `width` and a `height`. We insert the following definition into `NimBag` (anywhere we like).

```
public Dimension getPreferredSize()
{
  return new Dimension(450,350);
}
```

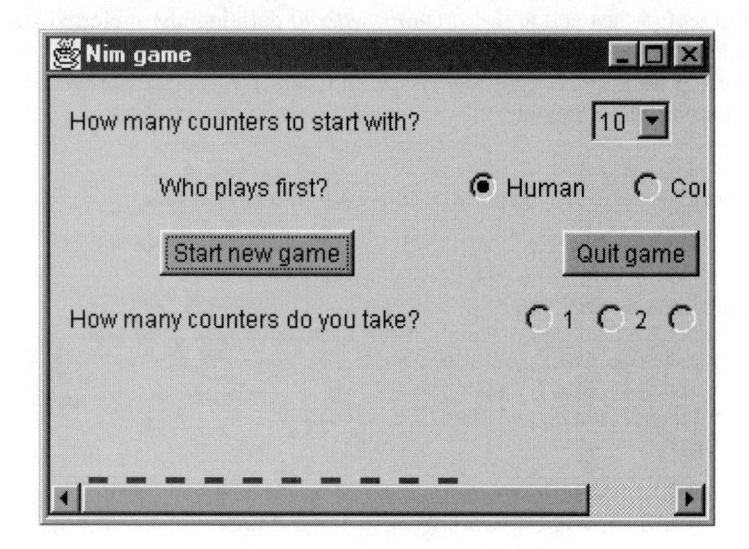

Figure 8.5. An initial attempt at using a `ScrollPane` in the nim game.

The `getPreferredSize()` method is called by the `ScrollPane` when it sets up its contents, and now it will know that we want the `NimBag` object to have a width of 450 pixels and a height of 350 pixels. The result is in Figure 8.6. We now have a vertical scrollbar which allows us to scroll over the controls *and* the drawing of the counters at the bottom.

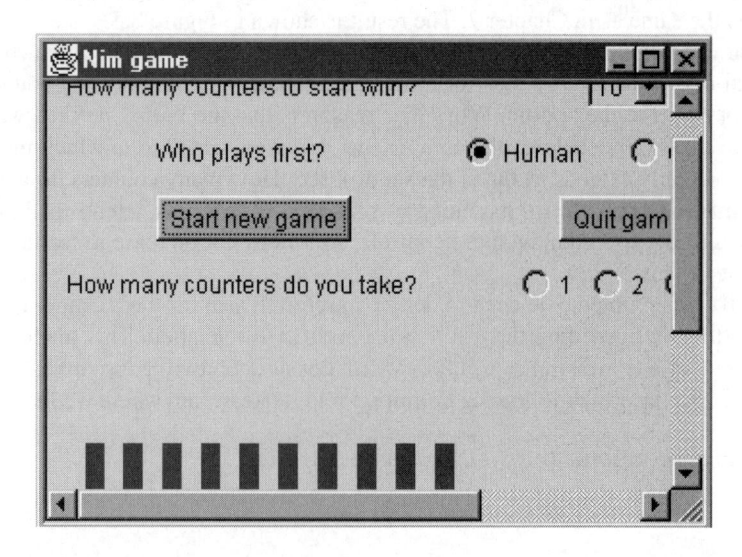

Figure 8.6 The effect of using the `getPreferredSize()` method.

Try resizing the enclosing `Frame` and you will see that when one of the two dimensions gets large enough, the corresponding scrollbar disappears.

The original `Scrollbar` class from Java 1.0 still exists in Java 1.1, but unless you want a scrollbar for some special purpose that is not connected with scrolling a `Panel` inside a frame, you are encouraged to use the `ScrollPane` instead. For example, you may want to create a standalone scrollbar that changes some of the properties of the applet (the background colour, say) without actually changing the position of what is viewed. As this is a rather specialized use of scrollbars, we won't cover it here.

Canvases

The `Canvas` class in the AWT is derived from the `Component` class directly, and contains only a `paint()` method in addition to the methods it inherits from `Component`. The `Canvas` can therefore accept drawing commands through its own graphics context, which is independent of the graphics context of any other `Canvas` object, and of the background `Frame`. To make use of a `Canvas`, you must derive a new class from it and override the `paint()` method so that it actually draws something. You will also need to give the class derived from `Canvas` a size, since the `Canvas` base class has a width and height of zero by default. This is best done by using the `getPreferredSize()` method, just as we did in the last section when loading a `Frame` into a `ScrollPane`.

For example, a simple class derived from `Canvas` is as follows.

```
class LineCanvas extends Canvas
{
  LineCanvas()
  {
    setBackground(Color.red);
  }

  public void paint(Graphics canvasG)
  {
    canvasG.drawLine(0, 50, 100, 50);
  }

  public Dimension getPreferredSize()
  {
    return new Dimension(100, 100);
  }
}
```

This produces a square 100 pixels on each edge, with a red background and a black line drawn across the middle of the square. A `LineCanvas` object can now be declared and added to a layout along with other AWT components such as `Buttons`, `TextFields` and so on.

Since a `Canvas` is derived from the `Component` class (and not from `Container`), you cannot attach a layout manager to it, nor can you add any components to it. As its name implies, it serves only as a canvas on which drawing may take place.

A class derived from `Canvas` can, of course, add methods beyond those shown in the `LineCanvas` class above. These methods may allow dynamic updating of the graphics being displayed in response to user input, either by clicking the mouse directly over the `Canvas` area, or by transmitting commands received from other components to the derived `Canvas` by calling one of its methods. We'll see an example of this below when we implement a `Canvas` containing a checkerboard.

As of Java 1.1, it is possible for the programmer to derive a user-defined class directly from `Component`, rather than using the `Canvas` class. For the purposes of this book, the effect is much the same either way, so we won't dwell on the finer distinctions.

Menus

Java allows a menu bar to be attached to the top of a `Frame`, as in Figure 8.7. The `Checkers` program (to be described in the last section of this chapter) contains a menu bar with two menus ('Game' and 'Colours'). Figure 8.7 shows the 'Colours' menu opened. This menu consists of two main items, allowing the user to select the colour of the dark and light squares on the checkerboard. Each of these items contains a sub-menu, allowing the choice of the actual colour.

A menu has a layered structure. At the top level, the menu bar itself is created as a `MenuBar` object, which is added to the `Frame` that is to contain it. A `MenuBar` on its own doesn't display anything except a blank bar at the top of the window.

At the next layer down, one or more `Menu` objects are attached to the `MenuBar`. A `Menu` object provides the title for a menu that appears in the `MenuBar`, but does not contain any actual items that may be selected. In Figure 8.7, for example, the `Menu` objects containing the labels 'Game' and 'Colours' are attached to the `MenuBar`, but at this stage, neither of these headings would have any items attached to them.

The final layer consists of one or more `MenuItem` objects attached to each `Menu`. Each `MenuItem` acts much like the AWT `Button`, in that it has a label and, when selected by the user, generates an `ActionEvent` that may be caught by an `ActionListener`. In fact, events generated by `MenuItems` are handled in exactly the same way as `Button` events.

We will examine a complete program containing menus when we introduce the `Checkers` example at the end of this chapter. For now, we will show a fragment of code from that program to illustrate the procedure for adding a menu to a window. The following code, taken from the `main()` method, creates a `MenuBar`, a single `Menu` and two `MenuItems`, and shows how all these are joined together.

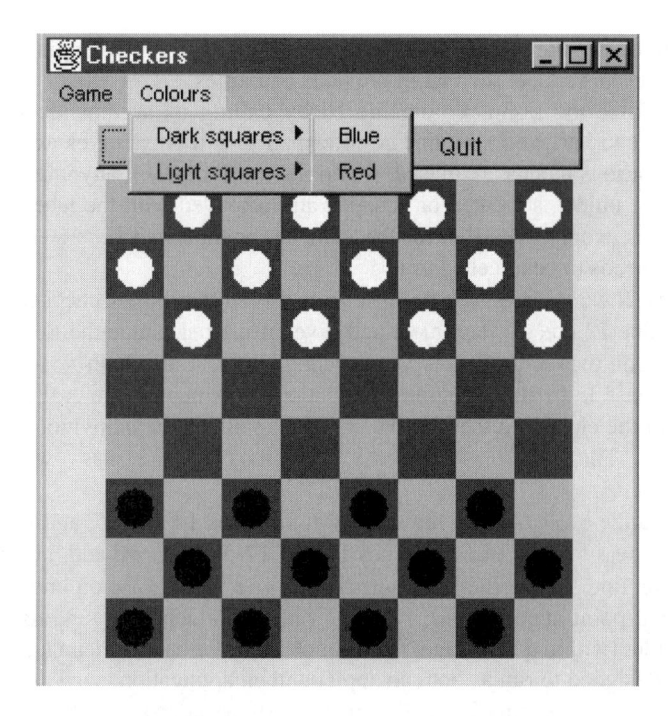

Figure 8.7 A menu attached to a frame.

```
1    MenuBar gameMenuBar;
2    Menu gameMenu;
3    MenuItem newGameItem, quitItem;
4
5    Frame checkersFrame = new Frame("Checkers");
6    Checkers checkersApplet = new Checkers();
7
8    // Initialization code for checkersFrame removed
9
10   gameMenuBar = new MenuBar();
11   gameMenu = new Menu("Game");
12   newGameItem = new MenuItem("New game");
13   newGameItem.addActionListener(checkersApplet);
14   quitItem = new MenuItem("Quit");
15   quitItem.addActionListener(checkersApplet);
16   gameMenu.add(newGameItem);
17   gameMenu.add(quitItem);
18
19   gameMenuBar.add(gameMenu);
20   checkersFrame.setMenuBar(gameMenuBar);
```

The components of the menu are declared on lines 1 to 3. The Frame and the applet to be contained within it are created on lines 5 and 6, in the usual way. We have omitted the code for initializing the frame and applet between lines 6 and 10, as it is the same as we have seen in all previous examples.

We initialize the `MenuBar` on line 10 by calling its argumentless constructor. Since the menu bar itself contains no information and only serves as a container in which the various menus are placed, we do not need to pass it any information.

The `Menu` object is created on line 11, and provided with the label 'Game'. The `Menu` itself acts only as a label for the items it contains, and generates no events, so no listener needs to be attached to it.

On line 12, we initialize the `MenuItem` that is to start a new checkers game when selected. Line 12 creates the object and gives it a label. Since the `MenuItem` is the part of a menu that actually generates events, we must attach an `ActionListener` to it on line 13. In this program, we have implemented the `ActionListener` interface in the class (see Chapter 5), rather than attach an anonymous class to each menu item. The `actionPerformed()` method in the class will handle all `ActionEvents`.

We initialize `quitItem` in the same way on lines 14 and 15, and then add these two `MenuItems` to `gameMenu` on lines 16 and 17. Finally, we add `gameMenu` to the `MenuBar` on line 19, and then add `gameMenuBar` to the `Frame` on line 20.

One final point about menus: they can only be attached to `Frames`. This means that an applet (within a web page, for example) *cannot* have a menu attached to it. In programs designed to run as both an applet and an application, such as most of those we have presented in this book, the menu must be attached to the `Frame` created within the `main()` method. Since the `main()` method is ignored when the program is run as an applet, the menu is also ignored and will not be created.

A menu *can* be attached to a popup `Frame` that is created in response to an event within an applet, however. For example, in the tic-tac-toe game from Chapter 7, a `Frame` pops up at the end of each game stating who won. This `Frame` could have a menu attached to it, and the menu would still function even if the main program was run as an applet within a web page.

Popup menus

Menus attached to menu bars have been available since Java 1.0. A new type of menu has been added in Java 1.1: the *popup menu*. A popup menu is a floating menu (that is, it can appear anywhere within the window) that is made visible by clicking the mouse at some point within the window. The mouse operation that causes a popup menu to appear varies from one platform to another, but on a PC, it is usually the *right* mouse button that creates a popup menu. Figure 8.8 shows a popup menu associated with the `Checkers` program.

A popup menu is constructed in much the same way as an ordinary menu, and the events generated by its `MenuItems` are handled in the same way as well. The main difference, as you might expect, is that code must be provided to specify when and where the popup menu is to appear.

Since a popup menu appears in response to a mouse event, but the actual event varies from computer to computer, Java must handle the popup menu in a device-independent way. This is done by associating a method called isPopupTrigger() with the MouseEvent class. The isPopupTrigger() method returns a boolean value which is true if the type of MouseEvent that has just occurred is recognized as a trigger for displaying a popup menu on that particular computer. For example, on a PC, clicking the right mouse button is such a trigger, so isPopupTrigger() will return true if called for a right mouse click. On some UNIX systems supporting three-button mice, the middle button brings up a popup menu, so isPopupTrigger() would return true on such a system. The main point is that the isPopupTrigger() method is tailored to the particular computer platform.

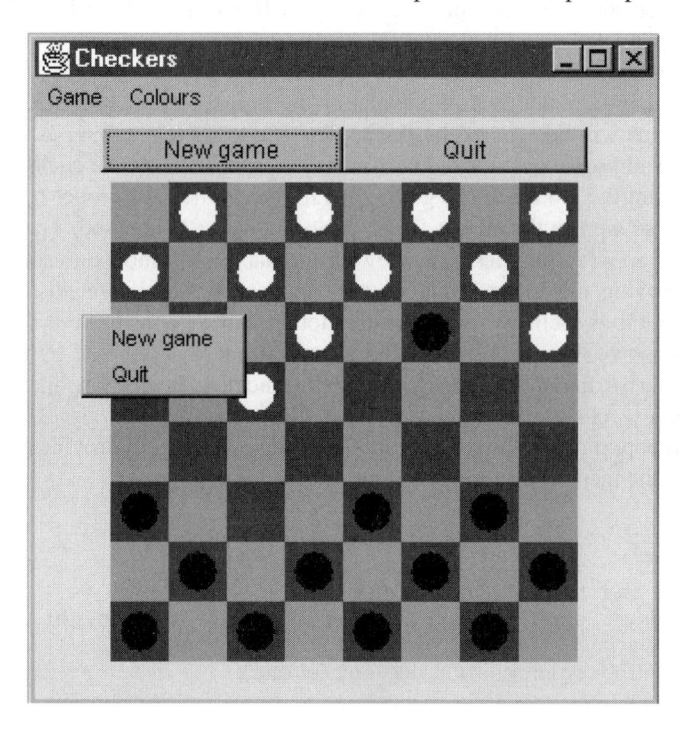

Figure 8.8 A popup menu.

The other main difference between a popup menu and a fixed menu is that popup menus may be attached to any component (not just a Frame). This means that they are useable within applets as well as applications.

To give an example of the use of a popup menu, we will again steal some code from the forthcoming Checkers application. The code below defines a popup menu that holds the two MenuItems shown in Figure 8.8, and is an excerpt from the init() method of the applet class.

```
1       PopupMenu gamePopup = new PopupMenu();
2       newGamePopup = new MenuItem("New game");
3       newGamePopup.addActionListener(this);
4       quitPopup = new MenuItem("Quit");
5       quitPopup.addActionListener(this);
6       gamePopup.add(newGamePopup);
7       gamePopup.add(quitPopup);
8       this.add(gamePopup);
9       this.enableEvents(AWTEvent.MOUSE_EVENT_MASK);
```

Line 1 uses the `PopupMenu` class to create a popup menu. Lines 2 through 7 define a couple of `MenuItem`s, attach an `ActionListener` to them, and add them to the popup menu in the same way as for a fixed menu. Line 8 adds the popup menu to the applet.

Line 9 is a special call that enables the detection of mouse events. Unless either a `MouseListener` is added to the applet or the `enableEvents()` method is called, mouse events will be ignored by the applet. The `MouseListener` is only added if we wish to add some customized behaviour in response to mouse clicks. In this case, we only want the mouse to bring up a popup menu when the proper trigger event is generated, so we use the 'lower level' `enableEvents()` method. The argument of `enableEvents()` specifies that we wish to enable only mouse events that do not involve moving the mouse (that is, only mouse clicks). If we wished to handle mouse motion as well, we would need another call to `enableEvents()` with the argument `AWTEvent.MOUSE_MOTION_EVENT_MASK`.

The code so far creates the popup menu and lets Java know that we wish to handle mouse clicks, but we haven't yet given any instructions as to when and where the popup menu should appear. To do this, we need to provide an overridden version of the method `processMouseEvent()`, as follows.

```
public void processMouseEvent(MouseEvent event)
{
  if (event.isPopupTrigger())
    gamePopup.show(this, event.getX(), event.getY());
  else
    super.processMouseEvent(event);
}
```

This method is called for all mouse clicks provided that the `enableEvents()` method has been called earlier. It tests the current `MouseEvent` with the `isPopupTrigger()` method and, if the current event is a popup menu trigger on the current platform, the `show()` method is called for the popup menu. The `show()` method takes three arguments. The first argument specifies the component over which the popup menu is to appear, and the last two arguments give the position relative to the origin of that component. In this case, we display the menu over the main applet at the location where the mouse was clicked. Although this is the most common behaviour, you may wish the popup to appear at the same place (no matter where the mouse was clicked) to avoid obscuring some part of the window, for example.

If the present mouse event is not a popup trigger, the `processMouseEvent()` method of the superclass is called to do whatever processing is required.

Example – a checkers game

As an extended example of the use of some of the graphics features in the AWT, we will write a program that allows two human players to play a game of checkers (or draughts, in the UK) on a graphical checkerboard. This is the first version of the program – a second version later in this chapter will illustrate the use of animation.

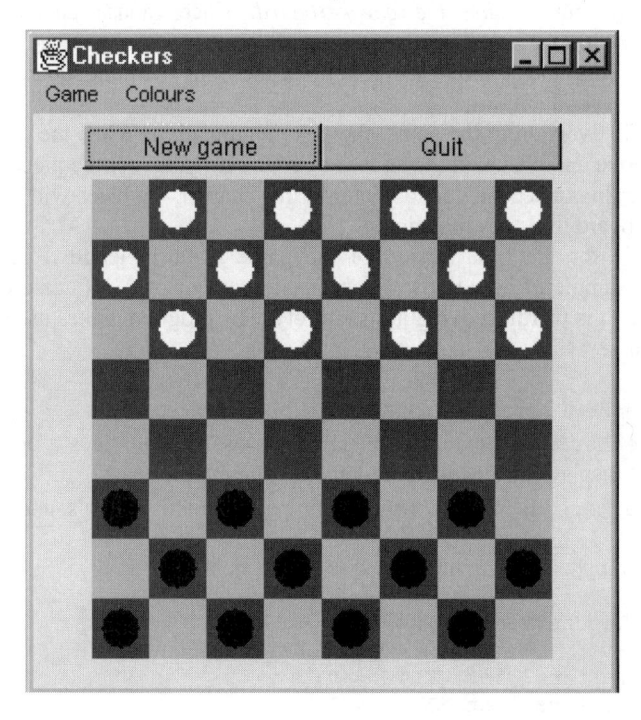

Figure 8.9 The opening window of the checkers game.

The opening window appears as in Figure 8.9. The main area is occupied by the checkerboard with the pieces set up for the beginning of a game. To make a move (black moves first), the player clicks with the left mouse button on the piece that is to be moved, then clicks on the square to which to move.[1] A piece can be removed

---

[1] A quick summary of the rules of checkers for anyone who hasn't played before: a piece is allowed to move diagonally forward (that is, up the board for black, down the board for white) onto an empty square. If a piece finds an enemy piece directly in front of it, and the square on the other side of the enemy piece

from the board by clicking on it with the *right* mouse button. Thus to perform a capture, the player would click on the friendly piece with the left button, click on the vacant square to which the friendly piece is to move (also with the left button), then click on the captured enemy piece with the right button to remove it.

In this version of the game, we will not check for illegal moves (except that we do not allow a move onto an occupied square). We also do not implement *kings* (but see the exercises at the end of the chapter).

There are two menus in the menu bar. The 'Games' menu contains two menu items: the 'New game' item allows a new game to be started (the board is set up to start a new game), and the 'Quit' item quits the program. These two commands are also available via a popup menu. The popup menu may be created by clicking with the right mouse button (or whatever the popup trigger is on your computer) within the window, but *outside the checkerboard*, since mouse clicks are handled separately within the board area.

The 'Colours' menu allows the colours of the light and dark squares of the board to be set to several options.

In this first version of the game, there is no animation. When the player selects a piece to move and clicks on the square to which it is moved, the piece jumps to the new square. In our second version, later in this chapter, the piece will appear to slide across the board to its new position.

The code for the first version of the game is fairly lengthy, but provides a complete example of how to use a reasonable number of AWT features in a single program, so it is worth studying in its entirety. The program makes use of three user-defined classes:

- `CheckerPiece`: represents a single playing piece.
- `CheckerBoard`: extends the `Canvas` class and provides a new component that displays the checkerboard and its playing pieces.
- `Checkers`: the main `Frame` containing the board, controls, and menu bar.

We begin by examining the `CheckerPiece` class.

```
class CheckerPiece
{
   static final int WHITE = 0;
   static final int BLACK = 1;

   int colour;
   int rank, file;
   boolean captured;
```

---

is empty, the enemy piece may be captured by jumping over it and landing in the empty square on the opposite side. If another capture is possible after the first capture, it may be made on the same move. If a capture is available to the side whose turn it is, it *must* be made. The winner is the first person to capture all the enemy's pieces.

When a piece reaches the opposite end of the board, it becomes a *king*. Kings move in the same way as ordinary pieces, except they can move backwards as well as forwards. We won't consider kings in this limited version of the game.

```
    CheckerPiece(int newColour, int newRank, int newFile)
    {
      colour = newColour;
      rank = newRank;
      file = newFile;
      captured = false;
    }

    public int getColour()
    {
      return colour;
    }

    public void setColour(int newColour)
    {
      colour = newColour;
    }

    // other set and get methods
}
```

The class defines a couple of constant parameters used to label the colour of the playing piece. The class variables include `colour` (WHITE or BLACK), the `rank` (row number) and `file` (column number) where the piece is found on the board, and a `boolean` parameter `captured`, which is `true` if the piece has been captured (and should not be shown on the board).

Apart from the class constructor, the only methods in this class are the standard 'set' and 'get' interface functions for accessing the variables.

The `CheckerBoard` class is derived from `Canvas`, and creates a new graphical component that may be added to layouts in other containers.

```
1   import java.awt.*;
2   import java.awt.event.*;
3
4   public class CheckerBoard extends Canvas
5   {
6     CheckerPiece[] whitePiece, blackPiece;
7     CheckerPiece pieceToMove;
8     Color darkColour, lightColour;
9     int squareSize;
10    int moveRank, moveFile;
11    boolean moveStarted;
12
13    CheckerBoard(int newSquareSize, Color newDark,
14      Color newLight)
15    {
16      whitePiece = new CheckerPiece[12];
17      blackPiece = new CheckerPiece[12];
18      darkColour = newDark;
```

```
19        lightColour = newLight;
20        squareSize = newSquareSize;
21
22        newGame();
23        addMouseListener(new MouseAdapter() {
24          public void mousePressed(MouseEvent event) {
25            if ((event.getModifiers() & InputEvent.META_MASK)
26                == InputEvent.META_MASK)
27              doCapture(event);
28            else
29              doMove(event);
30          }
31        });
32      }
33
34      void setDark(Color newDark)
35      {
36        darkColour = newDark;
37        repaint();
38      }
39
40      void setLight(Color newLight)
41      {
42        lightColour = newLight;
43        repaint();
44      }
45
46      void newGame()
47      {
48        int rank = 0, file = 0;
49        for (int piece = 0; piece < 12; ++piece) {
50          blackPiece[piece] =
51            new CheckerPiece(CheckerPiece.BLACK, rank, file);
52          whitePiece[piece] =
53            new CheckerPiece(CheckerPiece.WHITE, 7 - rank,
54              7 - file);
55          file += 2;
56          if (file > 7) {
57            rank++;
58            file = rank % 2 == 0 ? 0 : 1;
59          }
60        }
61        moveStarted = false;
62        pieceToMove = null;
63        repaint();
64      }
65
66      public Dimension getPreferredSize()
67      {
68        return new Dimension(8 * squareSize, 8 * squareSize);
69      }
```

```java
void drawBoard(Graphics g)
{
  int rank, file;

  Color squareColor = darkColour;
  for (rank = 7; rank >= 0; --rank) {
    for (file = 0; file < 8; ++file) {
      g.setColor(squareColor);
      g.fillRect(file * squareSize, rank * squareSize,
        squareSize, squareSize);
      squareColor = squareColor == darkColour ?
        lightColour : darkColour;
    }
    squareColor = squareColor == darkColour ?
      lightColour : darkColour;
  }
}

void drawPieces(Graphics g)
{
  for (int piece = 0; piece < 12; ++piece) {
    if (!blackPiece[piece].getCaptured())
      drawPiece(blackPiece[piece], g);
    if (!whitePiece[piece].getCaptured())
      drawPiece(whitePiece[piece], g);
  }
}

public void paint(Graphics g)
{
  drawBoard(g);
  drawPieces(g);
}

void drawPiece(CheckerPiece piece, Graphics g)
{
  Color drawColour = piece.getColour() ==
    CheckerPiece.WHITE ? Color.white : Color.black;
  int rank = piece.getRank();
  int file = piece.getFile();
  g.setColor(drawColour);
  g.fillOval(file*squareSize + 5, (7-rank)*squareSize + 5,
      squareSize-10, squareSize-10);
}

int findRank(MouseEvent event)
{
  int y = event.getY();
  return 7 - y / squareSize;
}
```

```
121
122      int findFile(MouseEvent event)
123      {
124        int x = event.getX();
125        return x / squareSize;
126      }
127
128      CheckerPiece findPiece(int rank, int file)
129      {
130        for (int piece = 0; piece < 12; ++piece) {
131          if (blackPiece[piece].getRank() == rank &&
132            blackPiece[piece].getFile() == file &&
133            !blackPiece[piece].getCaptured()) {
134            return blackPiece[piece];
135          }
136        }
137        for (int piece = 0; piece < 12; ++piece) {
138          if (whitePiece[piece].getRank() == rank &&
139            whitePiece[piece].getFile() == file &&
140            !whitePiece[piece].getCaptured()) {
141            return whitePiece[piece];
142          }
143        }
144        return null;
145      }
146
147      void doCapture(MouseEvent event)
148      {
149        int rank = findRank(event);
150        int file = findFile(event);
151        CheckerPiece piece = findPiece(rank, file);
152        if (piece != null) {
153          piece.setCaptured(true);
154          repaint();
155        }
156      }
157
158      void doMove(MouseEvent event)
159      {
160        moveRank = findRank(event);
161        moveFile = findFile(event);
162        CheckerPiece piece = findPiece(moveRank, moveFile);
163        if (moveStarted) {
164          if (piece == null) {
165            pieceToMove.setRank(moveRank);
166          pieceToMove.setFile(moveFile);
167          repaint();
168          }
169          moveStarted = false;
170        } else {
171          pieceToMove = piece;
```

```
172            if (pieceToMove != null)
173                moveStarted = true;
174        }
175    }
176 }
```

Although this class is fairly large, its function is simple – to provide an up-to-date picture of the checkerboard and the playing pieces, and handle the player's commands to move and capture pieces.

After initializing the class parameters in the constructor (lines 16 to 20), the newGame() method (lines 46 to 64) is called to set up the initial board position and display the board. The loop on lines 49 to 60 calculates the positions for the black and white counters to be placed, and creates a new set of pieces for a new game. Notice that in keeping with standard checkerboard notation, the rank is numbered from 0 at the bottom row to 7 at the top row. Files are numbered from 0 at the left to 7 on the right.

The purpose of the variables moveStarted and pieceToMove will be explained when we consider piece moves below.

The display of the board and pieces is handled by the paint() method (lines 99 to 103), where two methods are called: one to draw the board and the other to draw the playing pieces.

The drawBoard() method (lines 71 to 87) draws the eight-by-eight board using darkColour for the 'black' squares and lightColour for the 'white' squares.

The drawPieces() method (lines 89 to 97) loops through the two arrays of pieces, calling the drawPiece() method to draw each piece (if it has not been captured). The drawPiece() method itself (lines 105 to 114) extracts the colour, rank, and file of the piece and uses the fillOval() method to draw a circle at the correct location. We therefore need to invert the rank number on line 53 by using (7 - rank) to obtain the location to draw the piece.

The remainder of the class deals with handling the mouse events for moving and capturing pieces. The last section of the constructor (lines 23 to 31) adds a MouseAdapter to listen for mouse events. (Recall that the MouseAdapter class implements the MouseListener interface so that we need to define only those methods in the interface that we actually wish to use; see Chapter 5.)

The mousePressed() method (lines 24 to 30) must distinguish between the left and right mouse buttons. In doing this, however, we are assuming that the computer on which the program is run actually has a mouse with two buttons. This is not always the case – some computers only support mice[1] with a single button, others have mice with three buttons. As with the popup menu, the designers of Java have tried to implement the multiple-button mouse in as platform-independent a way as possible. Since users of a one-button mouse can usually mimic the effect of a second or third button by holding down one of the special keys on the keyboard while clicking their single mouse button, Java treats a mouse click with the right button on

---

[1] Some authors claim that the plural of a computer mouse is 'mouses'. We'll stick to the more conventional 'mice' in this book.

196 GRAPHICS AND ANIMATION

a PC as equivalent to clicking the single button on a one-button mouse, but with one of these special 'modifier' keys pressed at the same time.

The `mousePressed()` method on lines 24 to 30 shows how this is done. The `MouseEvent` class has a `modifiers` variable which contains information on any modifier keys that were pressed at the same time as the event was generated. On PCs with two-button mice, clicking the right button sets the META key flag in this `modifiers` variable. (On systems with a three-button mouse, the middle button is equivalent to setting the ALT key.) The `getModifiers()` method (line 25) retrieves an `int` that is composed of a series of bits, with each bit corresponding to one of the modifier flags that could have been set when the event was generated. We are interested only in one of these bits – the bit corresponding to whether the META flag was set. We can isolate this bit by using the logical AND operator (a single `&`) to *mask out* (basically, switch off, or set to 0) all the bits except the META bit. If the result of this operation produces an `int` with the META bit switched on (which we discover by comparing it with `InputEvent.META_MASK`), then we know that the right button was clicked. In that case, we call `doCapture()` (line 27) to remove a piece from the board.

If the META bit was not set, the left button (or at least *not* the right button) was clicked, and we do a piece move instead (line 29).

The `doCapture()` method (lines 147 to 156) extracts the rank and file of the square in which the mouse was clicked, then finds what piece is on that square (if any). If the right button was clicked when the mouse was over an empty square, `piece` will be `null`, so we do nothing. Otherwise, we mark `piece` as being captured and redraw the board. The `drawPiece()` method will not draw pieces that have been captured, so the effect is that the piece disappears from the board.

Moving a piece is a two-part operation. The first click must be on a square containing the piece to be moved, and the second click is on the square to which it is to move. Since the `doMove()` method is called in both cases, we must be able to tell which part of the operation we wish to perform. We do this by looking at the `moveStarted` flag – if it is `true`, we are in the middle of a move and the `doMove()` method is being called to complete the move operation by moving the piece to its destination square. If it is `false`, the `doMove()` method is being called to mark the piece which is to be moved.

In either case, the `doMove()` method starts by locating the square over which the mouse was clicked, and finding the piece (if any) on that square (lines 160 to 162).

Let us consider the first part of the move (when `moveStarted` is `false` – lines 170 to 174). We set the class variable `pieceToMove` to the piece that was on the clicked square (line 171). If the mouse was clicked over an empty square, this will set `pieceToMove` to `null`, and we obviously can only continue with the second half of the move operation if there really is a piece there to move. We therefore check this condition (line 172) and set the `moveStarted` flag to `true` (line 173) if there really is a piece there.

The second half of the move operation occurs if `doMove()` is called when `moveStarted` is `true`. In that case (lines 163 to 168) we check that no piece is present on the clicked square (since you cannot move a piece onto an occupied square), then set the rank and file of `pieceToMove` to the new location and redraw the board.

The final class required for the `Checkers` program to run is `Checkers` itself, to which we now turn.

```
1   import java.applet.Applet;
2   import java.awt.*;
3   import java.awt.event.*;
4     public class Checkers extends Applet
5        implements ActionListener
6   {
7     CheckerBoard board;
8     Button newGameButton, quitButton;
9     PopupMenu gamePopup;
10    MenuItem newGamePopup, quitPopup;
11    static final int DARK = 0;
12    static final int LIGHT = 1;
13
14    public static void main(String argv[])
15    {
16      MenuBar gameMenuBar;
17      Menu gameMenu, colourMenu, darkSquareMenu,
18        lightSquareMenu;
19      MenuItem newGameItem, quitItem, blueItem, cyanItem,
20        redItem, pinkItem;
21
22      Frame checkersFrame = new Frame("Checkers");
23      Checkers checkersApplet = new Checkers();
24      checkersApplet.init();
25      checkersFrame.add("Center", checkersApplet);
26      checkersFrame.setSize(600,500);
27      checkersFrame.setVisible(true);
28      checkersFrame.addWindowListener(new WindowAdapter() {
29        public void windowClosing(WindowEvent event) {
30          System.exit(0);
31        }
32      });
33      gameMenuBar = new MenuBar();
34      gameMenu = new Menu("Game");
35      newGameItem = new MenuItem("New game");
36      newGameItem.addActionListener(checkersApplet);
37      quitItem = new MenuItem("Quit");
38      quitItem.addActionListener(checkersApplet);
39      gameMenu.add(newGameItem);
40      gameMenu.add(quitItem);
41
42      colourMenu = new Menu("Colours");
43      darkSquareMenu = new Menu("Dark squares");
44      lightSquareMenu = new Menu("Light squares");
45      blueItem = new MenuItem("Blue");
46      blueItem.addActionListener(checkersApplet);
```

198 GRAPHICS AND ANIMATION

```
47      cyanItem = new MenuItem("Light blue");
48      cyanItem.addActionListener(checkersApplet);
49      redItem = new MenuItem("Red");
50      redItem.addActionListener(checkersApplet);
51      pinkItem = new MenuItem("Pink");
52      pinkItem.addActionListener(checkersApplet);
53
54      darkSquareMenu.add(blueItem);
55      darkSquareMenu.add(redItem);
56      lightSquareMenu.add(cyanItem);
57      lightSquareMenu.add(pinkItem);
58      colourMenu.add(darkSquareMenu);
59      colourMenu.add(lightSquareMenu);
60      gameMenuBar.add(gameMenu);
61      gameMenuBar.add(colourMenu);
62      checkersFrame.setMenuBar(gameMenuBar);
63    }
64
65    public void init()
66    {
67      newGameButton = new Button("New game");
68      newGameButton.addActionListener(this);
69      quitButton = new Button("Quit");
70      quitButton.addActionListener(this);
71
72      Panel buttonPanel = new Panel(new GridLayout(1,2));
73      buttonPanel.add(newGameButton);
74      buttonPanel.add(quitButton);
75      board = new CheckerBoard(30, Color.red, Color.pink);
76      Panel boardPanel = new Panel();
77      boardPanel.add(board);
78      Panel masterPanel = new Panel(new BorderLayout());
79      masterPanel.add("North", buttonPanel);
80      masterPanel.add("South", boardPanel);
81      add(masterPanel);
82
83      gamePopup = new PopupMenu();
84      newGamePopup = new MenuItem("New game");
85      newGamePopup.addActionListener(this);
86      quitPopup = new MenuItem("Quit");
87      quitPopup.addActionListener(this);
88      gamePopup.add(newGamePopup);
89      gamePopup.add(quitPopup);
90      this.add(gamePopup);
91      this.enableEvents(AWTEvent.MOUSE_EVENT_MASK);
92    }
93
94    public void processMouseEvent(MouseEvent event)
95    {
96      if (event.isPopupTrigger())
97        gamePopup.show(this, event.getX(), event.getY());
```

EXAMPLE – A CHECKERS GAME

```
 98          else
 99             super.processMouseEvent(event);
100       }
101
102       public void actionPerformed(ActionEvent event)
103       {
104          String command = event.getActionCommand();
105          if (command.equals("New game"))
106             board.newGame();
107          else if (command.equals("Quit"))
108             System.exit(0);
109          else if (command.equals("Blue"))
110             setColour(Checkers.DARK, Color.blue);
111          else if (command.equals("Light blue"))
112             setColour(Checkers.LIGHT, Color.cyan);
113          else if (command.equals("Red"))
114             setColour(Checkers.DARK, Color.red);
115          else if (command.equals("Pink"))
116             setColour(Checkers.LIGHT, Color.pink);
117       }
118
119       void newGame()
120       {
121          board.newGame();
122       }
123
124       void setColour(int darkOrLight, Color newColour)
125       {
126          if (darkOrLight == LIGHT)
127             board.setLight(newColour);
128          else
129             board.setDark(newColour);
130       }
131    }
```

There is very little to say about this class since its main purpose is simply to provide a Frame into which the checkerboard, a couple of Buttons, and the menus are placed. We have covered the techniques for doing all these things earlier.

Note that the fixed menus (attached to the MenuBar) are declared locally within the main() method (lines 16 to 20), while the popup menu is declared as a class variable (lines 9 and 10). This is because the MenuBar must be attached to the Frame contained within the main() method, while the popup menu is attached to the applet itself.

Apart from the usual initialization of the Frame and its applet in main() the rest of the method is occupied with creating the main menu. The technique is the same as that described in the section on menus above, except that we have added a few more items.

The init() method (line 65) creates and initializes the two Buttons and stores them in a GridLayout. A CheckerBoard object is created and the Buttons and

`CheckerBoard` are combined in a `BorderLayout`. Then the popup menu is created and added, and the `enableEvents()` method called to activate the mouse.

The `processMouseEvent()` method (line 94) is identical to the one described in the section on popup menus above.

The `actionPerformed()` method handles all the events generated by the menus and buttons. The events are sorted out by extracting their `ActionCommand` and comparing it with the various labels identifying the menu items and buttons. The `newGame()` and `setColour()` methods merely call the corresponding methods in the `CheckerBoard` class.

Animation

We have already seen a simple example of animation when we considered the `AlarmClock` class back in Chapter 2. Here we will expand the idea a bit, though we cannot fully understand animation until we study threads in Chapter 9.

The principle behind animation is the same as that used for television cartoons. To make an object move, we draw it in successive positions, repainting the screen between each pair of images. Thus to implement an animation in Java requires only that we recalculate the appearance of the applet for each frame in the applet and then call `repaint()` to refresh the image.

Although the principle is quite simple, there are a few practical difficulties. Apart from having to write the extra code to calculate the different positions of items in the display, the most noticeable problem, especially with larger applets or slower computers, is that the image can flicker quite badly as each repaint operation is done. The reason for this is that each time `repaint()` is called, it first calls `update()`, which blanks out the drawing area by repainting it with the background colour. Following the call to `update()`, `paint()` itself is called to redraw the new image.

There are several ways that flickering can be reduced, though in many cases it is not possible to eliminate it entirely. If the animation does nothing more than *add* something to the existing image at each step, there is no need to blank out the earlier image between redraws, so the call to `update()` can be skipped. The easiest way of doing this is to override `update()` in the class by a method of the form:

```
public void update(Graphics g)
{
   paint(g);
}
```

This makes `update()` call `paint()` directly without painting over the previous image with the background colour or resetting the drawing colour. (You can obtain the graphics context for the current component or container by using the `getGraphics()` method and then pass the result as the argument to the `update()` method.)

ANIMATION

In most cases, however, you do need to blank out at least part of the previous image before redrawing it. If the area on the image that actually changes between refreshes is fairly small, however, it is possible to *clip* the region that is drawn – that is, to restrict the area that is actually repainted to a small, rectangular section of the overall window.

To see how clipping can be useful, we will modify the CheckerBoard class above so that when a piece is moved, it appears to slide over the board rather than just jump directly to its final location. We will do this by calculating the path that the piece must follow and then calculating a series of positions that the piece must occupy along that path. Two adjacent frames in the animation will then consist of the piece at two neighbouring positions separated by a few pixels. The rest of the board remains unchanged, so we really only need to redraw the locations occupied by the piece before and after its move (see Figure 8.10).

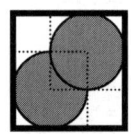

Figure 8.10 Two successive locations in the motion of a circle.

In Figure 8.10, the circle to the lower left represents the piece before its move increment, and the other circle is the piece after its incremental move. The two dashed rectangles around the circles show the rectangular areas that are affected by the move, and the heavy rectangle surrounding these two smaller rectangles represents the *union* of the two rectangles. This large rectangle contains the entire area that is affected by the incremental move, and is the only area that needs to be redrawn. Our goal, therefore, is to clip the drawing region to just this area when we repaint the board after each step in the animation.

To implement animation in the CheckerBoard class, refer to the class listing above and replace lines 165 to 167 by the line

```
animateMove(pieceToMove, moveRank, moveFile);
```

The animateMove() method should be added to the CheckerBoard class, and is as follows.

```
1    void animateMove(CheckerPiece startPiece, int toRank,
2       int toFile)
3    {
4       int fromRank = startPiece.getRank();
5       int fromFile = startPiece.getFile();
6       int stepSize = 3;
7       int signX = toFile > fromFile ? 1 : -1;
8       int signY = toRank > fromRank ? -1 : 1;
9       int steps =
10         Math.abs((toFile - fromFile) * squareSize) / stepSize;
```

```
11
12         int drawX = fromFile * squareSize;
13         int drawY = (7 - fromRank) * squareSize;
14         Color pieceColor = startPiece.getColour() ==
15            CheckerPiece.WHITE ? Color.white : Color.black;
16
17         startPiece.setCaptured(true);
18         Rectangle oldClip =
19            new Rectangle(drawX, drawY, squareSize, squareSize);
20
21         while (steps > 0) {
22            drawX += stepSize * signX;
23            drawY += stepSize * signY;
24            try {
25               Thread.sleep(50);
26            } catch (InterruptedException e)
27            { }
28            Rectangle newClip =
29               new Rectangle(drawX, drawY, squareSize, squareSize);
30            Rectangle clipArea = newClip.union(oldClip);
31            Graphics g = getGraphics();
32            g.clipRect(clipArea.x, clipArea.y,
33               clipArea.width, clipArea.height);
34            oldClip = newClip;
35            drawBoard(g);
36            drawPieces(g);
37            g.setColor(pieceColor);
38            g.fillOval(drawX + 5, drawY + 5,
39               squareSize - 10, squareSize - 10);
40            steps--;
41         }
42         startPiece.setRank(moveRank);
43         startPiece.setFile(moveFile);
44         startPiece.setCaptured(false);
45      }
```

The arguments of the method are the piece that is to be moved (startPiece) and the rank and file to which it is to be moved. The rank (row) and file (column) at which the piece is at the start are extracted on lines 4 and 5, and the step size (number of pixels to move at each increment in the animation) is set on line 6.

We must now work out what direction the piece is to move, and the number of steps it is to take. For a legal move in checkers, a piece must always move diagonally, which means that there will always be an equal number of pixels moved both horizontally and vertically on each step. However, there are four possible directions in which a piece may move (up and left, up and right, down and left, down and right). The approach we take here is to work out the horizontal and vertical directions separately. On line 7, we see if the destination file is greater than the starting file. If so, the piece moves to the right (in the positive x direction), so we set the signX variable to +1, otherwise we set it to −1.

For the vertical direction (line 8), we invert the condition since the rank number increases upwards, but in the pixel coordinate system, the *y* value increases *downwards*.

On lines 9 and 10, we work out how many steps are required in the animation to move the piece the required distance. The `Math.abs()` method is a static method from the built-in `Math` class, and calculates the *absolute value* of its argument. The absolute value of a positive number is the same number, while the absolute value of a negative number is the same number without the minus sign. For example, the absolute value of +5 is also +5, but the absolute value of −5 is +5. Using the absolute value ensures that we always get a positive value for the number of steps to move.

The number of steps is calculated as the total distance to move in the *x* direction (in pixels) divided by the step size. We could, of course, equally well have used the *y* direction to calculate the number of steps, since we always move the same distance in both the *x* and *y* directions.

Lines 12 and 13 calculate the initial position, in pixels, of the piece that is to move, and lines 14 and 15 find its colour. On line 17, we temporarily mark the piece as 'captured' in order to prevent it being drawn in its original location while the animation moves it to its destination. We restore it to being 'uncaptured' after the animation is complete, on line 44.

In order to implement the clipping, we must identify the rectangle enclosing the circle before and after each move. We use Java's `Rectangle` class to define a rectangle on lines 18 and 19, and set it equal to the starting square.

Line 21 begins the actual animation loop. We first increment `drawX` and `drawY` to identify the next position where the piece should be drawn. Lines 24 to 27 pause for 50 milliseconds (1/20 of a second). The syntax in these lines will be explained in Chapter 9, where we study threads.

Lines 28 and 29 find the rectangle that encloses the piece after its incremental move, and line 30 uses the `union()` method of the `Rectangle` class to find the union of the old and new clipping rectangles (equivalent to finding the solid box in Figure 8.10). The variable `clipArea` now contains the rectangle that needs to be redrawn.

In line 31, we obtain the graphics context for the board, and on lines 32 and 33 we apply the `clipRect()` method to clip the drawing area to the `clipArea` rectangle. (Paradoxically, `clipRect()` requires four `int`s as arguments, and will not accept a `Rectangle` object as its argument.) Then on line 34 we save the newest rectangle as the starting position for the next incremental move, and then draw the board and pieces on lines 35 and 36. Since we temporarily set the moving piece to be 'captured' on line 17, it will not be drawn as part of the `drawPieces()` call on line 36. Instead, we draw it in its current position on lines 37 to 39. The loop continues until `steps` is reduced to 0.

Finally, after the animation is complete, we set the piece's rank and file values on lines 42 and 43, and restore it to its uncaptured state on line 44.

You may find it slightly puzzling that we obtain the graphics context `g` every time we go through the loop on line 31, rather than just obtaining it once before the loop starts. The reason for this is that the `clipRect()` method works by intersecting the *current* clipping rectangle with the new rectangle passed to it as its arguments. If we had defined the graphics context outside the loop, then on each pass through the loop we would have to restore the clipping rectangle to the entire board before restricting it again with the call on line 32. By obtaining a fresh graphics context on each pass through the loop, we guarantee that it starts off with a clipping rectangle equal to the size of the entire board.

Exercises

1. Write an applet that allows the user to view a colour swatch when the RGB values of a colour are specified. The applet should contain a set of three `TextField`s, allowing entry of RGB values as `int`s (between 0 and 255), or `float`s (between 0.0 and 1.0). A pair of radio buttons should allow the user to specify which format is being used. Add a `Button` labelled 'View colour'. When the `Button` is pressed, the RGB values are read from the `TextField`s, and a filled rectangle is displayed showing the corresponding colour. As well, the RGB values of that colour are printed out in both `int` and `float` format.

2. Write an applet which allows the user to view some text in a font and style of their choice. The applet should contain `Choice` or `List` items offering the selection of available fonts (obtained from the `Toolkit` as in the text) and styles (normal, italic, bold, etc.). The user should also be able to specify the size of the font, for which you may wish to use a `TextField`. Another `TextField` should allow the user to enter the text that is to be displayed in the selected font. Add a `Button` which displays the text when pressed.

3. Write a Java component which displays *shadowed text* as in:

Shadowed text

The shadowing effect can be produced by first printing the shadow (in a lighter version of the same colour as the main text) and then printing the main text offset slightly to one side and upwards. The distance by which the offset is moved should be a constant fraction of the size of the font, so `FontMetrics` can be used to determine the offset. The component should also implement the `getPreferredSize()` method so that it can be placed in layout managers. Again, the overall size of the text can be obtained from `FontMetrics`.

4. Enhance the `TicTacToe` class from Chapter 7 by embedding it in a `ScrollPane`.

5. Further enhance the `TicTacToe` class by adding a menu bar. Add two menus to the menu bar. The first menu should allow the user to start a new game or quit the program. The second menu should allow the user to swap between the various layouts – the welcome screen, the main game panel, and the scores panel.

6 Add a popup menu to the `TicTacToe` game. The popup menu should duplicate all the functions in the two menus on the menu bar.

7 Write an applet which displays some text in a large, bold font (the text may be hard-coded into the applet, or you may provide a `TextField` allowing users to enter their own text). Add animation to the applet by slowly changing the colour of the text. You can start the applet by displaying the text in black, then gradually increasing the red component until it reaches 255, then the green and blue components. When the display becomes white, gradually reduce the red, then the green, then the blue components again until the text returns to black. (Note that unless you run this animation in a separate thread, as described in Chapter 9, you will only be able to stop the program by typing Ctrl-C in the command window.)

This animation is an example of a case where there is no need to clear the display before repainting it after each call to `Thread.sleep()`, so you can reduce flickering by overriding the `update()` method so that it does not clear the screen.

CHAPTER 9
Threads

Doing more than one thing at a time

If you run the final version of the checkers game from Chapter 8 (the one with the animation of the pieces), you will find that if you try to access a menu or push one of the Buttons while one of the pieces is moving across the board, nothing happens (or at least, nothing happens until the piece has stopped moving). If you have ever found a web page with some Java animation on it (many web pages use Java to provide an animated company logo which runs continuously), you will have been able to click on other parts of the applet and make something happen (unless the applet was very badly designed!). What, then, is wrong with the checkers game in the previous chapter?

The problem lies in the fact that when the checker piece is moving across the board, all the animation takes place within a single method which contains a loop to produce the animation. Once this method is called, it must run to completion before anything else can be done in the same Java program. This is because the program (and all the other programs we have studied so far) have been written so that they can handle only one thing at a time. To put it more technically, these programs only have a single *thread*.

To understand the idea behind threads, it is probably easiest to look at the general idea of *multitasking*. When you use a computer, you usually have several windows open at once – one window might be showing a list of your files, another might be a web browser, and yet another could be a word processor. You might start downloading a large file using the web browser, and while you're waiting for the file to arrive, you could go back to the word processor and continue writing your document.

It would appear that your computer is doing several things at once. However, if your computer is like most other desktop machines at the moment, it has only a single *processor*, which means that it can really only do one thing at a time. So how does the computer give the illusion of doing several things at once?

The trick is accomplished by *swapping* processes with each other. The underlying *operating system* (the program such as UNIX or Windows 95 that manages the operation of the computer) keeps track of the various programs that are running on the computer at any one time. If only one program actually needs any processor time, things are easy, since all the available time is allocated to that program. Once another program joins in, so that two or more programs are requesting computer time at once, the operating system partitions the available time between all the competing processes. Program 1 might get a few milliseconds (quite a long time by modern processor standards), then it is *swapped out* and the second program is given its share of time on the processor, and so on.

Since the slices of time that each program gets are all fairly small (by human standards) and the swapping occurs many times in each second, the illusion of several programs all running at the same time is achieved.

Just as it is possible to partition the processor's time among several distinct programs, it is also possible to divide up the time allocated to a single program so that the program itself can appear to do several things at once. This partitioning of time between different tasks within a single program is called *multithreading*. Each task within a program is called a *thread*.

Probably the biggest difference between multitasking and multithreading is that multitasking is done automatically by the operating system, while multithreading has to be explicitly programmed into the particular application. This distinction means that only programming languages that support the idea of a thread can be used to write multithreaded programs. Languages such as C cannot, on their own, be used to write multithreaded applications (though some systems provide libraries of pre-written code which allow threaded programs in C or C++). In Java, however, the ability to write multithreaded applications is built in to the language.

The Thread class and the Runnable interface

To see how to write a threaded program in Java, we will modify the `CheckerBoard` class from Chapter 8 so that the menu items and buttons are active even while a piece is sliding across the board. We will find, however, that allowing access to the menus and buttons during a move can cause problems. We will need to examine the rest of the class to ensure that the ability to access commands during a move doesn't cause any inconsistencies in the program.

Recall from Chapter 8 that the player moves one of the checkers by clicking on the piece to move and then clicking on the destination square. After the second mouse click, the `animateMove()` method is called, which draws the moving piece in several successive positions, giving the illusion of sliding the piece across the board. While `animateMove()` is running (in a single-threaded program), no other event handling takes place.

In order to allow access to the menus and buttons, we need to create a new thread in which the animation can run. Then, after the player clicks the mouse on the square to which the piece is to be moved, this thread is made active and the animation is run as an independent process, which shares processor time with the main program. This means that the computer will give the animation some of the processor time, but will also give the main program some processor time in which it can check for, and act on, events such as menu selections or button presses.

Java provides a Thread class (part of the java.lang default package) which allows the creation of a Thread object. A Thread object on its own, however, is powerless – it must be connected with another object which tells it when to start and stop, and what to do once it is running. The object to which a Thread is connected must implement the Runnable interface. Using an interface to define the type of object to which a Thread may be connected means that any class may be modified to accept a Thread merely by defining that class to implement the Runnable interface.

As you will recall from our discussion of interfaces in Chapter 4, any class that implements an interface must provide definitions for all of the methods in that interface. The Runnable interface contains only a single method: run(). Any class implementing Runnable must therefore contain a run() method. We will see a bit later how to use the run() method.

The steps required to use a Thread in another class are:

- Define the class so that it implements Runnable.
- Add a run() method to the class. This method will be called by the Thread when it starts.
- Declare a Thread variable in the class.
- Create and register the Thread variable so that it knows where to find the run() method that it is to call when it starts. The creation and registration procedures are usually combined, since the Thread is registered by means of one of the arguments passed to its constructor.
- Find the place in the class where the Thread is to start, and call the Thread's start() method at that point. This will cause the Thread to call the run() method of the class to which it was registered. All code in the run() method is now run as a separate thread to that in the main program.
- The Thread may be interrupted by calling interrupt().

All of this is difficult to follow without an example, so we will modify the CheckerBoard class from Chapter 8 so that it runs the animation in a separate Thread. To do this, refer back to the code for the CheckerBoard class, starting on page 191. Modify the class declaration on line 4 by adding the words implements Runnable. This declares the CheckerBoard class to implement the Runnable interface, which means we need to add a run() method to it. We will do this later.

Next, add a Thread object to the class by inserting the declaration

```
Thread moveThread;
```

after line 11. This is the Thread object in which the animation of the moving piece will be done.

Next, we can add the run() method to the class. The contents of the run() method should simply be whatever we want the Thread to do, once it starts. In this case, the only job the `Thread` needs to do is perform the animation of the piece, so insert the following `run()` method (anywhere in the class file) to do this.

```
public void run()
{
   animateMove(pieceToMove, moveRank, moveFile);
}
```

The only thing left to do is to create and register the `Thread`, and then start it up at the correct place. Where should we do this? Recall that we inserted the `animateMove()` command to replace lines 165 to 167 in the original listing of `CheckerBoard`. It is this location where we wish the `Thread` to start, so we replace lines 165 to 167 in the code on page 194 with the lines

```
moveThread = new Thread(this);
moveThread.start();
```

The first line creates `moveThread` by calling its constructor. The argument passed to the constructor is the `Runnable` object to which the `Thread` is to be attached. That is, it is the object which contains the `run()` method that the `Thread` is to run when it starts. Here, it is the `CheckerBoard` object itself which contains the `run()` method, so we pass `this` to the constructor.

The second line calls the `start()` method of the `Thread` class. This causes `moveThread` to call the `run()` method of the `CheckerBoard` class which, as we saw above, contains the call to `animateMove()`. At this point, the piece will start sliding across the board, as it did in the original animated version, except that here it will be doing so in a separate `Thread`.

At this point, you should run the program and experiment a bit. If you just move one of the pieces in the normal way, you will notice no difference between this version of the program and that at the end of Chapter 8. However, try setting a piece in motion and then clicking on the 'Quit' button before it reaches its destination. You should find that the program quits immediately, rather than waiting until the move is complete. If you're quick enough, try setting a piece in motion and then changing the colour of the squares on the board using the 'Colour' menu. (You will find it easier to do this if you slide one of the pieces over two squares, as in a capture.) You should find that the colour of the squares changes while the piece is still moving.

Has this solved all our problems? It may allow us to access the menus and buttons while a piece is moving, but it has also introduced some new problems. To see why, try starting one piece in motion and then, before it has finished, try moving another piece. You may find that both pieces move at once, but you may also find that one of these pieces seems to duplicate itself by leaving a copy behind on the original square. Obviously, we don't want this to happen, but we also don't want one player making a move before the first player's piece has finished its move. You may also find some strange behaviour if you press the 'New game' button while a piece is moving. Have we simply made things worse by introducing a `Thread`?

As we will see, it is relatively easy to fix these problems, but the situation does illustrate an important point. When you use a `Thread`, you are allowing at least two parallel tracks in your program to run at the same time. If one of these tracks can influence the other one, you must make sure that your code allows for the interaction and avoids any conflicts between the two tracks of execution.

In the checkers example, we have two main problems to fix:

- It is possible to move two or more pieces at once;
- The motion of a piece interferes with the 'New game' command.

To fix the first problem, we can introduce a `boolean` variable called `moveInProgress` which is `true` whenever an animation is occurring. If `moveInProgress` is `true`, we should not allow any other animations to start. We therefore add `moveInProgress` to the `boolean` declaration on line 11, and initialize it to be `false` in the constructor (following line 20, say). Since we wish to ignore any mouse events while an animation is taking place, we can insert the lines

```
if (moveInProgress)
   return;
```

in the `mousePressed()` method, following line 24.

Finally, we modify the `run()` method above to set and clear the `moveInProgress` flag:

```
public void run()
{
  moveInProgress = true;
  animateMove(pieceToMove, moveRank, moveFile);
  moveInProgress = false;
}
```

After these modifications, you should now find that it is impossible to start up a second move while one piece is in the middle of its animation.

However, the animation still interferes with the 'New game' command. The problem here is that, when we start a new game, all activity from the current game should stop. In other words, if a `Thread` is currently running when 'New game' is selected, it should be interrupted before the `newGame()` method is called. We can solve this problem by inserting the following code at the start of the `newGame()` method, following line 47.

```
if (moveThread != null && moveThread.isAlive()) {
  moveThread.interrupt();
  moveInProgress = false;
}
```

We first test `moveThread` to see if it has been created (that is, not `null` – we need to do this since `newGame()` is called by the `CheckerBoard` constructor as soon as the board is set up, which is before any Thread has been created). If moveThread does exist, we call the isAlive() method of the Thread class to see if the Thread is currently running. If it is, we interrupt it using the interrupt() method, and then set the moveInProgess flag to false. After doing this, we reset the board to its initial state as before.[1]

You can see that using a Thread is fairly straightforward – you simply decide which part of your code should be run in the Thread and then arrange for that part of the code to be called from the run() method rather than directly from the main class. However, you can also see that you must be careful to allow for side effects that may occur when you allow this parallel processing.

Multithreading example – the clock revisited

As an example of a program containing two Threads, we return to the clock program that was first introduced back in Chapter 1. This time, however, we include two clocks which may be run independently of each other. As well, the interface is entirely graphical, doing away with the need to enter the time parameters on the command line. The window appears as shown in Figure 9.1.

Figure 9.1 Using threads to run two clocks independently.

The window contains two clock displays at the bottom, each of which shows an independent time. Each clock may have its time set, and may be started and stopped

---

[1] The interrupt() method is only available in Java 1.2. In Java 1.1, you must use the stop() method instead. The stop() method is not recommended in Java 1.2 for technical reasons beyond the scope of this book.

by pressing the buttons in the control panel above the display. The clock on which a button acts is selected from a pair of radio buttons at the top. The values to be used in setting the time on one of the clocks are entered in three text boxes. When a clock is running, its display is updated once per second. As you can see in Figure 9.1, the clocks use a 24-hour notation, rather than 12-hour with an AM/PM marker. The top clock in Figure 9.1 was started at a time of 14:30:12 and had been running for 19 seconds when the image was captured.

As you have probably guessed, each clock display is run as a separate thread, so that there are two Thread objects used in the program. Both of these Threads are handled using a single run() method, however. The main purpose of this example program is to illustrate how several Threads can be handled in the same program.

We make use of two classes. One class, derived from Canvas, draws the clock numerals and handles the painting of these numerals. The other class handles the overall display of the controls and the two clock faces. The first class is as follows.

```
 1   import java.awt.*;
 2
 3   public class Clock extends Canvas
 4   {
 5     private int timeHours, timeMinutes, timeSeconds;
 6     private Color displayColor;
 7     private int fontSize;
 8     private Font clockFont;
 9
10     Clock()
11     {
12       timeHours = 12;
13       timeMinutes = timeSeconds = 0;
14     }
15
16     Clock(int newTimeHours, int newTimeMinutes,
17         int newTimeSeconds,
18         Color newDisplayColor, int newFontSize)
19     {
20       timeHours = newTimeHours;
21       timeMinutes = newTimeMinutes;
22       timeSeconds = newTimeSeconds;
23       displayColor = newDisplayColor;
24       fontSize = newFontSize;
25       clockFont = new Font("sansserif", Font.BOLD, fontSize);
26     }
27
28     public void paint(Graphics g)
29     {
30       g.setFont(clockFont);
31       g.setColor(displayColor);
32       String currentTime;
33
34       currentTime =
```

```
            (getTimeHours() < 10 ? "0" : "") + getTimeHours() +
            ":" + (getTimeMinutes() < 10 ? "0" : "") +
            getTimeMinutes() +
            ":" + (getTimeSeconds() < 10 ? "0" : "") +
            getTimeSeconds();

         FontMetrics metric = g.getFontMetrics(clockFont);
         g.drawString(currentTime, 0,
            metric.getAscent() - metric.getLeading());
      }

      public Dimension getPreferredSize()
      {
         Graphics g = getGraphics();
         FontMetrics clockMetrics = g.getFontMetrics(clockFont);
         int width = clockMetrics.stringWidth("88:88:88");
         int height = clockMetrics.getAscent();
         return new Dimension(width, height);
      }

      public void updateTime()
      {
         timeSeconds++;
         if (timeSeconds >= 60) {
            timeSeconds = 0;
            timeMinutes++;
            if (timeMinutes >= 60) {
               timeMinutes = 0;
               timeHours++;
               if (timeHours >= 24) {
                  timeHours = 0;
               }
            }
         }
         repaint();
      }

      // set and get methods omitted
   }
```

The design of this class is similar to that of the CheckerBoard class in Chapter 8. It provides a reusable component that can be used to display a digital clock face. We allow the hours, minutes and seconds to be specified, and the constructor (line 16) also allows the colour of the display and the size of the font to be specified when a Clock object is created. We have fixed the font style to be sans-serif.

The paint() method (line 28) draws the current time on the background in the format shown in Figure 9.1. The rather convoluted expression on lines 34 through 39 ensures that every number is drawn using two digits, even if the number is less than 10. If a value is less than 10, an extra 0 is inserted before the number itself is drawn.

The last lines of the paint() method (lines 41 to 43) extract the FontMetrics describing the current font, and use it to position the String in the centre of the canvas. Refer back to Chapter 8 for the meaning of the terms 'ascent' and 'leading'.

A FontMetrics object is also used to define the preferred size of the component on lines 46 to 53. We define the width to be the size required to hold the String 88:88:88 in the current font, and the height to be the ascent of the font. Recall that the preferred size is used by layout managers to allocate space for the component when it is inserted into a larger container along with other components.

The updateTime() method is the same as that used in the various clock classes in Chapter 2. At the end of the class we have omitted all the various 'set' and 'get' interface methods which allow the various parameters to be set and retrieved by external objects.

The other class that is used in this program is the one that manages the display of the various controls and also contains the Threads in which the clocks are run. Its code follows.

```
1   import java.applet.*;
2   import java.awt.*;
3   import java.awt.event.*;
4
5   public class ClockDisplay extends Applet
6      implements ActionListener, Runnable
7   {
8      Clock[] clock;
9      Checkbox[] clockBox;
10     TextField hoursText, minutesText, secondsText;
11     Button stopClock, startClock, setTime;
12     Thread[] timeThread;
13     boolean[] running;
14
15     public static void main(String argv[])
16     {
17       Frame clockFrame = new Frame("2 Clocks");
18       ClockDisplay testClock = new ClockDisplay();
19       testClock.init();
20       clockFrame.add("Center", testClock);
21       clockFrame.setSize(250,250);
22       clockFrame.setVisible(true);
23       clockFrame.addWindowListener(new WindowAdapter() {
24         public void windowClosing(WindowEvent event) {
25             System.exit(0);
26         }
27       });
28     }
29
30     void tellTime(int clockNum)
31     {
32       while (true) {
33         try {
```

MULTITHREADING EXAMPLE – THE CLOCK REVISITED

```
34            Thread.sleep(1000);
35         } catch (InterruptedException e) {
36         }
37         if (!running[clockNum])
38            return;
39         clock[clockNum].updateTime();
40      }
41   }
42
43   public void run()
44   {
45      Thread currThread = Thread.currentThread();
46      if (currThread == timeThread[0])
47         tellTime(0);
48      else
49         tellTime(1);
50   }
51
52   public void init()
53   {
54      GridBagLayout layout = new GridBagLayout();
55      GridBagConstraints constraints = new
56 GridBagConstraints();
57      setLayout(layout);
58
59      running = new boolean[2];
60      clockBox = new Checkbox[2];
61      CheckboxGroup clockGroup = new CheckboxGroup();
62      clockBox[0] = new Checkbox("Clock 1", true, clockGroup);
63      clockBox[1] = new Checkbox("Clock 2", false,
64 clockGroup);
65      Panel boxPanel = new Panel(new GridLayout(1,2));
66      for (int box = 0; box < 2; ++box)
67         boxPanel.add(clockBox[box]);
68      constraints.gridx = 0;
69      constraints.gridy = 0;
70      layout.setConstraints(boxPanel, constraints);
71      add(boxPanel);
72
73      Panel buttonPanel = new Panel(new GridLayout(1,3,5,5));
74      startClock = new Button("Start");
75      startClock.addActionListener(this);
76      buttonPanel.add(startClock);
77      stopClock = new Button("Stop");
78      stopClock.addActionListener(this);
79      buttonPanel.add(stopClock);
80      setTime = new Button("Set time");
81      setTime.addActionListener(this);
82      buttonPanel.add(setTime);
83      constraints.gridy = 1;
84      layout.setConstraints(buttonPanel, constraints);
```

```
85        add(buttonPanel);
86
87        Panel textPanel = new Panel(new GridLayout(2,3,5,5));
88        textPanel.add(new Label("Hours:"));
89        textPanel.add(new Label("Minutes:"));
90        textPanel.add(new Label("Seconds:"));
91        secondsText = new TextField(2);
92        minutesText = new TextField(2);
93        hoursText = new TextField(2);
94        textPanel.add(hoursText);
95        textPanel.add(minutesText);
96        textPanel.add(secondsText);
97        constraints.gridy = 2;
98        layout.setConstraints(textPanel, constraints);
99        add(textPanel);
100
101       clock = new Clock[2];
102       clock[0] = new Clock(12, 0, 0, Color.red, 48);
103       clock[1] = new Clock(0, 0, 0, Color.blue, 48);
104       Panel clockPanel = new Panel(new GridLayout(2,1));
105       clockPanel.add(clock[0]);
106       clockPanel.add(clock[1]);
107       constraints.gridy = 3;
108       layout.setConstraints(clockPanel, constraints);
109       add(clockPanel);
110
111       timeThread = new Thread[2];
112     }
113
114     int checkValue(int value, int minValue, int maxValue)
115     {
116       while (value < minValue)
117         value += maxValue - minValue + 1;
118       while (value > maxValue)
119         value -= maxValue - minValue + 1;
120       return value;
121     }
122
123     public void actionPerformed(ActionEvent event)
124     {
125       int hours, mins, secs;
126       String command = event.getActionCommand();
127       int clockSelected = clockBox[0].getState() ? 0 : 1;
128
129       if (command.equals("Start")) {
130         timeThread[clockSelected] = new Thread(this);
131         timeThread[clockSelected].start();
132         running[clockSelected] = true;
133       } else if (command.equals("Stop")) {
134         if (timeThread[clockSelected] != null)
135           timeThread[clockSelected].interrupt();
```

```
136            running[clockSelected] = false;
137        } else if (command.equals("Set time")) {
138            if (timeThread[clockSelected] != null)
139                timeThread[clockSelected].interrupt();
140            running[clockSelected] = false;
141            try {
142                hours = Integer.parseInt(hoursText.getText());
143            } catch(NumberFormatException e) {
144                hours = 0;
145            }
146            try {
147                mins = Integer.parseInt(minutesText.getText());
148            } catch(NumberFormatException e) {
149                mins = 0;
150            }
151            try {
152                secs = Integer.parseInt(secondsText.getText());
153            } catch(NumberFormatException e) {
154                secs = 0;
155            }
156            clock[clockSelected].
157                setTimeHours(checkValue(hours, 0, 23));
158            clock[clockSelected].
159                setTimeMinutes(checkValue(mins, 0, 59));
160            clock[clockSelected].
161                setTimeSeconds(checkValue(secs, 0, 59));
162            clock[clockSelected].repaint();
163        }
164    }
165 }
```

The `ClockDisplay` class illustrates that a class may extend one other class (in this case `Applet`), but may implement more than one interface (in this case, `ActionListener` and `Runnable`). The class implements `ActionListener` since it handles three `ActionEvents` generated by the `Buttons`, and it implements `Runnable` since it manages two `Threads`.

The various components are declared on lines 8 to 13. Note that we use arrays to store the `Clock` objects and the `Threads` that will run them. The `running` array declared on line 13 is used to indicate whether or not the corresponding thread is running.

The `init()` method (lines 52 to 110) creates the components and arranges them using a combination of `Panels`, `GridLayouts`, and a `GridBagLayout` for the overall layout. We have covered all the techniques used here in previous chapters. The array of two `Threads` is created on line 109.

Most of the substance of the class takes place in the `actionPerformed()` method starting on line 121. This method handles `ActionEvents` generated by all three `Buttons`, so we extract the label on the `Button` on line 124. We also determine which of the radio buttons is selected on line 125, since this determines which of the two clocks any action should affect.

218 THREADS

First, we deal with the 'Start' Button (lines 127 to 130). In this case, we create a new Thread for the corresponding clock and register the current class as the object which contains the run() method that the Thread will call when it is started. We then call its start() method, which in turn calls the run() method on line 43. Since we have two Threads in this class, we cannot just insert a line of code that is to be run into the run() method. We must first determine which of the two Threads is calling the run() method.

This is done on line 45 by calling the currentThread() method, which is a static method in the Thread class. This returns a Thread object (which we have stored in the local variable currThread) equal to the object that called the run() method. We can then compare currThread to the Thread responsible for running the first clock. If this is the Thread that called the run() method, we call the tellTime() method with an argument of 0, indicating that clock number 0 should be the one that is started. Otherwise, we start clock number 1. The tellTime() method (lines 30 to 41) starts an infinite loop consisting of one-second sleep() calls, followed by a check to see if that clock is running. If not, the method returns, but if the clock is running, a call is made to the updateTime() method for the corresponding clock. Because we are running this loop as a separate Thread, it will not lock up the program and prevent access to the controls.

Note that the run() method cannot be passed any arguments, since it must have exactly the same form as that specified in the Runnable interface. If we need access to any parameters within the run() method (as we do here, with the number of the clock that we should be starting), we must either extract this information from the identity of the Thread that called the run() method (as we do here), or else set a class variable before the Thread is started. Since the run() method belongs to the ClockDisplay class, it has access to all the class variables.

The second event to which actionPerformed() may respond is that generated by the 'Stop' Button (lines 131 to 134). We test the Thread corresponding to the selected clock to see if it has been created, and if so, we interrupt[1] it, and set the corresponding element in the running array to false. Note that merely interrupting the Thread doesn't erase the time values stored in the corresponding clock, so pressing the 'Start' button after pressing 'Stop' will restart the clock from the same time it had when it was stopped.

Finally, the 'Set time' Button is meant to read in the values entered by the user into the three TextFields and use them to set the time on the selected clock. We first interrupt any Thread that may be running for that clock and switch off the running array element (lines 137 and 138). We then read the values that have been entered for hours, minutes, and seconds. We have used the try...catch syntax that belongs to Java's exception syntax, which we will consider in Chapter 10. For now, it is enough if you believe that what is happening on lines 139 to 142, for example, is that the String entered into the hoursText text box is extracted and, if

---

[1] In Java 1.1, you must use the stop() method instead of interrupt(), as described in the previous footnote.

it is not a valid integer (that is, it contains some characters other than numbers), this is 'caught' by the exception handler, and the value of hours is set to 0 in this case. Otherwise, hours is set to the value specified by the user. The process is repeated for the minutes and seconds.

Finally, we store the entered values in the corresponding clock on lines 154 to 159, after calling the checkValue() method to ensure that the numbers are in the correct range for each component of the time. On line 160, the clock is repainted so that the new value is displayed.

Running the two timers in their own Threads thus creates a display with two clocks that can independently be started, stopped, and set.

Synchronization

The ability to write multithreaded programs in Java is a powerful addition to the language. However, we have already seen that introducing Threads into a program can cause as many problems as it solves. This is especially true whenever several Threads must cooperate with each other.

A detailed treatment of the problems associated with Thread cooperation (a topic known as *concurrent programming*) is beyond the scope of this book, but we will present a simple example here to illustrate the problem.

The following code is a command-line Java application that prints out two longish Strings with one word on each line. To illustrate the problems with Thread cooperation, we have started up two Threads, with each Thread having the job of printing out one of the Strings.

```
1   import java.util.*;
2
3   public class Unsync implements Runnable
4   {
5     String str1, str2;
6     Thread thread1, thread2;
7
8     public static void main(String argv[])
9     {
10      Unsync unsync = new Unsync();
11      unsync.init();
12    }
13
14    Unsync()
15    {
16      str1 = "This is the first string which is sent to a
17   thread for printing out on the screen, one line at a time,
18   in order to test whether synchronization is necessary.";
19      str2 = "THIS IS THE SECOND STRING WHICH IS SENT TO A
20   THREAD FOR PRINTING OUT ON THE SCREEN, ONE LINE AT A TIME,
21   IN ORDER TO TEST WHETHER SYNCHRONIZATION IS NECESSARY.";
```

```
22        thread1 = new Thread(this);
23        thread2 = new Thread(this);
24      }
25
26      public void init()
27      {
28        thread1.start();
29        thread2.start();
30      }
31
32    void printWords(String str)
33    {
34      StringTokenizer strToken = new StringTokenizer(str);
35      while (strToken.hasMoreTokens())
36        System.out.println(strToken.nextToken());
37    }
38
39    public void run()
40    {
41      Thread current = Thread.currentThread();
42      if (current == thread1)
43        printWords(str1);
44      else
45        printWords(str2);
46    }
47  }
```

The `main()` method (lines 8 to 12) creates an `Unsync` object and calls the `init()` method. The constructor (lines 14 to 24) defines two lengthy `Strings` and creates the two `Threads`, and the `init()` method starts the `Threads`.

The `run()` method detects which `Thread` has called it and then calls `printWords()` to print out the `String`, one word per line, using a `StringTokenizer` (see Chapter 6).

This may look straightforward enough, but what will probably happen if you run this program on your computer is that the output will start off something like this:

```
This
is
the
first
string
which
is
sent
to
THIS
a
IS
thread
THE
```

You can see that what is happening is that the first `Thread` got enough time to itself to print out the first nine words of its `String` (up to "This is the first string which is sent to"). At this point, the second `Thread` was started, and the thread management system started swapping time slices between the two `Threads`. From this point on, the two `Threads` alternate, with one word from each `String` being printed.

This is similar to the problem we encountered when introducing a `Thread` into the `CheckerBoard` class in order to allow access to menus and buttons while an animation was in progress – it was possible for a player to start moving a second piece before the first piece had finished. We solved the problem in that case by introducing a `boolean` variable called `moveInProgress`, which was tested whenever a request was made for a piece to be moved. If a move *was* in progress, the request was simply ignored, and the human player had to wait for the move to finish, and then try again to move the second piece.

If we tried setting a `boolean` flag in the string-printing program, we could allow access to the `printWords()` method only when no string was currently being printed. However, what do we do with a request to print a string if the `printWords()` method is busy? In the checkers game, we just ignored the request and waited until the player tried again. If we did that here, the second string would not get printed at all, since there is no external user making the request. We need some way of telling the second `Thread` to wait (rather than just kill itself) until the first `Thread` has finished.

Java neatly solves this problem by allowing a method to be specified as `synchronized`. If you insert the keyword `synchronized` at the beginning of line 32 above (if a method has an accessibility specifier such as `public`, the `synchronized` keyword goes between the `public` and the `void`) and rerun the program, you will find that the first string is printed out completely before the second string starts.

How does the addition of a single keyword cause such a profound change in the way the `Threads` are managed? Suppose we have a class in which one or more of the methods are declared as `synchronized`. When an object is created from that class, and any one of the `synchronized` methods is called, a *lock* is placed on that object. The lock prohibits any other `Thread` from running *any* of the `synchronized` methods in that object until the first `synchronized` method finishes. A `Thread` that attempts to access a locked object is placed in a *wait set*, which is just a collection of `Threads` that have attempted to access `synchronized` methods that were locked at the time.

When the `synchronized` method finishes, the lock on the object is released and a notice is sent to the wait set that the object is now available. If more than one `Thread` was waiting for access to that object, one of the `Threads` is chosen at random and allowed access to the object.

Synchronization is used primarily for situations where two or more `Threads` are doing different tasks, and the results of one task are required for the performance of another. A common application is the so-called *producer-consumer* task, where one `Thread` is the *producer* of some data which is *consumed* by another `Thread`. Clearly the consumer cannot do its job until the producer generates the data that is to be consumed. In this situation, the methods used to produce and consume the data would both be marked as `synchronized`, and any attempt by the consumer to access its method before the producer had finished with the production method would need to be blocked.

One problem that can occur with improperly synchronized methods is that of *deadlock*. Suppose we have a chain of `Threads` where each `Thread` consumes some data from the previous `Thread`, and produces some data that is consumed by the following `Thread`. If the first `Thread` is a producer only, and the last `Thread` is a consumer only, a synchronization mechanism can be worked out so that all the `Threads` cooperate. However, if the loop is closed by having the last `Thread` produce data that is required by the first `Thread`, it is possible for all `Threads` to be waiting for data from their predecessors before they can do anything. In such a situation, the program is completely locked, and nothing happens. This is a deadlock.

Deadlocks can only be avoided by careful planning of the algorithms used in writing multithreaded programs.

Exercises

1 Write an applet with a single `TextField` and a `Button`. When the user presses the `Button`, any text entered in the `TextField` is drawn in the frame as if being uncovered slowly from left to right. In order to do this, you should use `FontMetrics` to work out the width of the string when it is written in the current font (make it a large font to see the effect better). Then, use a clipping rectangle to restrict the portion of the string that is drawn at each stage. Arrange the timing so that 50 pixels are revealed per second.

Write the animation in a separate thread, so that the user may enter new text in the `TextField` and press the `Button` to stop any animation in progress and start a new animation with the new text.

2 Add a new thread to the checkers program and use it to run a clock that shows the time elapsed since the 'New game' button was pressed, thus keeping track of the total time spent on the game. You should be able to borrow most of the clock code from the `Clock` class in this chapter. Display the clock using a smaller font in a corner of the main window.

CHAPTER 10
Exceptions

Dealing with errors

There are two main types of errors that can occur when you are writing a program: *compile-time errors* and *runtime errors*. A compile-time error is something that stops your program from compiling – it could be a syntax error in the code, a reference to an undefined method, or a failure of the computer to find all the components required to build the final compiled version. Programs that have no compile-time errors can be run, either by embedding them as applets within a web page, or by running them as applications. A runtime error is something that goes wrong with the program while it is running. Runtime errors include such things as errors that cause the program to 'hang' (refuse to do anything, and possibly lock the entire computer up), attempt to access non-existent files for reading or writing, or simply cause the program to do something it wasn't intended to (such as produce the wrong answer to a calculation or draw things in the wrong place on the screen).

Usually, compile-time errors are easier to fix, since you have the compiler to help you by telling you what the error is and where it occurs in your source code. The sources of runtime errors, especially ones that cause the computer to crash or lock up with no other information, can be very hard to locate.

One way of dealing with runtime errors is to get hold of a Java development package that includes a *debugger*. Debuggers are tools that allow you to trace through the source code while the program is actually running and examine things like the values of variables at certain points and the path the program takes through your code.

The standard JDK (Java Development Kit) contains no debugging features beyond the JDB (Java DeBugger) package, which is not easy to use, being a command-line tool. Various commercial Java packages do provide debuggers, if you can afford them.

What the Java language *does* provide, however, is a feature which allows error 'hot spots' in your code to be tagged, so that they will produce helpful error messages, and sometimes take action to avert disaster. This feature is the Exception class (and its many descendants).

Java's built-in exceptions

According to the Java documentation, Java 1.1.5 supports 22 specialized exception classes in addition to the top-level Exception class. When would these classes be used, and do you ever have to use them yourself?

We have already seen some of Java's built-in exceptions in some of the example code in previous chapters. When studying animation, we had to enclose the Thread.sleep() method call inside a pair of statements with the keywords try and catch, and as part of the catch statement, an InterruptedException was mentioned.

If you have been experimenting with the Java code and trying the exercises at the ends of the chapters, you may well have seen other exceptions mentioned in error messages that appear in the command window where you start up the Java program. One of the more common exceptions is the NullPointerException, which occurs when you declare an object and forget to create it (using new, for example) before attempting to use it. If you have ever tried to access an array outwith its declared range (for example, trying to access element 20 in an array of size 10), you will have seen an ArrayIndexOutOfBoundsException (you can see that the designers of exceptions in Java didn't skimp on the names).

Let us take a closer look at some code that will generate an exception. Consider the class that follows.

```
1   import java.io.*;
2
3   public class TestArray
4   {
5     int[] square = new int[10];
6
7     public static void main(String argv[])
8     {
9       TestArray testArray = new TestArray();
10      System.out.print("Enter a number: ");
11      int number = testArray.readData();
12      while (number >= 0) {
13        System.out.println("The square of " + number +
14          " is " + testArray.getSquare(number));
15        System.out.print("Enter a number: ");
16        number = testArray.readData();
17      }
18    }
19
20    TestArray()
21    {
22      for (int num = 0; num < 10; ++num)
23        square[num] = num*num;
24    }
25
26    int readData()
```

```
27    {
28        int timeData = 0;
29        String timeString;
30
31        BufferedReader readData =
32           new BufferedReader(new InputStreamReader(System.in));
33        try {
34           timeString = readData.readLine();
35           timeData = Integer.parseInt(timeString);
36        } catch (IOException e) {
37           System.out.println("Read error: " + e.toString());
38        }
39        return timeData;
40    }
41
42    int getSquare(int number)
43    {
44        return square[number];
45    }
46 }
```

The `TestArray` class declares an array of `int`s and initializes the array to contain 10 elements. The constructor (lines 20 to 24) stores the squares of the numbers from 0 to 9 in the array, and the `main()` method contains a loop in which users are prompted to enter a number. The `readData()` method on line 26 is the same as the `readTimeData()` method used back in Chapter 2 to set up the time in the alarm clock example. The `getSquare()` method (lines 42 to 45) is called to retrieve the corresponding array element, and a message stating the square of the entered number is printed. The loop continues until the user enters a negative number.

If you run this program and enter any number less than 10, the program works as it should: a message is printed if the number is between 0 and 9, and the program stops if the number is less than 0. However, if you enter a number larger than 9, an error message is printed in the command window, stating that an `ArrayIndexOutOfBoundsException` has occurred, and giving the value of the offending array index.

The reason this happens is that, besides just carrying out the steps specified by your program code, Java also does a lot of internal checks on the commands before it executes them. If an error of a particular type is spotted (such as an out-of-bounds array index), program control passes to an *exception handler*, and the normal flow of your program is interrupted. In the case of a command-line program such as this, an exception actually kills off the program, but in an event-driven program (such as any program using a graphical interface) most exceptions will be ignored and the program will return to listening for the next event.

In some cases, ignoring an exception will make no difference to the running of the program, but in other cases it can be disastrous. In either case, a properly written program should ensure that either no exceptions occur, or, if they do, that they are handled properly. Since handling an exception does involve writing extra code, it is preferable to avoid cases where they occur, if possible.

In the TestArray program above, for example, we could easily avoid the exception by testing the value of number entered by the user on line 11. If number is larger than 9, we do not call getSquare(), thus avoiding any attempt to access the square array with an index that is too large.

However, to illustrate how an exception can be handled explicitly in a Java program, we will add some code to deal with large array indexes. Replace the while loop in the main() method above with the code:

```
while (number >= 0) {
  try {
    System.out.println("The square of " + number +
      " is " + testArray.getSquare(number));
  } catch (ArrayIndexOutOfBoundsException e) {
    System.out.println("The number is too large.
      Please try again.");
  }
  System.out.print("Enter a number: ");
  number = testArray.readData();
}
```

If you run the program again, you will find that entering a number larger than 9 causes the message 'The number is too large. Please try again.' to be printed, followed by a prompt to enter another number. In other words, entering an out-of-bounds array index no longer causes the program to crash – we have 'caught' the exception and handled it gracefully.

Exception handling is done using two Java keywords: try and catch. The statements that may cause a particular type of exception are surrounded by a try block, as we have done here with the statement containing the call to getSquare(). The idea is that these statements are tried out, but the program is warned that they might cause an exception by enclosing them within a try block. If an exception *does* occur, the catch block following the try is examined. If an exception of the type that has actually occurred is listed there (more than one type of exception can be caught, as we'll see below), the code within that catch block is executed. Execution of the program then continues normally with any code that follows the catch block.

If no exception occurs, or the type of exception that does occur doesn't match any of those listed in the catch block, then the catch block is skipped, and execution resumes with the code that follows the catch block (provided the exception doesn't cause a crash).

Throwing exceptions

The example in the previous section showed how to `try` a block of code and `catch` an exception of a specific type that may have been generated by that code. In this case, the exception was generated, or *thrown*, by the underlying Java machine when an error was found. It is also possible to create and `throw` one of the built-in exceptions at any point in your own code. For example, we could modify the example above as follows. First, in the `while` loop, we replace the line in the `catch` block:

```
System.out.println("The number is too large.
   Please try again.");
```

with:

```
System.out.println(e.toString());
```

We also change the `getSquare()` method to:

```
int getSquare(int number)
{
  if (number > 9)
    throw new ArrayIndexOutOfBoundsException
      ("The number is too large. Please try again.");
  return square[number];
}
```

That is, rather than relying on Java's underlying exception handler to throw the exception, we do the check on the array index ourselves and throw an exception if the index is out of bounds. Note that the constructor for the exception object contains a `String` as an argument − this `String` is passed to the exception object and becomes the message that is printed by the `println()` method back in the `while` loop. The `toString()` method, when applied to an exception, generates the exception's name along with the message.

Runtime and non-runtime exceptions

There are actually two main types of exceptions in Java: *runtime* and *non-runtime* exceptions. A runtime exception is an instance of the `RuntimeException` class (or a class derived from it). Runtime exceptions are caused by some invalid data, such as an out-of-bounds array index or a division by zero, being produced during the execution of the program. In other words, they are exceptions arising from erroneous data that has been produced *within the program*.

Non-runtime exceptions are faults caused by factors outside the control of the program. Typical causes of non-runtime exceptions are interruptions to the program caused by the operating system, and errors in attempting to read from or write to the disk.

The reason the distinction between these two types of exceptions is important is that *non-runtime exceptions must always be handled*, while runtime exceptions can be ignored. It is for this reason, for example, that we must always enclose the call to Thread.sleep() within a try...catch block that catches an InterruptedException – this exception is a non-runtime exception that deals with external interruptions to the program. Since the Thread.sleep() method may throw this exception, we must handle it.

Exceptions such as ArithmeticException and ArrayIndexOutOfBoundsException are runtime exceptions, and need not be caught. This is fortunate, since if we did need to catch all exceptions of this type, we would need to enclose every arithmetic expression and array operation within try...catch blocks.

The Java documentation provides a complete list of exceptions and states which ones are derived from RuntimeException and which are not.

If a runtime exception that is generated within one method is not caught in that method, it is passed up to the method from which the first method was called. This continues along the chain of method calls until either the exception is caught along the way, or the main() method is reached. If main() does not catch the exception, it is passed along to the operating system itself, which may either ignore it or be affected by it in a way that causes the program to crash. We saw this effect earlier when we did not bother to catch an ArrayIndexOutOfBoundsException – the result was that the program crashed.

Although an exception may be caught at some point in the program, it need not be caught within the method in which it arises. For example, suppose we introduced a 500 millisecond delay into the getSquare() method by inserting the line Thread.sleep(500) at the start of the method. Since Thread.sleep() can throw the non-runtime InterruptedException, we must catch this exception in our program. Ordinarily, we would do this by enclosing the call to Thread.sleep() within a try...catch block directly. However, another option is to declare the getSquare() method so that it throws an InterruptedException itself:

```
int getSquare(int number) throws InterruptedException
{
  Thread.sleep(500);
  return square[number];
}
```

Doing this simply passes the responsibility for catching the exception to the method that calls getSquare(). This method, in turn, has the option of catching the exception itself, or passing it along again. In an application, we can declare main() itself so that it throws the exception, thus passing the responsibility right out of the program and onto the operating system. Doing so, of course, means that we cannot recover from the exception and if it occurs, the program will probably crash.

Suppose we decide to catch in `main()` both the `ArrayIndexOutOfBounds-Exception` and the `InterruptedException` that may be thrown by `getSquare()`. As mentioned earlier, we may catch more than one exception after a single `try` block. To do so, we just add an extra `catch` block for each exception we wish to catch. Thus, we can modify the `while` loop in `main()` as follows.

```
while (number >= 0) {
  try {
     System.out.println("The square of " + number +
        " is " + testArray.getSquare(number));
  } catch (ArrayIndexOutOfBoundsException e) {
     System.out.println(e.toString());
  } catch (InterruptedException e) {
     System.out.println("Sleep interrupted.");
  }
  System.out.print("Enter a number: ");
  number = testArray.readData();
}
```

If an exception is thrown, it is first checked to see if it is an `ArrayIndexOutOfBoundsException`, then to see if it is an `InterruptedException`, with the appropriate action taken in each case. If the first `catch` block is activated, all remaining `catch` blocks for that `try` are skipped without being checked.

Defining new exception classes

Explicitly throwing one of the built-in Java exceptions is likely to be fairly rare, however, since most of the cases where such exceptions would be thrown are already handled by Java itself. It is more likely that the programmer will wish to define a new type of exception for use in some specialized case. This is easy to do by using inheritance to extend one of the existing exception classes.

For example, we might wish to distinguish between array indexes that are too low (that is, negative) and those that are out of bounds at the other end. We can derive two new exception classes from `ArrayIndexOutOfBoundsException`, as follows.

```
class LowArrayException extends
   ArrayIndexOutOfBoundsException
{
   LowArrayException(String message)
   {
      super(message);
   }

   LowArrayException()
   {
      super();
```

```
      }
    }

    class HighArrayException extends
      ArrayIndexOutOfBoundsException
    {
      HighArrayException(String message)
      {
        super(message);
      }

      HighArrayException()
      {
        super();
      }
    }
```

All that is needed to derive a new exception class is to provide the two forms of the constructor, one of which takes a `String` argument, and the other of which takes no arguments. We simply call the constructor of the super-class in both cases.

These new classes obviously don't add any functionality to that of the base class, but they do add two new exception types which may be used to distinguish between different types of error in the program. We can modify the `getSquare()` method to throw the right kind of exception:

```
      int getSquare(int number)
      {
        if (number < 0)
          throw new LowArrayException();
        if (number > 9)
          throw new HighArrayException("Array index too large.");
        return square[number];
      }
```

Since a negative value for `number` will be used to stop the program, we don't define a message when we create a `LowArrayException`.

We can now modify the `while` loop yet again so that these two exceptions are caught.

```
1       while (true) {
2         try {
3           System.out.println("The square of " + number +
4               " is " + testArray.getSquare(number));
5         } catch (LowArrayException e) {
6           System.exit(0);
7         } catch (HighArrayException e) {
8           System.out.println(e.toString());
```

```
9            } catch (Exception e) {
10               System.out.println(e.toString());
11           }
12           System.out.print("Enter a number: ");
13           number = testArray.readData();
14       }
```

Here, we have removed the termination condition from the `while` loop on line 1. This is because we now rely on one of the new exceptions to stop the program. If a `LowArrayException` is caught (line 5), the user has entered a negative number and the program exits. Otherwise, a `HighArrayException` prints out the message 'Array index too large.'

The final `catch` block on line 9 illustrates another feature of exception handling. Both `LowArrayException` and `HighArrayException` are derived from `ArrayIndexOutOfBoundsException`, which is in turn derived from the `Exception` class. In a sequence of `catch` blocks such as those on lines 5 to 10, a given `catch` will catch any exceptions of that type *and all exceptions of classes derived from that type*. So, if we had derived another type of exception from `LowArrayException`, the first `catch` block would catch that derived type as well.

The final `catch` block on line 9 will therefore catch all exceptions that are not of class `LowArrayException`, `HighArrayException` or any class derived from either of them. Note that if we had placed the `catch (Exception e)` statement *before* the other two, the other two `catch` blocks would never be executed since all exceptions would be caught by the first block.

A more general exception class

As a final example of what can be done with exceptions, we consider another extension to the out-of-bounds array index. This time, however, the exception allows the offending array index to be stored as part of the exception class itself.

```
class SaveIndexException extends
  ArrayIndexOutOfBoundsException
{
  private int errorIndex;

  SaveIndexException(int index, String message)
  {
    super(message);
    errorIndex = index;
  }

  SaveIndexException(int index)
  {
    super();
```

```
      errorIndex = index;
    }
    public int getErrorIndex()
    {
      return errorIndex;
    }
}
```

The `SaveIndexException` class contains two constructors, one of which saves only the offending index, while the other saves a message `String` as well. The class also includes an interface method for retrieving the value of `errorIndex`.

Rewriting the `while` loop in `main()` yet again shows how the new exception class may be used.

```
while (true) {
  try {
    System.out.println("The square of " + number +
        " is " + testArray.getSquare(number));
  } catch (SaveIndexException e) {
    if (e.getErrorIndex() < 0)
      System.exit(0);
    else
      System.out.println
        ("Array index " + e.getErrorIndex() +
        " too large.");
  } catch (Exception e) {
    System.out.println(e.toString());
  }
  System.out.print("Enter a number: ");
  number = testArray.readData();
}
```

This time, we catch a `SaveIndexException`, retrieve `errorIndex`, and stop the program if the index is negative. Otherwise, we print out an error message that includes the actual value of the offending array index.

When to use exceptions

As you can see from the preceding examples, exceptions can be used in a variety of ways, but perhaps a more important question is when they should be used at all. After all, we could equally well have coped with all the situations in the preceding examples by using a few `if` statements to do some simple checks on the array index that was typed in.

In principle, if you were supremely confident in your coding ability and were absolutely certain that you could account for all possible errors using a few checks on input, you would never need exceptions. The point of using exceptions is that even the most careful programmer will occasionally overlook a situation where erroneous data will creep into a method. By providing a few checks at the source of the data, as we did above with the `getSquare()` method, we will get some meaningful error messages if at some point an error *is* made, and some rogue data infiltrates another part of the program.

This doesn't mean that you should define an exception for every little error that is possible in your program. In many cases, a simple test of a value is all that is needed, and you should be content with that. Timing studies have shown that exceptions take considerably more time to process than simple comparisons. However, if you are writing a class or component that will be frequently used in other settings, and you have identified a place in the class where users can insert external data, perhaps a `try...catch` block or two at that point could be helpful to programmers (possibly including you!) who fail to put in the proper checks when they use your code.

Exercises

1   Write a command-line program containing a `main()` method and another method named `init()` in which an array of `String`s named `test` is declared. Initialize the array variable by assigning it to `new String[10]`, but do *not* actually create any of the array elements. Immediately after this, try printing out (using `System.out.println()`) the length of `test[0]`. What sort of error message is printed?
    Enclose the `println()` statement in a `try...catch` block to catch this exception. Have the `catch` block print out the message 'String has not been initialized'.
2   Rather than catching the exception directly in `init()` as in exercise 1, have the `init()` method `throw` the exception and catch it in `main()` instead.
3   Define a new exception class called `NullStringException`. This class should extend the `Exception` class, and contain just the two constructors as shown in the `LowArrayException` class in the text. Starting from the first version of the program in question 1, check to see if the value of the `String` `test[0]` is `null` before attempting to print its length. If it is, throw a `NullStringException` with the message 'String is null'. In `main()` enclose the call to `init()` in a `try...catch` block to catch this exception and print its message using the `toString()` method.
4   Modify the `NullStringException` class (or else derive a new version from the existing one) so that it has a `String` variable named `calledFrom`. This `String` is to contain the name of the method where the exception occurred. Modify the existing constructors for `NullStringException` to initialize `calledFrom` (it should have a default value of `null`, since it should be possible to throw this exception without providing the name of the method

where the exception occurred). Provide an interface method allowing `calledFrom` to be retrieved.

Modify the `init()` method so that the name of the method ('init') is passed to the exception when it is thrown, and modify the `catch` block in `main()` so that it retrieves and prints this information when a `NullStringException` is caught.

CHAPTER 11

Saving, loading, and printing

Saving your work

None of the Java programs we have studied so far has allowed you to save your work, either as a file on disk or as printout on paper. For some programs, such as the alarm clock, saving data in a file is not terribly useful, but for other programs it would certainly be convenient, if not essential.

In Java 1.0.2, saving data in a disk file was not particularly easy, and printing anything on paper was impossible. Java 1.1 has greatly eased the saving and loading of data, and has provided a reasonably easy-to-use way of printing on paper what you see on the screen. We will illustrate both of these features in this chapter by adding saving, loading, and printing options to the checkers game from Chapter 8. We will consider saving and loading disk files first.

Serialization

Java 1.1 allows data to be *serialized*, which means that the data can be read from and written to objects called *streams*. A data stream is basically any object which accepts data from (or passes it to) a running program. The most common stream is probably that which allows data to be stored on and loaded from a disk, but other types of stream exist. For example, two different programs (either on the same computer or on two separate computers connected by a network) may communicate with each other through streams, even though nothing is actually written to disk.

In Java 1.0.2, only primitive data types (`ints`, `floats`, and so on) could be serialized directly, which meant that if you needed to save all the variables in a user-defined object, you needed to write a method in the corresponding class that read and wrote each primitive variable separately. Java 1.1 introduced *object serialization*, which allows entire objects to be serialized with a single method call. What's more, if one of the variables in a class is itself an object from another user-defined class, this object is automatically serialized when the object containing it is serialized.

There are two main steps required to serialize an object. First, the class of which the object is an instance must implement the `Serializable` interface. This interface is a bit odd in that it contains no method definitions at all (so that a class that implements it need not define any extra methods). The `Serializable` interface thus serves only as a tag that labels the class as one whose objects may be serialized. For various reasons, it may be desirable to prevent some objects from being serialized. Some classes, for example, represent objects that have different forms on different types of computers. If an object of that type were saved in a file on a PC and then loaded back on a UNIX system, the result may be incomprehensible to the UNIX computer. Such objects should always be recalculated whenever the program is run.

Any class that implements `Serializable` may be written to and read from a stream using the classes found in the `java.io` (the 'io' stands for 'Input Output') package, so this package must be imported into a class file where serialization occurs.

To make things more concrete, we will concentrate on the procedure for saving data to and reading it from a disk file, but the principles for other types of serialization are similar.

Let us return to the checkers program from Chapter 8, and add options allowing a game to be saved and loaded. In order to save a game, we need only save the two arrays of `CheckerPiece` that store the locations of the checkers, and whether or not each piece has been captured. We therefore need to modify the definition of the `CheckerPiece` class so that it implements `Serializable`. Refer back to the definition of this class on page 190. The first line of the class must be changed to:

```
class CheckerPiece implements Serializable
```

This change means that objects of class `CheckerPiece` may now be saved to disk using a serialization command, as we will see below. No other changes are required to the `CheckerPiece` class.

The `CheckerBoard` class (see page 191) contains the arrays of white and black pieces, so it is the appropriate place to insert methods for saving and loading a game. The classes that are needed to save and load data are found in three built-in packages, so at the beginning of the `CheckerBoard` definition, we need to add some `import` statements.

```
import java.io.*;
import java.util.*;
import java.util.zip.*;
```

We may now add a `save()` method to the `CheckerBoard` class to save the data contained in the `whitePiece` and `blackPiece` arrays of `CheckerPiece`. Since an array in Java is an object in its own right, it is automatically serializable, provided that the data type of which the array is built is also serializable. The method's code is as follows.

```
1    void save()
2    {
3       FileDialog saveDialog = new FileDialog(frame,
```

```
4            "Save game", FileDialog.SAVE);
5            saveDialog.show();
6            String filename = saveDialog.getFile();
7            if (filename != null) {
8              try {
9                FileOutputStream fileOut =
10                   new FileOutputStream(filename);
11               GZIPOutputStream zipOut =
12                   new GZIPOutputStream(fileOut);
13               ObjectOutputStream objectOut =
14                   new ObjectOutputStream(zipOut);
15               objectOut.writeObject(whitePiece);
16               objectOut.writeObject(blackPiece);
17               objectOut.flush();
18               objectOut.close();
19             }
20             catch (Exception e) {
21               System.out.println(e.toString());
22             }
23           }
24         }
```

The code may look fairly involved, but it follows a series of obvious steps that should be familiar to anyone who has used a commercial application that offers a file-save option. The code here may be copied almost in its entirety to other applications, with only the actual data that is being saved (lines 15 and 16) needing to be changed in each case.

Lines 3 and 4 create the standard 'File save' dialog that should be familiar to most readers (see Figure 11.1). The first argument in the `FileDialog` constructor must be a `Frame` object which is the owner of the dialog. For the checkers program, this will be the `Frame` object `checkersFrame` created in the `main()` method of the `Checkers` class (see page 197). We will see how to pass this object to the `CheckerBoard` class a bit later. The second argument is a `String` which appears in the title bar of the dialog (see Figure 11.1), and the third argument is a constant indicating which type of dialog is to be created.

Once the dialog has been created, it is made visible on line 5, and the filename entered by the user is retrieved on line 6. If the user clicked the 'Cancel' button, the `filename` will be `null` and no further action should occur, so this is checked on line 7.

The code in the `try` block (lines 8 through 19) does the actual serialization. First, we create a `FileOutputStream` object (line 9) connected to the `filename` entered by the user. On line 11, we use a `GZIPOutputStream` (from the `java.util.zip` package) to *compress* the data before it is written to the file. This is an optional step, but it doesn't hurt to put it in, especially if you are saving a lot of data. (The curious name – GZIP – comes from a freely available package from the Free Software Foundation, and is part of the GNU package. GZIP is the GNU zip package, and zip itself is a standard data compression method.)

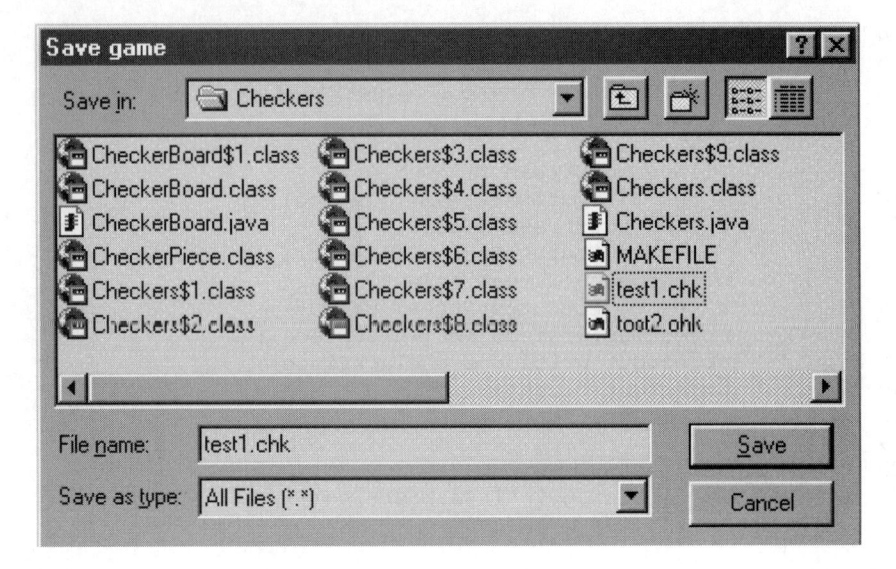

Figure 11.1 The standard 'File Save' dialog.

Finally, we create an `ObjectOutputStream` (line 13), which is the object that actually starts the serialization process. This stream takes the raw data and passes it to the `GZIPOutputStream`, which compresses the data and passes it to the `FileOutputStream`, which writes the compressed data to the file.

Lines 15 and 16 write the two arrays of `CheckerPieces` to the `ObjectOutputStream`. Line 17 *flushes* the stream (makes sure that all the data that was put into the stream is pushed out the other end), and finally, line 18 closes the stream. The whole process contains several methods which may throw non-runtime exceptions and as we saw in Chapter 10, such exceptions must be handled, so we must enclose all these statements inside a `try` block. We use the generic `Exception` class to catch all possible exceptions. These exceptions arise mainly from problems in accessing the disk file.

If you look at the file (in a text editor, for example) that is created by the serialization process, it will probably appear as gibberish, especially if it is has been compressed. But never fear, the format of the file is understandable by the `load()` method, which we examine now.

```
1    void load()
2    {
3      FileDialog loadDialog = new FileDialog(frame,
4        "Load game", FileDialog.LOAD);
5      loadDialog.show();
6      String filename = loadDialog.getFile();
7      if (filename != null) {
8        try {
9          FileInputStream fileIn =
```

```
10                new FileInputStream(filename);
11            GZIPInputStream zipIn =
12                new GZIPInputStream(fileIn);
13            ObjectInputStream objectIn =
14                new ObjectInputStream(zipIn);
15            whitePiece = (CheckerPiece[])objectIn.readObject();
16            blackPiece = (CheckerPiece[])objectIn.readObject();
17            objectIn.close();
18            repaint();
19        }
20        catch (Exception e) {
21            System.out.println(e.toString());
22        }
23    }
24 }
```

The `load()` method is very similar to the `save()` method, so we will just point out the differences.

On line 3, the `loadDialog` is created using a `FileDialog` but with the third argument set to `FileDialog.LOAD`. Lines 9 through 14 are similar to the corresponding code in the `save()` method, except that `Output` is replaced by `Input` in all the class names.

Lines 15 and 16 illustrate how the `whitePiece` and `blackPiece` arrays are loaded from the file. The `readObject()` method of the `ObjectInputStream` class is called to read in the next object in the file. This method cannot, on its own, determine the type of object that it has just read, so we need an explicit *cast* to do the conversion. The cast is the name of a data type, enclosed in parentheses, that is placed in front of the method call. On line 15, for example, the cast is `(CheckerPiece[])`, which tells the compiler that the data is to be interpreted as an array of `CheckerPiece` objects.

Line 17 closes the input stream (there is no need to flush an input stream). Line 18 repaints the display after the data has been read into the two arrays, so the loaded game is now visible on screen.

Before we leave this section, we need to consider the `Frame` object that is the first argument in the `FileDialog` constructor on line 3 of both the `save()` and `load()` methods. Where does it come from?

As mentioned above, the `Frame` must be the parent frame of the object calling the `FileDialog`. This is necessary because a dialog box needs to know what frame it is attached to so that it can be displayed in the right place. Since the checkers game is controlled from the `Frame` that is created in the `main()` method (see page 197), we must arrange for that `Frame` object to find its way down to the `CheckerBoard` class.

The easiest way of doing this is to pass the parent `Frame` as an argument to the `CheckerBoard` constructor. That is, we add a `Frame` variable to the `CheckerBoard` class, and add an argument to the constructor to allow this variable to be initialized. So, we add the line

```
   Frame frame;
```

to the declarations at the start of the `CheckerBoard` class on page 194, and change the constructor to:

```
   CheckerBoard(int newSquareSize, Color newDark,
     Color newLight, Frame newFrame)
   {
     frame = newFrame;
     // Other statements unchanged
   }
```

Similarly, we need to add a `Frame` variable to the `Checkers` class and add a `Frame` argument to its constructor so that the `Frame` defined in the `main()` method on page 197 can be passed to the `Checkers` class.

Of course, we also need to add in menu items or buttons which call the `save()` and `load()` methods, but as this requires no new techniques, we leave this as an exercise for the reader.

One final note about saving and loading data: for security reasons, it is not possible to save or load data to and from disk (at least, not directly) if your program is being run as an *applet* (that is, from within a web browser). If this were possible, an applet could wreak havoc on the hard drive of a computer that happened to load the web page in which it was embedded. There are various security measures that have been included in some Java packages that do allow applets to access the hard drives of both the client and server computers, but these are beyond the scope of this book.

Printing

As of Java 1.1, it is possible to produce *hardcopy* or printed output from an application. (As with saving and loading, it is not possible to print an applet from a web page, unless the browser itself initiates the printing request. Again, this is for security reasons – if an applet could print itself without the approval of the client, the possibilities for electronic junk mail don't bear thinking about.) Printing a single-page copy of the window that you see on the screen is no more difficult than saving or loading some data.

If you think about it, printing onto paper is essentially the same thing as drawing to the screen, so you might expect that printing would make use of the `Graphics` class. This is in fact what is done, except that the `Graphics` object that is used is actually a subclass which inherits the main `Graphics` class that contains extra code for dealing with the peculiarities of printing. The `Graphics` object can be sent directly to the `print()` method of the `Component` class (which is the ancestor of all components and containers in Java). The `print()` method then calls the `paint()` method of the corresponding component, which just draws exactly the same graphics to the printer as it would draw to the screen in response to a `repaint()` call (but without the initial call to `update()`, since there is no point in attempting to 'clear the screen' before printing).

It is also possible to draw some additional graphics (beyond what is in the `paint()` method) to the printer by just using ordinary method calls from the `Graphics` class, in just the same way as you would draw to the screen. If you add in these extra commands before calling `Component`'s `print()` method, the printer will print a combination of the two.

To illustrate Java's printing capabilities, we will add a `print()` method to the checkers game which allows the current board position to be printed, just as it appears on screen. As with saving and printing, the addition of a menu item or button to trigger printing is left to the reader. The following `print()` method is added to the `Checkers` class.

```
1   void print()
2   {
3     Toolkit toolkit = getToolkit();
4     PrintJob job =
5        toolkit.getPrintJob(frame, "PrintBoard", printProps);
6     if (job == null)
7        return;
8     Graphics page = job.getGraphics();
9     Dimension size = this.getSize();
10    Dimension pageSize = job.getPageDimension();
11    page.translate((pageSize.width - size.width)/2,
12       (pageSize.height - size.height)/2);
13    page.setClip(0, 0, size.width, size.height);
14    print(page);
15    page.dispose();
16    job.end();
17  }
```

Most of this method may be transplanted directly from one program to another, as the steps to be followed in implementing printing are fairly constant. We begin by obtaining the `Toolkit` for the current component (line 3). We discussed the `Toolkit` class in Chapter 8 when we considered the `FontMetrics` class.

The `toolkit` object is used on lines 4 and 5 to obtain a `PrintJob` object. The `PrintJob` object opens the printer dialog box, which allows the user to set various properties of the printer before any actual printing (see Figure 11.2). The first argument of the `getPrintJob()` method is the `Frame` object that contains the component to be printed. This is obtained in the same way as with the `save()` and `load()` methods above. The second argument is a `String` that provides a title for the printing job. This does not appear on the printout, but can be used elsewhere in the program, if needed.

The third argument is a `Properties` object which, in theory at least, allows the properties of the printer to be stored between printing requests. In order to supply an argument here, you need to declare a `Properties` object as a `static` variable (that is, one that is not attached to any specific instance of the class), at the beginning of the class, as in:

```
static Properties printProps = new Properties();
```

The effect of the `Properties` object, if any, seems to vary with the computer system, so you may find it more trouble than it is worth. If so, it is acceptable to just pass `null` as the third argument to `getPrintJob()`.

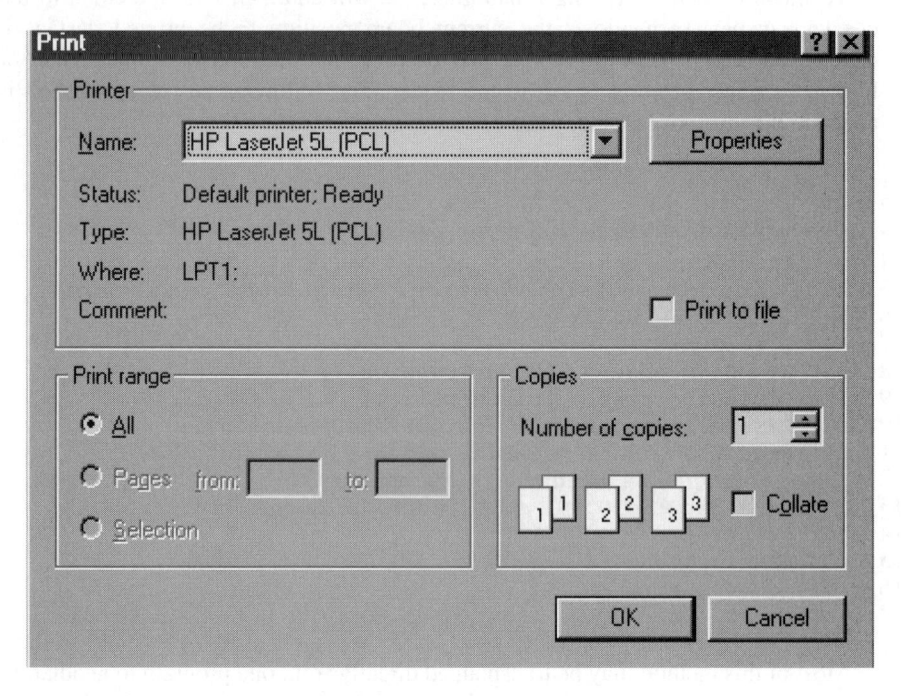

Figure 11.2 The printer dialog.

If the user presses 'Cancel' in the printer dialog box, `job` will be `null`, and no further action is taken (lines 6 and 7). Otherwise, we extract a `Graphics` object from `job` (line 8). This object can be used just like the `Graphics` object that we have been using to draw to the screen, except that all drawing commands will appear on the printer instead.

Line 9 extracts the dimensions of the component that is to be printed, using the `getSize()` method, while line 10 extracts the size of the physical paper sheet onto which printing will occur. Lines 11 and 12 use these two dimensions to centre the image on the paper, both horizontally and vertically. If we omitted this statement, the image would appear in the upper left corner of the paper. Obviously, you can alter this command to place the image wherever you like.

We can insert other graphics commands after line 12 if we like. For example, we might draw a border around the image with the statement

```
page.drawRect(-1, -1, size.width+1, size.height+1);
```

It is important that all specialized graphics commands that draw outside the boundaries specified by `size` are inserted *before* the call to `setClip()` on line 13. Otherwise, the clipping command will just chop them off again.

Line 13 clips the image around its edges. This may seem unnecessary if we are printing an image, such as the checkerboard, which has a well-defined size, but it is a good idea to put this statement in anyway, especially if the component you are printing contains nested components. Failure to do so can cause problems with some of the library methods that are called to process the image.

The `print(page)` command on line 14 sends any specialized drawing commands that may have been inserted after line 12 to the printer, and then calls the `paint()` method of the current component. Thus all drawing commands attached to `page` will be drawn, together with all the drawing commands found in `paint()`. Note that the `print(page)` method on line 14 actually calls the `print()` method that is inherited from the `Component` class, and not the `print()` method defined in the `Checkers` class. The compiler can tell the difference since the `print()` method in the `Checkers` class takes no arguments, whereas the `print()` method in the `Component` class takes a `Graphics` object as an argument.

The call to `dispose()` on line 15 is analogous to the `flush()` command we used when saving data to a file – it ensures that all the data is cleared and sent to the printer.

As of line 15, the printing of a single page is complete. If we wanted to print another page, we would repeat the process to build up a `Graphics` object containing the information required for the next page and send it off. Java itself provides no help in determining where page breaks occur – it is up to you to work out which data should be printed on each page, construct the `Graphics` object for each page, and send it to the printer using the `print()` and `dispose()` methods.

When all pages have been sent to the printer, call the `end()` method (line 16) to stop printing.

The `print()` method given above will print out the entire display of the `Checkers` program, which includes the board diagram *and* the two `Buttons` above it (see Figure 8.9). This is because the method appears within the top-level class of the program. If we wanted to print out *only* the board diagram, we could insert the `print()` method above into the `CheckerBoard` class and arrange for a menu item to call that method instead. The method can be inserted exactly as is, since there is nothing in the method that is specific to either class.

Lightweight and heavyweight components

If you run the `print()` method above from within the `Checkers` class, you may find that the output from the printer contains a double image of the board, with one image shifted slightly, and overlapping the first image. (Printing the board alone from the `CheckerBoard` class doesn't show this effect.) The technical explanation of why this happens is rather involved, but it illustrates a principle that needs to be understood if you want to produce good-quality printouts. The principle concerns the method by which user-defined components are created.

In Java 1.0.2, a custom component (such as the `CheckerBoard` class) could be produced only by deriving a new class from the `Canvas` or `Panel` classes. These two classes (the `Canvas` being used for creating components containing only graphics, and the `Panel` being used to create a container) have an opaque, rectangular window associated with them, which serves as the background on which drawing takes place, or into which components are placed. The window requires an extra level of management, and therefore more computing time to draw on the screen. Such components are now known as *heavyweight* components.

As of Java 1.1, it is possible to produce custom components in two ways – the traditional heavyweight method, and a new *lightweight* technique. A lightweight component can be derived directly from the `Component` class (rather than having to use `Canvas`), and a lightweight container can be derived directly from `Container`, rather than having to use `Panel`. Although in many cases there will be no visible difference, the lightweight technique eliminates the extra background window, allowing faster handling of the component. (It also allows some impressive graphical effects such as non-rectangular components through the use of transparent backgrounds.)

What does all this have to do with printing? If you are printing a simple component that has no other components embedded within it, there is nothing to worry about. However, if you are printing a component with more than one layer (as with the `Checkers` class, which consists of a `Panel` containing two `Buttons` and an embedded `CheckerBoard` component), the printing command starts at the top layer and then calls the printing command for the components that are embedded within that layer. (The process continues recursively if the internal layers themselves have embedded layers.)

The point is that the command to print embedded components is only guaranteed to work properly if the these internal components are lightweight. In our original definition of the `CheckerBoard` class back in Chapter 8, we derived it from the `Canvas` class, thus making it a heavyweight component. It is easy enough to change `CheckerBoard` to a lightweight component, however – simply extend it from `Component` rather than `Canvas`. All the code inside the class remains the same. Making this single change will now allow the compound diagram to print properly.

Exercises

1   Write an applet which contains some components into which the user can enter some personal information such as their name, age, and address. Add 'save' and 'load' options (using buttons or menus) which will save the current information to a file and load information from a file. When information is loaded, it should be displayed in the applet.

2　In most commercial applications, if you attempt to quit the program before saving any changed data (or load in some data that overwrites unsaved data), a small dialog box (often called a *confirmation box*) will pop up asking if you wish to save your changes. Add this feature to your applet from question 1.

To do this, add a `boolean` variable called `modifiedData` which should be `false` initially, but should be set to `true` whenever the user types anything into any of the `TextFields` (add a listener for keyboard events to all `TextFields`). If the user attempts to either quit the program or load in some new data when `modifiedData` is `true`, create a popup frame asking if the user wishes to save the current data. If the response is 'yes', go through the usual saving procedure as described in the text. The `modifiedData` flag should be set to `false` after a save.

3　Add in the menu items that will allow a user of the checkers game to activate the saving and loading methods given in the text.

4　Add printing capabilities to the `TicTacToe` game from Chapter 7. Print the game panel on one page and the scores on a second page.

APPENDIX
Further reading

General

The main source for anyone interested in the latest developments in Java should be the Javasoft website, run by Sun Microsystems, the inventors of Java. The site contains free downloads of all the software and documentation you need to start writing Java programs, along with a lot of other useful material and news. The URL is:

    http://www.javasoft.com/

Java is still evolving and growing, so it is difficult to recommend printed (as opposed to electronic) material that is not out of date by the time you read it. However, the 'essence' of Java, as covered in this book, is not likely to change much in future versions of Java. Many of the references given below cover Java 1.1 rather than 1.2, but they still provide useful material.

The basics of Java

- A comprehensive introduction (more than 1000 pages!) to programming with Java can be found in Deitel & Deitel, *Java: How to Program*, 2nd edition, Prentice Hall, 1997; ISBN 0-13-899394-7. (Make sure you get the second edition, which covers Java 1.1.)
- A more compact survey of Java 1.1 may be found in Flanagan, *Java in a nutshell*, 2nd edition, O'Reilly, 1997; ISBN 1-56592-262-X. Again, make sure you get the second edition for Java 1.1. This book is *not* a beginner's book, however. It is a very useful reference after you have some experience as a programmer.
- Introductory books on programming that emphasize the importance of classes and objects from the start are, regrettably, still quite rare. Besides the present book, another good reference for novices is Culwin, *Java: An Object First Approach*, Prentice Hall, 1998; ISBN 0-13-858457-5.

- The reader who wishes to learn about data structures using Java could consult Rowe, *An Introduction to Data Structures and Algorithms with Java*, Prentice Hall, 1998; ISBN 0-13-857749-8. This book also uses an 'objects first' approach.
- A massive compendium of information (1400 pages) on Java 1.2 may be found in *Java 1.2 Unleashed*, by Jamie Jaworski, Sams Publishing, 1998; ISBN 1-57521-389-3. This is definitely *not* a beginner's book, but contains almost anything you could wish to know about Java 1.2, with plenty of examples.

The Sun Microsystems library

Sun Microsystems Press has produced a number of books that cover various aspects of Java programming. Some of these are as follows:

- Pew, *Instant Java*, 2nd edition, ISBN 0-13-272287-9.
- Horstmann and Cornell, *Core Java 1.1; Volume 1: Fundamentals*, ISBN 0-13-766957-7
- and *Volume 2: Advanced Features* ISBN 0-13-76696-58
- Geary, *Graphic Java 1.1 – Mastering the AWT*, 2nd edition, ISBN 0-13-863077-1
- van der Linden, *Just Java 1.1*, 3rd edition, ISBN 0-13-784174-4
- van der Linden, *Not Just Java*, ISBN 0-13-864638-4
- Jackson and McClellan, *Java by Example*, 2nd edition, ISBN 0-13-272295-X
- Weaver and Jervis, *Inside Java Workshop*, ISBN 0-13-858234-3
- Morris and Hinrichs, *Web Page Design – A Different Multimedia*, ISBN 0-13-239880-X

Index

-- operator, 42
% operator (modulus), 43
?: operator, 53
++ operator, 42

absolute value, 203
abstract class, 83, 169
Abstract Windowing Toolkit, 19
ActionEvent, 95, 97, 104
ActionListener, 97, 104, 217
actionPerformed(), 98, 100, 217
actions, 2
adapter classes, 101
add(), 21, 144
addActionListener(), 98
addItem(), 112
addition, 41
address in memory, 37
adventure games, 133, 141
algorithm, 26
ALT key, 196
American spelling, 170
  color, 78
anchor, 164
and (&&), 44
AND operator (&), 196
animation, 200
anonymous classes, 103, 113
append(), 139
applets, 11, 20, 25
  and files, 240
  HTML tag, 25
appletviewer, 25
applications, 11
argument (of a method), 8, 14
argument list, 14
argv[], 141
arithmetic operators, 41

ArrayIndexOutOfBoundsException, 224
arrays, 119
  length, 121
  of objects, 125
  syntax, 121
  two-dimensional, 157
ascent, 214
  of a font, 176
ASCII code, 34, 132
assignment operator (=), 39
associativity (of operators), 38
autoexec.bat, 81
AWT, 19

base class, 73
baseline (of a line of text), 176
binary data, 34
binary operators, 39
Boole, George, 34
boolean (data type), 6, 34
Boolean logic, 44
BorderLayout, 148
braces, 5
break, 52
Button, 104
byte, 34, 35, 132
byte code, 93

C language, 169
C++, 169
call (a method), 6
Canvas
  heavyweight component, 244
CardLayout, 149
case, 52
case-sensitive, 5
cast, 90

casting, 80, 239
catch, 224
    and inheritance, 231
char, 34, 133
Checkbox, 104, 112
CheckboxGroup, 104, 112
checkers, 189
Choice, 104
class, 5
    compared with object, 13
class files, 11, 93
CLASSPATH, 81
clipping, 201
clipRect(), 203
close() (a stream), 237
Color, 78, 171
Color (Java AWT class), 170
colors. *See* colours
colours, 171
    number of, in Java, 171
    primary, 171
command-line arguments, 141
comments, 16
compile-time errors, 223
compiling Java programs, 10
Component, 92, 105
    inheriting directly, 244
component classes, 92
ComponentAdapter, 105
ComponentEvent, 105
ComponentListener, 105
compressing data, 237
concatenation (of Strings), 130
concurrent programming, 219
conditional expressions, 27, 45
confirmation box, 245
constant, 35
constant parameters, 124
constructors, 13, 66
    in inheritance, 75
Container, 92, 143
    inheriting directly, 244
conversion (of data types), 42
Courier, 173
cryptogram, 142

curly brackets, 5
currentThread(), 218

data compression, 237
deadlock, 222
deallocation of memory, 71
debugger, 223
declaration
    purpose of, 37
declaration (of a variable), 35
declaring objects, 13
default, 53
delimiters, 133
derived class, 73
descent (of a font), 176
development environment, 8
device driver, 168
Dialog font, 174
DialogInput font, 174
Dimension, 181
dispose(), 243
division, 41
    of ints, 41
do...while, 56
double, 34, 35
draughts, 189
drawString(), 22, 176
dynamic binding, 79
dynamic memory allocation, 65

else, 46
emacs, 9
enableEvents(), 188
encapsulation, 4
encryption, 142
end(), 243
environment variable, 81
equal to (==), 44
equals()
    applied to Strings, 99
event handlers, 94
event listener, 95
event model, 95
events, 94
Exception, 223

exception handler, 225
exceptions, 218
  defining new, 229
  multiple, 229
exit(), 52
exponent, 35
extends, 21, 74

false, 6
FileDialog, 237, 239
FileOutputStream, 237
fill, 165
fillOval(), 195
flickering (reducing), 200
float, 34, 35
floating point, 35
FlowLayout, 144
  and stretching, 159
flushing output, 238
FocusAdapter, 105
FocusEvent, 105
focusGained(), 105
FocusListener, 105
focusLost(), 105
Font, 77, 173
  constructor, 174
font.properties, 173
FontMetrics, 176, 214
fonts, 173
  adding, 173
  bold, 174
  bold italic, 174
  constant spacing, 174
  italic, 174
  normal, 174
  proportional spacing, 174
for, 57
Frame, 19
Free Software Foundation, 9

garbage collection, 70
getActionCommand(), 99
getBytes(), 138
getFont(), 178
getFontList(), 178

getFontMetrics(), 178
getGraphics(), 200
getLabel(), 129
getModifiers(), 196
getPreferredSize(), 181, 183
getPrintJob(), 241
getSelectedCheckbox(), 115
getSize(), 242
getState(), 129
GNU software, 9, 237
Graphical User Interface, 18
Graphics, 21, 168
  in printing, 240
graphics classes, 92
graphics context, 168, 170
greater than (>), 44
greater than or equal to (>=), 44
GridBagConstraints, 161, 164
GridBagLayout, 161
GridLayout, 147
gridwidth, gridheight, 165
gridx, gridy, 165
GUI, 18
GZIPOutputStream, 237

hardcopy, 240
hasMoreTokens(), 134
HCI, 47
heap, 37
heavyweight components, 244
height (of a font), 176
Helvetica, 173
HTML, 25
human-computer interaction, 47
human-computer interface, 47
HyperText Markup Language, 25

if statement, 46
if statement (pseudocode), 28
implements, 88
import, 12, 81
indentation, 28, 31
infinite loops, 30, 54
inheritance, 21, 72
init(), 24

INDEX 251

inner classes, 103
input/output, 23, 236
insets, 165
int, 34
int data type, 5, 35
integer, 5
interfaces, 4, 88
internationalization, 173
interrupt(), 208, 211
InterruptedException, 224, 228
ipadx, ipady, 165
is a type of, 80
isAlive(), 211
isPopupTrigger(), 187
ItemEvent, 95, 104, 114
ItemListener, 104

Java AWT, 92
Java DeBugger, 223
Java Development Kit, 9, 223
Java Virtual Machine, 93
java.applet, 20, 92
java.awt, 19, 92
java.awt.event, 95
java.awt.peer, 94
java.io, 23, 236
java.lang, 92, 208
java.util, 133
java.util.zip, 237
javac (Java compiler), 10
JDB, 223
JDK, 9, 223
JVM, 93

KeyAdapter, 105
keyboard (handling events from), 100
KeyEvent, 95, 100, 105
KeyListener, 100, 105
keyPressed(), 100, 105
keyReleased(), 100, 105
keyTyped(), 100, 105
keywords, 5

Latin alphabet, 174
layout managers, 93, 143

layoutContainer(), 147
leading, 176, 214
length (of array), 122
length() (String method), 131
less than (<), 44
less than or equal to (<=), 44
lightweight components, 244
List, 104
load(), 238
loading from a file, 235
local classes, 103
local variables, 36
lock, 221
logical operators, 44
long, 34, 35
loops, 27, 54
    nested, 160

main(), 11, 15
mantissa, 35
masking, 196
Math.abs(), 203
Math.random(), 125
Math.sqrt(), 86
member classes, 103
memory management, 37
Menu, 184
MenuBar, 184, 199
MenuItem, 184
menus, 184
    popup, 186
META key, 196
method, 6
Microsoft Windows, 169
modifiers, 196
modulus operator (%), 43
Monospaced font, 174
Motif, 94
mouse
    right button, 195
MouseAdapter, 106, 195
mouseClicked(), 105
mouseDragged(), 105
mouseEntered(), 105
MouseEvent, 95, 105

mouseExited(), 105
MouseListener, 105, 195
MouseMotionAdapter, 106
MouseMotionListener, 105
mouseMoved(), 105
mousePressed(), 105, 195
mouseReleased(), 105
multiple inheritance, 87
multiplication, 41
multitasking, 206
multithreading, 207

nested loop, 160
new, 13, 65
new (for creating arrays), 124
newline, 129
nextToken(), 134
nim (game of), 106
non-runtime exceptions, 227
not (!), 44
not equal to (!=), 44
noughts and crosses, 151
null, 66
NullPointerException, 224

Object (Java base class), 93
object-oriented language, 2
ObjectOutputStream, 238
objects, 2
   initializing, 64
   serialization, 235
operands, 38
operating system, 37, 206
operators, 38
or (||), 44
overriding methods, 76

packages, 81
   as visibility modifer, 83
   default (nameless), 82
paint(), 21, 170
   in printing, 241
Panel, 117, 151
   heavyweight container, 244
   stretching components, 159

parentheses, 7
parseInt(), 114
passing by reference, 70
passing by value, 69
pixel, 168
platform-independence, 93
pointers, 65
points (font size), 174
popup menus, 186, 199
portability, 169
postfix operator, 42
precedence (of operators), 38
preferred size, 180, 214
prefix operator, 42
primary colours, 171
   in painting, 171
primitive data types, 34
   passed by value, 69
print(), 241
printed output, 240
PrintJob, 241
private, 5, 83
   in inheritance, 74
processMouseEvent(), 188, 200
processor, 206
producer-consumer task, 222
properties, 2
Properties (Java class), 242
protected, 74, 83
pseudo-code, 27
pseudo-random numbers, 125
public, 5, 83
Pythagoras, 86

random numbers, 124
random(), 124
readInt(), 24
readObject(), 239
Rectangle, 203
remainder operator (%), 43
repaint(), 31, 170
return, 7
return type, 15
return value (of operators), 38, 40
returning (from a method), 7

RGB (red-green-blue), 171
round brackets, 7
run(), 208, 209, 218
Runnable, 208, 217
run-time errors, 223
runtime exceptions, 227

SansSerif font, 174
save(), 236
saving in a file, 235
scope, 36
   class-wide, 36
   method-wide, 36
scrollbars, 179
ScrollPane, 180
Serializable, 235
serialization, 235
serif, 174
Serif font, 174
setClip(), 243
setColor(), 173
setConstraints(), 161
setEnabled(), 115
setFont(), 174
setHgap(), 147
setLayout(), 146
   (in ScrollPane), 180
setSize(), 180
setVgap(), 147
setVisible(), 117
short, 34, 35
show(), 149
   popup menus, 188
sleep(), 30, 218
square root, 86
start(), 209, 218
statement, 7
static, 16, 124
   methods, 124
stop(), 211
streams, 235
String, 130
   constructor, 130
   operators, 130
StringBuffer, 139

StringTokenizer, 133, 220
stringWidth(), 179
substring(), 131
subtraction, 41
Sun Microsystems, 9
super, 76
super(), 75, 229
swapped out, 207
swapping processes, 206
switch, 50
synchronized, 221
syntax, 33
System.exit(), 52, 113, 158
System.out.print, 15
System.out.println, 15

television, 171
ternary operator (?:), 53
text encryption, 142
TextArea, 129
this, 98
Thread, 208
Thread.sleep(), 228
threads, 206, 207
   multiple, 212
throw, 227
throwing exceptions, 227
throws, 228
TicTacToe, 151
TimesRoman, 173
tokenizing a String, 133
toLowerCase(), 138
Toolkit, 178
   in printing, 241
toString(), 93
toString() (for exceptions), 227
toString() (for fonts), 179
true, 6
truth table, 45
try and catch, 224, 226
two-dimensional arrays, 157

unary operators, 39
Unicode, 35, 132
union (of rectangles), 201

union(), 203
UNIX, 169
update(), 170
   overriding, 200

variable, 35
visibility modifiers, 83
void, 7

wait set, 221
weightx,weighty, 165

while, 54
while loop (pseudo-code), 27
white space, 134
WindowAdapter, 158
windowClosing, 158
writeObject(), 237

X Windows, 169

zero-based arrays, 121
zip compression, 237